Abundance

THEORY Q   A series edited by
————   Lee Edelman, Benjamin Kahan,
and Christina Sharpe

ANJALI ARONDEKAR

Abundance

Sexuality's History

DUKE UNIVERSITY PRESS · DURHAM AND LONDON · 2023

© 2023 DUKE UNIVERSITY PRESS
All rights reserved

Project Editor: Jessica Ryan
Designed by Matthew Tauch
Typeset in Garamond Premier Pro by Westchester Publishing Services

Library of Congress Cataloging-in-Publication Data
Names: Arondekar, Anjali R., [date] author.
Title: Abundance : sexuality's history / Anjali Arondekar.
Other titles: Theory Q.
Description: Durham : Duke University Press, 2023. | Series: Theory Q |
Includes bibliographical references and index.
Identifiers: LCCN 2022048860 (print)
LCCN 2022048861 (ebook)
ISBN 9781478019909 (paperback)
ISBN 9781478017240 (hardcover)
ISBN 9781478024484 (ebook)
Subjects: LCSH: Sex—Historiography. | Sexual minorities—Historiography. |
Decolonization—Social aspects—South Asia. | Devadāsīs—India—Velha Goa—History. |
Queer theory. | BISAC: HISTORY / LGBTQ | SOCIAL SCIENCE / Gender Studies
Classification: LCC HQ12 .A76 2023 (print) | LCC HQ12 (ebook) |
DDC 306.7—dc23/eng/20230302
LC record available at https://lccn.loc.gov/2022048860
LC ebook record available at https://lccn.loc.gov/2022048861

Cover art: Cover page of the *Samaj Sudharak*, September 1940.
Gomantak Maratha Samaj Archives, Mumbai, India.

*For Aai, Baba, and all
the kalavantins . . .*

CONTENTS

INTRODUCTION · 1
Make. Believe. Sexuality's Subjects

CHAPTER ONE · 33
In the Absence of Reliable Ghosts: Archives

CHAPTER TWO · 63
A History I Am Not Writing: Sexuality's Exemplarity

CHAPTER THREE · 90
Itinerant Sex: Geopolitics as Critique

CODA · 112
I Am Not Your Data. Caste, Sexuality, Protest

Acknowledgments · 129
Primary Sources · 135
Secondary Sources · 139
Index · 163

INTRODUCTION

Make. Believe. Sexuality's Subjects

To "write" a history of sexuality, or so the story goes, is to embrace the chimeric prose of paucity and plentitude. If the present is marked by an inescapable surfeit of evidence, the past is haunted by an unremitting loss of materials.[1] Marginality and loss, paucity and disenfranchisement: these are the hermeneutical forms that have become the common currency of histories of sexuality. The missing amphora of sexuality is recovered from the archival detritus of hegemonic histories of slavery, colonialism, and nationalism to showcase more liberatory narratives of emancipation, liberation, and rights.[2] Even scholars of precolonial histories of sexuality in South Asia, for example, who rightfully bemoan the temporal focus on nineteenth-century European colonialism, call on a similar language of loss as they lament the postcolonial erasure of a historical archive resplendent with evidence of sexuality's past.[3] This orientation to loss, mutatis mutandis, surfaces most vividly within sexuality studies in the Euro/American academy, where the current invocation of negativity, failure, even utopia, still tethers histories of sexuality to forms of loss, lack, and failure in the face of, or rather because of, our embattled political horizons.[4] The appeal to psychoanalysis as the privileged language of critique further solidifies an attachment to sexuality as loss, phantasmatic, protean, or otherwise.[5] Tropes of loss especially abound in historiographical work where sexuality's (putatively) pathologized pasts and archives are recuperated as reparative sources of sanctuary/*jouissance* rather than despair.[6] Sexuality thus endures as an object of historical recovery, it follows, through a recursive and iterative poetics of melancholia, an irresolvable longing for loss that eschews all forms of consolations.[7]

To note the orthodoxy of such theorizations about histories of sexuality is not to dismiss the considerable productivity of such thinking, or to re-create yet again the (false) divide between historicist and psychoanalytical thinking; if anything, it is more gestural of a larger and robust critical ecology, as evidence and evocation of the collective pull of loss across geo/political landscapes. Indeed, any effort to chart or critique such a broad swath of intellectual currents is, as one well knows, ipso facto reductionist. After all, narrative economies of loss are always already at work in the worlds we seek to enter, as an excruciating double bind that indentures us to the very historical holdings we seek to release.[8] We redeem the deficit of our minoritized histories through concerted acquisitions of lost pasts. Queer/trans subjects (especially in elusive subaltern pasts) remain in the stranglehold of such constant loss even as they stumble toward pragmatic, entrepreneurial (often legal) structures of survival.[9] In the face of the casual brutality of dispersed global suffering, there is, as Elizabeth Povinelli writes, "nothing spectacular to report" about loss anymore. Indeed, any epistemological privileging of loss (past or present) assumes an "eventfulness" that flounders in the face of the "ordinary, chronic and cruddy" syncopations of everyday subaltern life.[10] As Geeta Patel reminds us, the alluring double bind, that "ethical habit we refuse to release," is also "the ultimate place where recursivity resides,"[11] where our attachments to loss return and reset in an endless spiral of recuperative historiographies (from savage to salvage).[12]

My book challenges such an epistemological preoccupation with loss as the structuring mode of narration for histories of sexuality. Instead, I call for a historiography of sexuality that pushes against the binding energies of such "melancholic historicism," of an origin-mythos, as Stephen Best notes, that anchors us to scripted itineraries of loss and recovery.[13] To fix sexuality within such vernaculars of loss (while politically exigent) is to refuse alternative historiographical models, to bypass imaginative histories of sexuality, full of intrepid archives and acts of invention. I wish to set the two terms—*history* and *sexuality*—both alongside and athwart one another to stage a different story, one that seeks to discover what each of these terms might do to the other, without assuming a position of negation from the outset. At its most ambitious, my book invites two sets of ruminations: (1) What if we shift our attention from the recuperation of sexuality as loss to understanding it as a site of abundance? (2) What archival forms and effects emerge from such a coupling of sexuality and abundance? To enter histories of sexuality through an imaginary of abundance is not to invest in and stabilize a new knowledge economy of plenitude, or to slide into plodding literalization (ah, there is more, more, more), mislaying in the process the messy misalignments the concept of abundance lugs along. Bypassing salvific modes, underwritten by loss as value, abundance serves more as a theoretical than descriptive supplement, as a concept-metaphor that moves us away from the incessant shuttling between the sated fulfillment and avid impoverishment of historiographical ambitions. Simply stated, the concept of abundance I am proposing does not replace paucity with overflow but, rather, unravels a set of archives that are fertile ground for producing and contesting attachments to history-writing.[14] Rather than resolve abundance into a concept that will be portable to other geopolitical contexts, I propose a messier experiment, an open-ended inquiry that travels between a difficult present and an unfinished past, a reeling spiral of flight and return, approaching histories of sexualities aslant. To speak of a history of sexuality from the *Ansatzpunkt* of abundance is to emphasize both the efflorescence of the past and to attend to its strategic and active mobilization within the politics of the present. One way to parse the concept of abundance I am proposing here is to see it as inextricably linked to the histories of subordinated collectivities, as a historiographical orientation that challenges the narratives of their constant devaluation. What historical forms does abundance take when we turn to subaltern peoples and pasts? How do such forms of abundance fall outside historical interest and preservation? How might a turn to abundance work against the imperative to fix sexuality within wider historical structures of vulnerability, damage, and loss?

In my previous work, I have grappled with these thorny concerns by writing about a pressing impasse in our recuperation of the historical archive, about the hermeneutical demands placed on histories of sexuality such as those in South Asia, which are entangled with questions of colonialism and race, and about the multiple double binds and possibilities that emerge from it. I have argued that the promise of archival presence as future knowledge is always circulated in relation to historical desire, a desire for lost bodies, subjects, and texts, and for the evidentiary models they enable.[15] My efforts here, however, are drawn especially to how such recuperative historiographical methods assume their more salutary forms of loss precisely in the service of collectivities tallying up what they do not yet have in relation to other constituencies. Far from repudiating such salvific historical forms (instantiated as they routinely are in the language of lost rights and representation), I would like to ask (1) how minoritized conclaves wrestle with the evidentiary genres that such models of devaluation demand, and, in doing so, (2) how they assemble historical archives that self-consciously activate the compensatory mechanisms that such losses should or will produce. More broadly, I am interested in thinking through how the absence and/or presence of archives secures historical futurity, and what proceeds from an unsettling of that attachment, from a movement away from the recursive historical dialectic of fulfillment and impoverishment. The challenge here is to engage a historiography of sexuality that paradoxically adds value to a sedimented historical form (lost archives must be resurrected, found, produced for future gains) precisely by staging interest in its modes of reproduction (found archives must be disseminated, digitalized, and memorialized).

Such challenges are especially heightened, as I have suggested above, when geopolitics enters the diversified holdings of such historical work through languages of capitalization that shift the value of loss into the content of incommensurability. Thinking sex with geopolitics makes it a concept ineluctably linked to asymmetry, whereby a geographical location garners (lost) historical value through its (untranslatable) relationship to the West—in other words, through the labor of incommensurability.[16] Even as histories of sexuality appear provisional, open to transformation and to the velocities and inscriptions of *other* worlds, geopolitical sites (particularly in the global South) continue to be hailed as obdurately and enticingly incommensurate—literally ungraspable, undecipherable forms. Incommensurability generates a positive value here by promising to carry meanings beyond the failures of the present, to transport histories of sexuality into the future.[17] Indeed, the seductions of such incommensurability (often cast in the broad languages of divergent spatialities and temporalities) accrue a further political value where you cede to geopolitical difference precisely to lay aside the epistemic work such difference does.[18] Thus, as scholars repeatedly gesture toward the vastness of geopolitical landscapes (the required self-reflexive move that marks a reading as limited to the West while more knowledge awaits us in the "Rest"), or to the persistence of geopolitical asymmetries, little effort is made to translate those gestures to the *content* of episteme. References to knowledge elsewhere may abound in the requisite listings and bibliographies that accompany most studies of/on sexuality, but they remain largely a noninterventionist counterpoint to Euro-American epistemologies.[19] As

Neferti Tadiar reminds us, "In this endeavor, anti-European, anti-colonial critiques have not lost their pointed relevance"; rather, they have become suitably bracketed, akin to "third-string guests in a crowded party, nodded to in passing," while academic shareholders make their way to topics with "the highest profit margin."[20] In so doing, we recast, as it were, over and over again, the early debates inaugurated by Gayatri Spivak's seminal essay "Can the Subaltern Speak?" as histories of elsewheres perform necessary scenes of nonrepresentability and reprieve (recall her opening invocation of the conversation between first-world intellectuals, Deleuze and Foucault). What is often elided in readings of Spivak's essay is her emphasis on forms of learning from below that must flourish precisely because of such incommensurability.[21]

Given such a conceptual quagmire, then, how do we harness the tremendous generative potential of incommensurability, and think sex with geopolitics, without ceding meaning *and* value?[22] How do we mark the incommensurability of geopolitics with the simultaneous plaint that such opacity is irrevocably compromised, interrupted, even staged? How do we generate geo/histories of sexuality through different economies of presence, through sight lines of abundance?[23] Given this book's indebtedness to knowledge formations in South Asia, how does one then translate the richness of a region's myriad politics, theoretical nuances, and multilingual aesthetics without falling prey to historical habits of legibility? To answer these questions and more, I want to step away from the acrimony of current debates, or from narrative conventions that impute "radical" critique. I want to bypass (or at least attempt to) settler-colonial habits of analysis that emphasize "new" discovery and capture, even as we tread shared, inherited modes of reading. Indeed, if the rich efflorescence of scholarship in transgender studies can be our guide, we are now more than ever in need of an ethos of theoretical and political generosity. For example, translation, decolonization, and trans/historicity are just some of the themes that animate recent special issues of *TSQ: Transgender Studies Quarterly*, all foci that call for theoretical vernaculars bold enough to galvanize and evoke situated knowledges.[24]

Setting aside privileged citations and methods, as well as critical priorities that have accrued to historical practices founded on the recuperation, reproduction, and reparation of a lost and/or erased past, let us commit instead to thinking sex and geopolitics not just as abstract concepts but as the substance and condition of our engagements.[25] To do so, I draw here from intellectual traditions within two entangled and often segregated historiographies, one in South Asian/area studies and the other in sexuality studies, to ask: What would histories of sexuality look like if interrogated as histories of regions and/or "areas"?[26] As Keguro Macharia trenchantly asks, How does thinking in place, thinking with a geo/history, produce knowledge?[27] Such an invocation would, *eo ipso*, attempt to perform at the level of text the myriad epistemological forms such engagement can take. To that end, I have also deliberately turned to the term *sexuality* in lieu of *queer* to gather epistemologies and interlocutors across geopolitical sites that are not always poised to offer political salvation, or even configure as "queer." "Sexuality" here is not staged as a counternarrative or corrective to "queer"; rather, it serves more as an itinerant heuristics that gathers a density of narrative genres across divergent histories and spatialities.[28]

To flesh out these compacted observations and more, let me turn to some possible pathways to such abundance.

RIP: RETURN(S) IF POSSIBLE

July 14, 2009.[29] "Tumhi kai karta, madam?" (What are you doing, madam?) This was the question that the caretaker of the Gomantak Maratha Samaj archives in Panaji, Goa, quizzically asked me as I painstakingly placed a fragile document into one of many ziplock bags. The Gomantak Maratha Samaj (henceforth the Samaj) is a prominent lower-caste devadasi collectivity hailing from colonial Portuguese and British India. *Devadasi* is a Sanskrit term literally meaning "slave" (*dasi*) of a god/master, often falsely read as interchangeable with terms such as *courtesan*, *sex worker*, and *prostitute*. *Gomantak* speaks to geographical roots in Goa, *Maratha* is both a caste and regional term, and *Samaj* translates to "collectivity," "society," and/or "community." Bemused by my attempts to preserve rare archival materials that I perceived as being damaged or open to loss, the caretaker's question signaled an unforeseen twist in my orientation to archival research. For her, the preservation of these rare archival materials was of little consequence; after all, as she sternly reminded me, this was an oversaturated archive, so full at its seams that it struggled to manage the constant production of new and diverse materials. Here the return to a history of sexuality was not through a call to loss (of object and/or materials) but, rather, through ordinary surplus. When asked about the potential loss of valuable historical materials, the response from the archival custodian was one full of mirth and consternation. For her, the risk of loss is more *ek hasaichi gosht* (a laughable matter), where the preservation of rare archival materials is of little consequence. We have more materials than we need (*zaroori peksha jasht*), she added, shaking her head in amused exasperation at my continued insistence on the looming dangers of archival loss. To this day, she reminded me proudly, new materials continue to enter the Samaj archives, with little effort being expended to either digitalize or republish older, more fragile materials.

July 20, 2014. On a rainy monsoon afternoon, a woman rushes into the Mumbai branch of the same Gomantak Maratha Samaj, where I am again busy wading through boxes of archival materials. A sheaf of papers in hand, the woman frenetically approaches the general factotum on call and demands to see the institution's *chitnis* (secretary). She is in urgent need of a written affidavit from the Samaj, an evidentiary marker, she states, that can then be used to procure an OBC (Other Backward Caste) certificate for her son to attend university on a seat reserved for lower-caste communities. The secretary arrives, listens patiently to her request, and gently reminds her that a letter from the Samaj no longer carries much legal weight, due to stricter regulations on caste verification materials. The rise in cases of false caste certificates, he tells her, has made collectivities such as the Samaj suspicious recordkeepers of caste histories, open to charges of caste fabrications. After all, he tells her with some amusement, we have trouble proving who we are.[30] Yet the woman insists that a letter authenticating her son's lower-caste status will help, so the secretary pulls out the requisite form and begins to fill out the necessary information. But surely, the woman asks, you must want to see my son's birth certificate. Surely, she asks, you must want some evidence of my claims. Ah, says the secretary, we don't need to see any evidence, nor your papers. All we ask, he adds, is your permission to list your name in our annual published record of members. "Aamche karya, tumcha vishwas" (We make, you believe), he notes, with a wry smile. The woman listens to the secretary's request, pauses, gathers her papers, and quietly walks out the door. No caste certificate is exchanged.[31]

TRANSLATION AS TRANSACTION

The two archival encounters described above animate, in many ways, the historiographical ambitions of this book: What are the evidentiary mandates that provoke histories of sexuality into presence? And what happens when such mandates go awry, flouted by the radical pragmatism of subaltern evidentiary practices? Bear in mind that in both scenes, there is no renunciation or refusal of the evidentiary value of archives, or of the historiographical demands placed on minoritized communities. After all, the caretaker of the Goa branch acknowledges the Samaj's commitment to archival production (we keep producing, she states), just as the secretary of the Mumbai branch cannily speaks to the necessary visibility that such evidentiary forms can produce (the published list of Samaj members in exchange for the caste certificate). Together the archival events foreground (1) the compensatory economies of archival formations (archives as guarantors of presence, rights, representation), (2) the conventions of evidentiary genres (the caste certificate that we need to garner contractual rights and freedoms, a caste certificate that we have already noted is constantly under siege as a verifiable marker), and (3) the imaginative yet transactive refusal of such prescriptions (the epistemological liveness of the two scenes that speaks to riskier sorts of historical engagement).

In the first scene, we have the story of a collectivity that stubbornly refuses to move on from the ordinary plenitude of sexuality. Shorn of the aura of loss, we are confronted with a historiography that refuses to give up the paradoxes instantiated in its self-archiving: presence without preservation, production without reproduction. The very abundance of the archives directly kindles the nonrecuperation of its materials. As the caretaker of the Samaj archives reminded me, there is no dearth of materials and, as such, no inheritance of loss. Rather than safeguard against the (inevitable) destruction of fragile archival materials, the caretaker's obiter dicta folds archival surplus into an unexceptional consistency: more materials, we are told, keep coming in. Archival abundance here does not merely signify a surfeit of materials; it points more toward a deliberately embraced historical and pragmatic project. In all its ostensible substance (we have so much), the Samaj archive displays an errant materiality that remarkably eschews the exigency of preservation.

The caretaker's disinterest in the reproduction of the Samaj archives through digitalization equally stanches cherished archival routes of aspirational value. The digitalization of minoritized archives, we are endlessly reminded (and, for the most part, rightly so), safeguards against the risk of lost value, especially within the treacherous landscapes of post/colonial worlds.[32] As such, the Samaj's lack of investment in digitalized pasts and futures speaks further to an almost counterintuitive embrace of archival abundance: a refused relation to the valued reproductive imperative. In contrast to the imperative to immure and preserve materials through digitalization, the Samaj archives appear instead to be focused on the sustenance of a history of sexuality whose abundant productions negotiated an unexpected pathway to futurity. What remains instead is the promise and failure of archival recuperation, the looking for, and a queer historiography about, found archival objects that are so plentiful that one must look askance.

In the second archival encounter, conventions of verification are cast/e aside, the uncertainty of the "original" evidentiary value-form writ large, even as claims to the future are sought (by the secretary) and refused (by the woman). As Lawrence Cohen and Amrit Rai, have variously argued, the logic of the *jugaad* (flexible form) and the "duplicate" founds the very evidentiary models of the colonial/postcolonial state in South Asia. Even as colonial/postcolonial subjects recognize themselves through the evidentiary regimes of the bureaucratic "stamp-state," they equally understand those regimes to be flexible and inherently provisional. For Cohen, the copy/duplicate of the original evidentiary marker (instantiated in the sign of the birth certificate, the ration card, etc.) crucially becomes the bearer of value such that the distinction between the proper and the spurious is always held in abeyance. The original opens itself to the threat of destruction, whereas the copy, the duplicate, the *jugaad*, continues to accrue in value through its constant reproduction.[33]

In the second archival event, the secretary's caution around the inherent "falseness" of the caste certificate (we have trouble proving who we are, as the secretary notes) does not summon unreliability as a salvational resolution; rather, his provocation (we make, you believe) captures the transactive value immanent in the evidentiary form. As such, the call to make.believe seeks less to free the caste certificate from its evidentiary referent (caste) than to corrupt the referent with a mimicry that can then, when the Samaj asserts itself as lower caste, be revealed as a ruse. Caste emerges as an open-ended fiction, not of bounded life but of an ongoing oppressive present, full of imperfection and fantasy. It is solely through such an understanding that the desired caste certificate can perform its proper transactive function, which is to signify not just alliance but the deeper and more contradictory attachments to the institutions exemplified in that alliance: family and reproduction. When the secretary invites the woman into an imagined collectivity brokered through sexuality (we make, you believe), he scripts presence outside the bureaucratic forms of judicially sanctioned life. No proof needed—we make it up as we go. These observations take hold of caste in a new way: caste is achieved now by dissolution, by the very annulment of its form. The caste certificate becomes a radical invention of solidarity, an attachment to community, and an experimental vernacular of self-making.

The two archival events also speak directly to the ways that minoritized collectivities assemble archival technologies of presence and absence (what I am calling make.believe) to bypass our attempts to make coherent the heady confluence of uneven imaginings and longings that comprise the lives of caste and sexuality. After all, we live in a moment (especially in South Asia) where the 2018 repeal of Section 377 (the so-called antisodomy statute) and the 2014 NALSA (*National Legal Services of India v. Union of India*) judgment highlights the complex journey of gay, lesbian, and trans emergence.[34] That is, the success of these legal judgments foregrounds once more the maligned yet desired access-for-progress model (to have these rights we must cede to made-up judicial verities of identity (gay, lesbian, trans) that are rarely commensurate with lived experiences.[35] Juxtapose these efforts with the rising ranks of lower-caste/OBC communities (from the Bhandaris in Goa to the Marathas in Maharashtra and the Jats in Haryana, mockingly marked as the "haves who want more" or the "creamy layer") who clamor for rights that are currently reserved for ESBC classes (i.e., economic and socially backward classes) who in turn may or may not also be classified as OBC.[36] At the heart of these struggles is an uncertainty, a foundational unreliability in how evidentiary regimes guarantee forms of legal, economic, and social freedom. If we cannot prove (without legal doubt) the exchange value of caste and sex, how can we then transact a liberatory project? But before I delve any further, I need to first bring you closer to the historical stage on which my questions unfold. What and where is this subaltern archive of sexuality that promises abundance and courts the freedom of make.believe?

COME. AGAIN.

Even the most thorough historical study fears getting into trouble, less with the histories it is displacing or decentering than through what might be perceived as an overall lack of "proper" evidence. Nothing expresses this convention better within a history of a minoritized collectivity than an inherently paradoxical archival economy, at once empty and therefore full. An essential characteristic of such conventions is that the history far exceeds the official archives within which it is circumscribed. That is, the "absence" within official archives attests to the collectivity's enduring historical "presence" and necessitates the concomitant search for missing and lost archives. In what follows, I hope to recalibrate such habits of historical writing, to shift the emphases away from what is missing toward a recognition of what is. The history of the Samaj, I will offer here, satisfies a double exigency: how to produce abundance entirely outside any official and/or state archive and, at the same time, how to preserve the effects of that archive within its own productions.

Members of the Gomantak Maratha Samaj, also referred to as *kalavants* (literally, carriers of *kala* [art]), are a devadasi diaspora that shuttled between Portuguese and British colonial India for over two hundred years, challenging European epistemologies of race and rule through their inhabitation in two discrepant empires. For scholars such as Rosa Maria Pérez, there is much confusion around what constitutes a devadasi under Portuguese rule, especially given the variegated and often competing references to "*bailadeiras*" (dancing girls) and "devadasis" within largely Catholic Goan sources including ecclesiastical and administrative documents, travel accounts, essays, literature, and poetry.[37] Central to such formulations is the force of Portuguese conversion campaigns that often collapsed all Hindu ritual practices into a larger arena of excess and eroticism. However, in her rush to rescue devadasis from the detritus of Portuguese colonialism and to return them to their former (Hindu) histories and cultural formations, Pérez conveniently glosses over similar atrocities committed against devadasis by Hindu and other local elites.

Interestingly, one of the few substantial accounts of the Goan bailadeiras appears not in a Portuguese source but in an 1851 travelogue by the infamous British spy/ethnopornographer Sir Richard Burton. Burton's interest in the "beautiful *Bayaderes*" situates them in the famed town of "Seroda" (now Shiroda), within a climate of Portuguese imperial decline and moral excess.[38] These "Bayaderes" are lapsed "high caste maidens," who interestingly have no ostensible ties to deity or creed. As Burton writes: "Having been compelled to eat beef by the 'tyrannical Portuguese in the olden time,' [they] had forfeited the blessings of Hindooism, without acquiring those of Christianity."[39] Yet "Seroda" then (as today) is described as a "Hindoo town," containing "about twenty establishments, and a total number of fifty or sixty dancing girls," some of whom read and write "Sanscrit shlokas" and speak a "corrupt form of Maharatta called Concanee."[40] Throughout his descriptions of the "Bayaderes," Burton routinely uses the terms *bayadere*, "*nautch*" *girl*, and *dancing girl* interchangeably, thus effacing the distinctions between the different terms in Goa. *Bayadere* is a term exclusively used to describe Goan "dancing girls," whereas the terms *nautch* and *dancing girl* function more as pan–British Indian categories, covering a range of regions and linguistic cultures.⁴¹

On the one hand, Burton's account of the Goan "bayaderes" can be written off as yet another instance of his prurient interest in all things carnal and exotic. On the other hand, Burton's description of these "bayaderes" could also provide us with a complex prehistory to the emergence of the devadasi Gomantak Maratha Samaj in Goa. "Seroda"—or Shiroda, as the city is now known—was and continues to be one of the central locations for devadasi congregation in colonial and postcolonial India. At the center of this "Hindoo town" lies the temple of Kamakshi or Shanta Durga, the goddess of peace, which housed on its premises many generations of devadasis.⁴² Unlike the noted "bayaderes," the devadasis in Shiroda were not known for their dancing skills but were instead lauded for their prowess as musical kalavants (artists) and were never lapsed "high caste maidens." Whether the devadasis of Shiroda were distinct from the "bayaderes" of Burton's Seroda is of less consequence than their historical entanglement within a diverse range of colonial texts and sources.⁴³

Postcolonial histories of Goan devadasis rarely engage with the nominal replacement of *devadasi* with more fraught terms such as *nautch girl* and/or *dancing girl*. Instead, the focus is more on constructing genealogies of caste and labor that fix devadasis within a longer history of Brahminic despotism. As the story goes, the Goan Saraswats (a Brahmin subgrouping) were historically the primary patrons of the devadasis and devised a structure that demarcated kalavants who were either *ghanis* (singers) or *nachnis* (dancers) or both, *bhavnis* (women who attended to temple rituals), or *fulkars* (flower collectors). Of significance here is that *both* men and women did menial and physical labor on the farmlands of the Saraswat Brahmins and the Mahajans (elders associated with religious institutions) and were named *chede* or *bande*, literally bodies tied to the land. Included within the Goan devadasi structure were also *Chadde farjand* or *frejent*, a Persian term that literally means "boy" but is principally applied to sons of single mothers who had sex with their employers. These latter groups of boys were referred to as *deuli* (male members of the Bhavin class) and were situated lower than the kalavants within the devadasi substructures.⁴⁴

According to one theory, Goan devadasis were no different from their counterparts in the Deccan region in function and history. Another account provides a different history of enslavement and labor by suggesting that the devadasis were brought to Goa by the migration of Saraswat Brahmins who came in search of fertile lands and sustenance. The term *Gomantak*, for instance, is the Sankritized toponomic of the state of Goa and denotes the prosperity of its cattle herds. The irony, however, is that the region of Goa is geographically and topographically not suited for cattle rearing, and the term clearly references the nomadic Brahmins who came to its shores in search of lands and resources. Within the latter theory of enslavement and labor, devadasis were primarily "chattel," enslaved workers, whose services shifted into regimes of sex and art after their migration into foreign lands. The earliest official mention of the existence of devadasis as a social group appears in the Goa census of 1904. Of note is the careful demarcation of subgroups within the larger community; the first figure lists the number of males recorded under the category, and the second lists the number of females:

> Males: Females
> Kalavants 305: 420
> Devlis 4615: 4051
> Bhandis [Slaves] 3752: 4099
> Adbaktis [half slaves] 900: 1881[45]

The Gomantak Maratha Samaj, the focus of our study here, draws its members from such complex groupings of Goan devadasis. If the restoration of the devadasi archive has relied on a lost or maligned avatar of sexuality, the archive of the Gomantak Maratha Samaj, by contrast, denaturalizes any such presumptive understanding of the devadasi's customary forms, particularly under colonialism. In many ways, the Samaj turns to its own archives to articulate the question of sexuality, not by displacing it but by folding sexuality into the lineages through which it travels. Tracing its roots back to early eighteenth-century Goa, the Gomantak Maratha Samaj is an OBC (Other Backward Castes) community and was established as a formal organization in 1927 and 1929 in the western states of Goa and Maharashtra, respectively. It officially became a charitable institution in 1936. The Samaj continues its activities to this day and has from its inception maintained a community of ten thousand to fifty thousand registered members. Unlike oft-circulated histories of devadasis in South Asia that lament the disappearance or erasure of devadasis, the history of the Samaj offers no telos of loss and recovery. Instead, the Samaj, from its inception, has maintained a continuous, copious, and accessible archive of its own emergence, embracing rather than disavowing its past and present attachments to sexuality.

Counter to well-documented histories of reform, particularly in southern India, this community's story in Portuguese Goa underwent very little transformation and exposure until the early part of the twentieth century. Members of the Samaj, unlike the devadasi figurations in southern India, rarely wed deities and were not "prostitutes" in any conventional sense of the word. Rather, these devadasis were mostly female singers, classically trained, placed through ceremonies like *hath-lavne* (touching hands) into companionate structures with both men and women. Only occasionally do we find references to dedications to deities through rituals such as the *shens* ceremony. And even then, the ceremony appears more as a proxy wedding in which a girl who is to be dedicated to a god or goddess is wed to a (surrogate) groom, always represented by another girl dressed as a man and holding a coconut and a knife.

Portuguese colonial officials also granted Samaj members exemption from antiprostitution laws, primarily because they remained in structures of serial monogamy, supported by *yajemans*, both male and female, who functioned as patrons and partners through the life of the Samaj subject. The Samaj members were also crucially sworn to remain in the spatial proximity of temples, whether or not they performed ritual temple roles. One curious feature of such arrangements was that children born to Goan devadasis were often given gender-neutral names that made accession of inheritance (particularly land) less judicially contentious, especially after the death of a particular yajeman, or patron. With the passage of the antidevadasi acts, many members gradually made their way to urban spaces like Bombay in search of work in the newly emergent Hindi film industry. The success of the Samaj was not restricted to the arts; it extended to fields of science, literature, and philosophy.[46]

Often referred to as Bharatatil ek Aggressor Samaj (an aggressive community in India), this devadasi diaspora is now routinely lauded (by the left *and* the right in India) for its self-reform and progress. From the immortal Mangeshkar sisters (Lata and Asha) to the first chief minister of independent Goa, Dayanand Bandodkar, there are few sectors of Indian society where the presence of Samaj members cannot be felt.[47] In obvious ways, the presence of this vibrant devadasi diaspora in western India (spliced as it is between the borders of two competing colonial projects) disrupts established histories of sexuality through its survival and geography and holds great potential for a differentiated model of historiography. Devadasis are studied more in southern India, and rarely in western India. We have here the regional twist:[48] studies of sexuality and colonialism have overwhelmingly focused on the affective and temporal weight of British India, with Portuguese India lurking as the accidental presence in the landscape of colonialism (despite the startling fact that the Portuguese occupied Goa for nearly 451 years), so we have here a South-South colonial comparison.[49] And last but not least, Goan historiography itself, long written off as an underdeveloped and undertheorized kin of Indian historiography, could find new flesh within the lineaments of the radical history of the Samaj. As one scholar writes, it is time for Goan history to move beyond a "kind of absence," to brush aside the "shadows that obstruct our attempt to access, retrieve and understand" our past.[50] Yet even as such comparative modes (regional, South-South) enrich our understanding of sexuality's pasts, they could equally function in ways that are perilously additive, minoritizing the very histories they seek to make visible. That is, the story of the Samaj must not function as a singular parable of cathartic potentiality, nor of an abjured geopolitics, resolving historical ambivalence or loss through its success and emergence. Rather, I will argue, the archives of the Samaj must be read as examples of catachresis, as incitements to analytical reflection that produce more robust idioms of the historical.

It is important to note first that there are multiple registers of archival representation at work within the history of the Samaj. On the one hand, there are public archives of vocal performances (many Samaj members have been classical singers, and the group continues to constitute an impressive who's who of classical singers in South Asia) that are available and widely disseminated.[51] Yet such archives are largely generated by non-Samaj members and rarely include information or references on the membership of these singers to the Samaj, and they routinely elide any attachment to histories of sexuality. Mostly hagiographical in nature, these archives of voice and sound have been routinely utilized to address the centrality of the kalavants within traditions of Hindustani classical music. Indeed, the energetic circulation of these archives by scholars of South Asian classical music and music aficionados in general has guaranteed that the presence of the Samaj endures in public view.[52]

Alternatively, the Samaj's own archives are massively messy, and contain multiple genres of archival records in Marathi, Konkani, and Portuguese, ranging from minutes of meetings to journals, private correspondence, flyers, and programs, replete with the minutiae of everyday life in the Samaj.

Such efflorescence appears startling, almost jarring, pushing against archival expectations of absence and erasure. The Samaj archives are housed in open collections in brick-and-mortar buildings in Bombay and Panaji and have always been available for public viewing since their formation in 1929. I have spent the last fifteen years or so reading and sitting with the materials in the Samaj archives and have as yet read, at most, about 50 to 60 percent of the available materials.[53] In fact, the Samaj's incitement to archive, as previously mentioned, is surpassed only by its startling disinterest in the preservation and circulation of the very materials it continuously produces. A researcher's or even a curious visitor's request for rare materials is met with relative ease (a feat for anyone working in archives in India!), as one is directed to the archives without fanfare, and often with a cup of hot chai to accompany one's reading.[54]

A second key feature of the Samaj archives is the relative paucity of "veracity" genres such as memoirs, testimonials, and biographies. Indeed, the only available biography, to this day, remains Rajaram Rangoji Paigankar's *Mee kon (Who Am I?)* (1969), whose storyline (as we shall see in a later chapter) is itself mired in the production of a foundational fiction.[55] The privileged archival genre is fiction, written by Samaj members, in the form of short stories, serialized novels, and novellas that take center stage in the Samaj's self-fashioning project. Fiction provides the vitalizing properties of the archive, deliberately rerouting the demand for archival presence, from conventional evidentiary forms to more imaginative modes of representation. Here the "truth" of the Samaj is not what is at stake; rather, what matters are the genres of self-fashioning. These writings (mostly anonymous) appear in the monthly journal *Samaj Sudharak* (1929 to this day) and are heavily didactic in content, encompassing issues such as education, marriage, devadasi reform, the perils of prostitution, caste shame, travel, contraception, sports, and even the evils of gossip.[56]

More confounding still is the Samaj's relationship to principles of archival provenance and circulation. That is, how does the Samaj's archive become visible and gather value, mediating the imaginative leap, as David Squires points out in a different context, from "historical record to historical truth"? For Squires, even as histories of sexuality embrace the munificent returns of the archival turn, less attention is paid to the material organization of archives, their evidentiary genres, and the multiple problems of access and circulation.[57] As I noted earlier, the archives of the Samaj have not been read, circulated, or memorialized beyond a repeated reference to the glories of the Samaj's success as an aggressive, self-reforming collectivity. Such a historical elision is particularly telling because there is no mystery surrounding access to the archives, no governmental bureaucracies to accommodate. In the story of the Samaj, archival surplus repeats itself in a historical calculus so minor, so unspectacular, that it does not appear to excite historical recuperation. As a historian colleague once asked me with great exasperation, Why is this not just a failed archive? If it has not been read and is so evidently available, surely there must be nothing there. The Samaj's provenance thus marks both archival abundance and historical minoritization: it is both removed from the archival mandates that govern minoritized histories and, at the same time, intimately acquainted with them and their most subtle efforts on history-writing.

KEEPING COMPANY

My efforts amplify recent scholarship within caste, slavery, and Indigenous studies that has also chosen to refuse the mandate of a "show and tell" and/or "lost and found" historical script. That these trenchant challenges to our consumption of times past have overwhelmingly come from scholars working on histories of minoritization that are attentive to archival economies of loss, paucity, and/or devaluation is hardly surprising. Echoing early postcolonial and anti-imperial critique, much of this scholarship has pushed back against the repeated demands of a Manichean perspective by drawing attention to the dangerous consolations of a rhetoric of blame, or of a salvific nativism and/or identitarianism. The sterility of established formulations is jettisoned for an intellectual renewal that aspires to supplant a politics tied to structures of paucity and recovery. A runaway poetics is needed, Fred Moten writes, that challenges ascriptions of impoverishment, crafts "a resistance to constraint and instrumentalization," and refuses the constant demand to "perform how mad you are."[58]

At this point, I must underscore that my effort in bringing these divergent strains of scholarship together is openly directed at pushing us to examine our own critical genealogies, along with those we leave aside or dis/engage even in seemingly shared political projects. My assemblage of thinkers and field-formations is thus not meant to suggest compatibility between the works I cite; more than anything, one must mark the convergences and divergences within such an amalgam. For instance, histories of sexuality and slavery in North America engage unevenly with histories of sexuality and slavery in South Asia, despite the obvious convergence of historical and political antecedents. By this I mean not that there has been no acknowledgment of Indian Ocean histories of slavery and sexuality but more that such acknowledgment participates more in a structural economy of affiliation than in a robustly epistemological one. In other words, we understand that slavery existed across spatialities and temporalities, even as we elide what differences in form and content those variegated histories make to the very idea of who and what constitutes a slave. As Indrani Chatterjee reminds us, historians of slavery and sexuality need to liberate themselves from a Eurocentric racial imagination and cultivate "a vision larger than that which takes the plantation as its starting point for imaging slave lives."[59] To not do so is to surrender to the imperialist rhetoric of the nineteenth and twentieth centuries, whose Orientalism literally colors our narratives of the non-West.[60] Such an elision is equally seen within South Asia itself, whereby the Atlantic Ocean model of slavery still holds sway within much contemporary mobilizations of slave histories, complex local histories of slave emergence notwithstanding.[61] All this to say, let us not forge false equivalences between minoritized citational practices and ignore the asymmetries at work within and without.

Within South Asia, such pushback against the demand to proffer evidence of one's historical self is most notably seen within the vibrant field of Dalit studies. Dalit historiography, whether of Dalit actors or their archives, remains scripted, Milind Wakankar writes, as a heroic transition from silence (the horror of caste discrimination) to speech (empowerment as caste communities in electoral stakes). What happens, asks Wakankar, if we think instead on or/of "the cusp," of historiographical traditions? To think on the cusp is to catch a "a form of political will on the make," alluding to the retrospective movement that captures a moment of rupture "that was as yet open to transformation and change."[62] On the one hand, Wakankar argues, the recuperation of the Dalit radical medieval poet—Kabir, for example—installs him as a god, as an original prehistory that grants Dalit pasts a mighty presence, well before the emergence of colonial and/or nationalist caste formations. On the other hand, even as claims to Kabir restore Dalit histories, what falls away are Kabir's attachments to the now-defunct sect, the mythical Kapalikas, who, as silent figures of mourning, violence, and death, provide a more textured prelude to historical genealogies of caste. For Wakankar, to do Dalit historiography on the cusp is to suture speech and silence, to ask for divergence at the very moment of historical rupture and recuperation.

For more polemical scholars such as Kancha Ilaiah, the ascription of loss to Dalit histories derives more stridently from an upper-caste, hegemonic historiographical model that fosters elitist vernaculars of research and legibility, bypassing Dalit modes of historical writing. Illiah refuses such mandates of elitist nationalist historiography in most direct terms: "The methodology and epistemology that I use," Illiah writes in one of his oft-cited essays, "being what they are, the discussion might appear 'unbelievable,' 'unacceptable,' or 'untruthful' to those 'scholars and thinkers' who are born and brought up in Hindu families. Further, I deliberately do not want to take precautions, qualify my statements, footnote my material, nuance my claims, for the simple reason that my statements are not meant to be nuanced in the first place."[63] That Illiah's essay appeared in volume 9 of the heralded Subaltern Studies Series is hardly a coincidence, as its mocking foregrounds the disciplining and disciplinary proclivities of even that politically progressive intellectual project. To that point, Dipesh Chakrabarty (a founding member of the Subaltern Studies Collective and coeditor of that volume) acknowledges the difficulties the collective had in taking Illiah's work seriously: "I still remember the debate among the editorial members of Subaltern Studies that preceded our decision to publish this essay that deliberately—and as a political gesture—flouted all the disciplinary protocols of history and yet claimed to represent the past in a series that was, after all, an academic enterprise."[64]

A second key feature of Illiah's critique (which may in some ways pose even more of a disciplinary threat to Indian historiography) is his indictment of nationalism as the aspirational antidote to the evils of colonialism. Nationalism becomes the desired historical script that promises to restore and redeem the losses incurred (especially by subaltern subjects) through the brutalities of colonialism. Such a binary, Rawat and Satyanarayana remind us in their recent introduction to *Dalit Studies*, discourages any historical study of the vibrant Dalit social and religious reform movements that mobilized the promise of colonial modernity. From "antiuntouchability agitations to temple entry movements, to struggles for access to public space and representations,"[65] Dalit collective action (particularly in the nineteenth and early twentieth centuries), they note, foregrounds anticaste discrimination, often utilizing the colonial state and its frameworks to fashion its demands. Archives of such Dalit mobilizations and more exist across multiple registers, yet they remain unreadable within the annals of nationalist history. Thus, if Dalit histories are now produced as untold or lost in modern Indian history, it is more because they cannot be easily assimilated into the folds of a dominant anticolonial nationalist narrative. Instead, their abundance complicates our narration of the movement of a colonial to postcolonial history, provoking a different and difficult shift in our historiographical orientations to the past.[66]

In a similar vein, scholars of Adivasi and/or tribal historiography in South Asia, such as Prathama Banerjee, signal the paradox of even claiming such a lost history within current nationalist historiographical practices. Here the Adivasi appears as the missing link within narratives of counterinsurgency and policy, or to disappear within the folds of a flawed ethnographic imaginary. While such a historical calculus may well account for the "disappearance" of most subaltern subjects, Banerjee notes that the figure of the Adivasi and/or the tribal (distinct from the Dalit) poses an even more foundational agon. That is, if Adivasis or tribals are "an archaic embodiment of authenticity and radicality, outside of the realm of the modern, who is the subject around which a field such as adivasi studies might coalesce in the first place?"[67] What is there to recover or recuperate if the very historical category of the Adivasi was cultivated to fuel missionary and nationalist discourses of improvement and education? For the colonial and postcolonial state projects to flourish, the Adivasi must remain lost in time and space, enabling the reproduction of the modern as the tribe's necessary other. Yet Banerjee is quick to point out that it is no longer sufficient to simply invoke such a genealogy of construction. After all, construction or not, Adivasis or tribals have been disciplined and governed for over two centuries and have mobilized within the terms of the very category that erased them in the first place.

Similar imperatives surface within Indigenous histories (specifically in North America and Asia Pacific) where the recuperation of "Native" loss is seen as merely reproducing and replicating the homogenizing forces of settler colonialism. As Joanne Barker writes, it is time to suspend deluded forms of historical reading, to rail "against the idea of an indigeneity that was authentic in the past but is culturally and legally vacated in the present." Such ideas of indigeneity, Barker warns, hypostatize a modernist temporality whereby the celebration of a glorious past permits the dismissal and disavowal of a vivid and vast living present. As she says, "It is a past that even Indigenous peoples in headdresses are perceived to honor as something dead and gone."[68] Expanding on such pernicious historical fictions, James Clifford further cautions against the seductions of returns that incite claims of ownership to a past via a "logic of priority." To narrate Indigenous history, within such a logic of priority, is ironically to decenter Indigenous historical practices that "give shape to time that question and expand conventional assumptions."[69]

While Clifford's study roams over broader networks of what he calls a global "*présence indigène*," he foregrounds the urgent need for a different mode of historical "realism" (of ritual, memory, and affect) that engages the living present, provincializing, as it were, the dead language of lost records and archives.[70] Further to this project, scholars such as Audra Simpson have advocated for more foundational shifts in the very ethnographic and historical forms through which we articulate and recover allegedly lost Indigenous knowledge and lands. "To fetishize and entrap and distill indigenous discourses into memorizable, repeatable rituals for preservation against a social and political death that was foretold but did not happen," she writes, is to tread the territories of the (dangerously) familiar. Instead, Simpson invokes a different order of knowing, or what "no one seems to know," where the demands for recognition, political life, and identity were all instantiated in refusals.[71]

Nowhere has the recuperation for a lost past seemed more palpable than within histories of Atlantic slavery. As the editors of a recent *Social Text* special issue on the question of recovery and slavery note, the limits of recovery in "the field of Atlantic slavery and freedom" have reshaped the very parameters of historical methods and debate.[72] Indeed, nearly every theoretical account of Atlantic slavery stages the historiography of slavery as the place where absence and archive meet.[73] A similar reading of archival loss, paucity, and erasure even animates scholarship that challenges the foundationalism of Atlantic slavery as the "origin story" for the African diaspora.[74] For scholars such as Jennifer Morgan, the enduring seductions of statistical empiricism concatenate such attachments to loss. Even as Morgan lauds efforts to develop crucial research databases such as the Trans-Atlantic Slave Trade Database (TSTD) that have led to new research on the contours and dimensions of the slave trade, she also remains "troubled by this kind of archival construction."[75] After all, data accumulation and modes of quantification in general, Morgan cautions us, remain enmeshed within the logic of the very "technology by which Africans are rendered as outside the scope of Man." That historians still remain continually struck by the difficulty of accessing counterfactual "evidence" of the slave past puzzles Morgan, especially as the records we do have were created primarily to shore up the commercial aspects of the slave trade. Morgan reminds us that histories of gender and slavery are further erased in databases such as

TSTD because ship captains rarely kept records according to sex ratio. As such, the multitude of experiences women had on these slave ships remains unmapped, undocumented, and thus transacted as archival loss.[76]

The historical inheritance of loss, as is now obvious, is formidably recursive and iterative. Loss and paucity provide the warp and woof of a better future, all the more so when they carry the promise that if such deficits are erased, we, who are subjected to both, can somehow be redeemed. And in every plangent iteration of this promise, the burdens of minoritization paradoxically demand archives and histories that must equally proffer arguments for their own survival. Under these conditions, when minoritized subjects have so effectively absorbed *and* struggled with the lineaments of loss, it becomes even more urgent to ask: What kind of historiography do we want? A historiography, I would respond, that breaks with such moribund conventions and summons more abundant and joyful lineages of possibility and freedom.

MADE TO ORDER

My book refuses the conventional reading of South Asia as a region that provides local historical avatars for Euro-American histories of sexuality. Instead, I ask, what would histories of sexuality look like if interrogated as histories of regions and/or "areas"? As such, the book equally offers a broader meditation on the politics and poetics of sexuality, geopolitics, and historiography. Even as South Asia, a fabular geography, provisions the possibility of archival abundance, it remains convened through epistemology rather than exemplarity. Individual chapters thus are composed through the ambit of the archives of the Gomantak Maratha Samaj, its torsioned histories, summoning us into worlds of make.believe, than to readings of geopolitical certitude. Each chapter speaks to the places where historiographical conventions and genres get stuck, go awry, or simply fold back into recursive habits of search and rescue. The structure of the book is organized around three concepts that have increasingly become the foci of debates within histories of sexuality: archives (what constitutes historical evidence), exemplarity (how we read evidence), and geopolitics (where we read from).

My first chapter, "In the Absence of Reliable Ghosts," serves both as a summation of the issues outlined thus far and as a lead-in to the broader trajectories of the book. For anyone who works within historical archives, it would come as no surprise that any hegemonic text making confident claims to historical truth will be destabilized and exceeded by the operations of counter-archives, counter-stories that disrupt any and all ideological projects being advanced. Such a critical understanding, however, does not as easily extend to minoritized archives, where the "subversion/resistance hypothesis" (despite or perhaps because of the contaminations of Foucault and Subaltern studies) continues to function as difference's most consequential and enticing effect. The aura and/or seduction of resistance stubbornly lingers, suturing subaltern archives to an oppositional imperative. Even the most rigorous intentions to the contrary have not prevented the demand for a veracity archive that promises such desired radicality for histories of minoritized collectivities. What happens, I ask, if we are confronted instead with an archive of sexuality that eschews the consolations of veracity genres (such as memoirs, testimonials, and biographies), for the promise of more imaginative genres of representation? The orchestrated refusal of the Samaj to conform to representational archival forms, even as it continues to produce an efflorescence of materials, embraces the very paradox it engenders: the archive remains a central value-form, even as its radical transformation is continually demanded. The revelatory veracity of the archive gives way to a revelatory labor that eschews transparency and celebrates its own continuous (non)production.

My second chapter, "A History I Am Not Writing," explores what exemplifying readings of the Samaj records mean for the way we encounter archives, particularly archives of sexuality. What makes something an archival exemplar, adequate to the challenge of representation and study? Why does the writing of a history of sexuality take a particular narrative form (specifically in British and Portuguese India), and what creates obstacles to its seamless storytelling? I focus on one such narrative ritual that continues to inaugurate most historiographical projects of sexuality: the problem event, the detail, the legal case—in other words, an archival trace that compresses or even obfuscates historical content, legible only through reconstructive hermeneutics. For scholars working at the interstices of sexuality and subalternity, such as myself, the problem event could offer glimpses of a lost history, the scarcity of historical evidence countered by the hermeneutical performance of plenitude as you mine the archival trace for the promise of historical precedence and futurity. The incitement of my chapter title, "A History I Am Not Writing," calls for a more paradoxical labor: to read the archival exemplar precisely for what it cannot hold. What is on offer here is not a stabilizing recuperation of historical detail but more an exhortation to think the archival exemplar as an absorbing and abundant discursive presence, reassembled through our every reading. Bypassing the seductive heroics of recuperative historiography, this chapter proffers a different pathway to historical presence.

My third chapter, "Itinerant Sex," interrogates how histories of region constitute robust histories of sexuality and what critical lessons are to be learned from such a shift in historical orientation. How do histories of sexuality trouble the heightened divide between the de/colonial and the post/colonial turn? Eschewing the conventional segregation of spatialities (Latin American studies versus South Asian studies) that often undergirds the force of the decolonial turn, this chapter engages the emergence of the Samaj in the fraught contexts of colonial Portuguese India. In so doing, I pose one central historiographical question: How do the vernaculars, temporalities, and spatialities that make "sex" intelligible as object and archive summon itinerant geopolitical forms (Portuguese in South Asia) that are often left behind? Itinerant sex calls for historiographical forms that muddle the theoretical pathways that suture geopolitics to forms (refused or otherwise) of region, area, nation.

Spatially split between British India and Portuguese India, the available archival records of the Samaj outline the peculiar geopolitical challenges its members face as sex workers who travel between regions. Samaj members express concern with the demands for national belonging and wrestle more with their place within and outside such regional formations. Even as Samaj records (minutes, editorials, judicial and property records) demonstrate a resistance to upper-caste/Brahmin hegemony, there is no evidence of any involvement in the burgeoning liberation movements in British or Portuguese India (India gains independence in 1947, and Goa is liberated in 1961). Indeed, the early absence of any collective involvement by the Samaj in the resistance movements outside of their local interests speaks to yet another twist in the tale of the Samaj. In fact, one of the recursive and fascinating features of this Samaj's history of sexuality is its refusal or rather sidelining of any regional attachment, outside of its own formation. Instead of laying claim to geography as established historical value, the Samaj, as I will demonstrate, strategically mobilizes the politics, desires, and identities made possible by the reach of geopolitics.

The book ends with a short coda, "I Am Not Your Data: Caste, Sexuality, Protest," an experimental fragment that excerpts three scenes of abundant reading in postcolonial India: from recent protests by trans/queer activists in India against the 2019 discriminatory Citizens Amendment

Act, to the radical attenuation of caste amid the dogged brutality of the current pandemic. Each scene translates histories of caste and sexuality as remaindered evidentiary forms, ongoing refutations of clarity and easy categorization.

IMPERATIVE

My meditations do not focus, as is clear by now, on archives that can be considered explicitly homosexual or transgender. Neither am I invested in extracting queer value from lost histories of sexuality within the sprawling landscape of an ever-changing South Asia. Rather, my turn to abundance as heuristic speaks to a nonrecuperative history of sexuality that embraces presence without return or the fear of loss. To theorize a history of abundance is not to be restored to value but, rather, to be set adrift upon more intrepid economies of meaning—sometimes harmonious, sometimes dissonant—that come together to upend genealogies of historical recuperation and representation.

And finally, this book, more than anything I have previously written, is the thick subjective effect of a history as it has been lived. The past is not only usable here but always somewhere close at hand. I grew up within the bawdy, colorful, and expansive lower-caste politics of the Gomantak Maratha Samaj, and it is those familial genealogies that first opened me up to the urgencies of archives and politics. My questions thus emanate from those intimacies; they are of them, but not about them. Contravening the protocols of reproduction (whether of collectivity, family, caste) was not just a familiar feature of my Samaj life but also a profoundly political matter. One's history was not a place of capture; it was a compositional lexicon of self-making, to be continuously taught, modulated, inhabited, and shed. I can do no better than to tell that story.

NOTES

1. I borrow the phrase "inescapable surfeit" from Teju Cole's focus on the constant incitement to photograph, to document the surfaces of the worlds we inhabit. "Take lots of photographs," he writes, is the mantra of a good account. See Cole, "Finders Keepers," 176–80.
2. Some sample texts include Arunima, *There Comes Papa*; Kapur, *Erotic Justice*; and Dave, *Queer Activism in India*.

3   See Chatterjee, "When 'Sexualities' Floated Free of Histories in South Asia."
4   I am imputing a certain relationality to the thinkers named, even though they may not always conceive themselves as constituting a cohort. I do not mean to suggest here that Edelman, Love, and Halberstam are uncritically recuperating languages of loss, lack, and failure, or that they are to be read as simply fungible within my conceptual formulation. Edelman, for instance, continually emphasizes a nonredemptive understanding of sex through his theorizations of negativity and the antisocial. My point here is each of their projects speaks (with varied degrees of success) to new imaginaries within queer theorizations of temporality and affect. I mean to draw attention more to the persistence of dominant forms of queer reading circulating around structuring tropes of loss, lack, and failure. See Edelman, *No Future*; Edelman, "Ever After"; and Halberstam, *Queer Art of Failure*. José Muñoz's landmark *Cruising Utopia*, for example, draws on queer of color critique to fashion imaginaries of reparation and renewal, distinct from a teleology of redemption, that would allay the injuries of the past through a "utopian" memorialization. See Muñoz, *Cruising Utopia*.
5   There is a literal cottage industry of texts on the potentiality of melancholia as a productive conceptual structure for thinking gender, sexuality, and difference. For example, see Eng and Kazanjian, *Loss*.
6   See Goldberg and Menon, "Queering History"; Love, *Feeling Backward*; Freeman, *Time Binds* and "Still After."
7   Fuss, *Dying Modern*, 4.
8   When I first began to give public talks on this project, I was often reminded by well-meaning and often concerned colleagues in the US academy that I was speaking from a privileged position—that as a tenured professor in a research institution, I had no idea of how people suffered in those distant elsewheres. To dismiss loss was to dismiss the very persistence of economic inequities, I was told. The irony of such presumptions about myself notwithstanding, I was struck by how the very insistence of such reminders was precisely the point I was trying to make. But more on that later . . .
9   Berlant, *Cruel Optimism*. Berlant's opus, among many other weighty questions, speaks to the ethical conditions of nonpossibility under which minoritized subjects carve their relationship to the world. For a careful genealogy of the proliferation of the concept of precarity, see also Nyong'o, "Situating Precarity between the Body and the Commons."
10 See Povinelli, *Economies of Abandonment*, 3–4, and "The Woman on the Other Side of the Wall." See also Deer, "Beyond Recovery."
11 Patel, *Risky Bodies and Techno-Intimacy*, 18, 48. Patel writes that "double binds . . . show up with such assiduous, diligent, banal consistency, like

the old uncle who always arrives at every wedding with the same parcel of ageing hoary jokes."

12   I am of course drawing from James Clifford's important argument around modes of "salvage ethnography" in his essay "On Ethnographic Allegory."

13   Stephen Best makes an exemplary case for pushing against the melancholic attachments to the history of slavery. See Best, "On Failing to Make the Past Present." See also Crawford, "The Twenty-First-Century Black Studies Turn to Melancholy."

14   Hannu Salmi calls for a "principle of plenitude" within historiographical writing, inspired through scientific models of "black-hole research." Drawing from such a model, a historian must speculate about the infinite traces surrounding a (lost but present) object that cannot be seen, but which must in many ways be "invented." See Salmi, "Cultural History, the Possible, and the Principle of Plenitude."

15   For an excursus on the relationship between sexuality and archival hermeneutics, see A. Arondekar, *For the Record*.

16   For more on the work of race, sexuality, and incommensurability within the United States, see Muñoz, "Race, Sex, and the Incommensurate."

17   For Subaltern studies scholars, such as Dipesh Chakrabarty, the subaltern's incommensurability emerged from their unreadability, from their "archaic" and "religious/mythical" attachments to nonelitist modes of historical survival. To attribute value to subaltern historiography was to make way for multiple modes of historical writing that would take such attachments seriously. See Chakrabarty, "Subaltern Studies in Retrospect and Reminiscence."

18   See A. Arondekar, "Thinking Sex *with* Geopolitics." The piece is a response to Traub, *Thinking Sex with the Early Moderns*.

19   Hayot, *On Literary Worlds*.

20   Tadiar, "Ground Zero," 174.

21   Spivak, *Critique of Postcolonial Reason*.

22   Arondekar and Patel, "Area Impossible."

23   Povinelli, "Radical Worlds."

24   See Gramling and Dutta, "Translating Transgender," special issue, *TSQ*, 3. See also DeVun and Tortorici, "Trans, Time, and History"; and Rizki, "Trans-, Translation, Transnational."

25   Reiter, *Constructing the Pluriverse*. See also Chen, *Asia as Method*.

26   See Chiang and Wong, "Asia Is Burning."

27   Macharia, "Queer African Studies."

28   I am thinking here of early feminist work in South Asia, which provided many of the theoretical vernaculars that have become the mainstay of histories of gender and sexuality for contemporary scholars. See, among others, Sinha, *Colonial Masculinity*; Visweswaran, *Fictions of Feminist Ethnography*; Tharu, "The Impossible Subject-Caste and the Gendered

Body"; Oldenburg, "Lifestyle as Resistance"; John and Nair, *A Question of Silence?*; Sangari and Vaid, *Recasting Women*; and Mani, *Contentious Traditions*.

29 There is a (bracketed) prehistory to my lifelong tussle with the logic of returns. As a child I often visited a Catholic cemetery near my grandmother's house in Girgaum in South Mumbai. Given the paucity of open spaces for children to play freely in that area, my cousins and I often wandered over to the cemetery, which provided us with the rare luxury of space and exploration. We were surrounded by headstones, marked by scattered details of the lives of strangers, always framed with the invocation "RIP." As lower-caste Hindus (lapsed or otherwise) and staunch converts to the doctrine of reincarnation, RIP always read to us as an active "Return If Possible," not the sanctuary of a place of rest!

30 Saksena, Seth, and Biswas, "Study on Issue of False Scheduled Caste / Scheduled Tribe Certificates," 102.

31 Gatade, "Phenomenon of False Caste Certificates."

32 There is of course much more to be said about debates around the push toward digitalization. On the one hand, as Brian Connolly asks (particularly in research on nineteenth-century North American history), does the digital availability of multiple archival genres of evidence produce a new and more problematic empiricism? Does the access to archives overdetermine the value ceded to written materials and more? On the other hand, literary scholars of early modern Europe, such as Elizabeth Williamson, speak to the limits of digitalization within early modern histories of accumulation and access: How does it cover over the gaps, or erase the abundance of multiple reading practices? While both Connolly and Williamson make sound cases for the limits of digitalization, I do have to note with some irony here that for most archives in the global South, digitalization is not even an option open for consideration. See Connolly, "Against Accumulation"; Williamson, "Abundance and Access"; and Balachandran, "Documents, Digitisation and History." For a discussion of the challenges of digitalization and access in South Asia, see "State of the Archive," *Archive and Access* (blog), https://publicarchives.wordpress.com/state-of-the-archive-2/.

33 Navaro-Yashin, "Make-Believe Papers, Legal Forms and the Counterfeit."

34 The 2014 NALSA case judgment led to the recognition of transgender people as the "third gender" by the Supreme Court of India, affirming that the fundamental rights granted under the Constitution of India would equally extend to them. However, the terms of such judicial recognition have yet to translate materially for most transgender subjects who continue to survive in conditions of economic and social precarity. See https://thewire.in/gender/over-two-years-after-landmark-judgment-transgender-people-are-still-struggling.

35 For excellent analyses, see Bhan, "For All That We May Become"; and Dutta, "Contradictory Tendencies."
36 To understand the complications of caste verifiability and discrimination in postcolonial India, see, for example, Daniyal, "As BJP MP Mounts 'Creamy Layer' Revolt against His Party, What Is Modi Government Thinking?"
37 Pérez, "The Rhetoric of Empire."
38 R. F. Burton, *Goa and the Blue Mountains*, 118–35.
39 R. F. Burton, *Goa and the Blue Mountains*, 119.
40 R. F. Burton, *Goa and the Blue Mountains*, 125.
41 See entries for "bayadere," "nautch girl," and "dancing girl" in Yule and Burnell, *Hobson-Jobson*.
42 Amita Kanekar provides a detailed demystification of the so-called pillage and rescue of Goan temples during Portuguese colonial rule and beyond. See Kanekar, "Architecture, Nationalism, and the Fleeting Heyday of the Goan Temple."
43 Sarkar, "Dedication to the Altar," 145–51.
44 Kakodkar, "The Portuguese and Kalavants." I am grateful to Dr. Kakodkar, senior librarian (retired) at Goa University, for her invaluable help in locating crucial sources on Kalavants in the Historical Archives of Goa. She is the only scholar who has yet worked extensively on cataloguing the history of the Gomantak Maratha Samaj.
45 Sa, "Here Lived Batabai."
46 Kakodkar, "Devadasis of Goa." While female singers such as Moghubai Kurdikar, Kesarbai Kerkar, Lata Mangeshkar, and Kishori Amonkar remain the best-known Gomantak Maratha Samaj members, others of note include the first composer of Marathi musical drama, Hirabai Pednekar; a former chief minister of Goa, Shashikala Kakodkar; and Sulochana Katkar, retired president of the Goa Congress.
47 For more historical detail on the emergence of the Samaj, see A. Arondekar, "Subject to Sex." Other texts that gloss briefly on the history of the Samaj include Bhobe, *Kalavant Gomantak*; Khedekar, *Gomantak Lok Kala*; and Satoskar, *Gomantak Prakriti ani Sanskriti*. For the most recent hagiographical study of the Samaj, see Verenkar, *Prerarna Rukh*.
48 There is a small and well-cited set of writings on the cultural history of devadasis in southern India. Some key texts include Srinivasan, "Temple 'Prostitution' and Community Reform"; Kersenboom-Story, *Nityasumaṅgalī-Devadasi Tradition in South India*; Kamble, *Devadasi ani Nagnapuja*; Shankar, *Devadasi Cult*; Marglin, *Wives of the God-King*; Chakraborthy, *Women as Devadasis*; Ramberg, *Given to the Goddess*; and Soneji, *Unfinished Gestures*.
49 Goa's official liberation came on December 19, 1961, when the Indian army moved in against the Portuguese garrisons as part of Operation

Vijay. Yet this late "liberation" by and into the Indian state did not come without a fair share of controversy and resentment. For many Goan historians and nationalists, Prime Minister Nehru's "soft policy" against the dictatorship of Portuguese rule provided late relief and relegated Goa to an extended state of historical stasis and neglect. See Shirodkar, *Goa's Struggle for Freedom*; Deora, *Liberation of Goa, Daman, and Diu*; and Rubinoff, *India's Use of Force in Goa*.

50   Trichur, "Politics of Goan Historiography," 268. For a further sense of the peculiarity of Portuguese colonialism and its afterlife within Goan historiography, see de Sousa Santos, "Between Prospero and Caliban."

51   A small sampling of notable singers from the Samaj between 1930 and 1959 (all women) would include Saroj Welingkar, Tarabai Shirodkar, Saraswati Rane, Kumodini Pednekar, Kesarbai Kerkar, and Mogubai Kurdikar.

52   An excellent example of such elisions is Bakhle's *Two Men and Music*.

53   My first serious research forays into the Samaj archives began in early 2008. I was eager to collect all necessary permissions and authorizations to quote from and/or reprint archival materials as needed. When I brought this question up to the Samaj's board of trustees, the response was again one of consternation. The question of ownership and copyright was not one they had considered, and as such, they were pushed to think of some process that would satisfy academic protocols. After some deliberation, I was asked to submit a letter of request to the Samaj collectivity at large, which would then be published in the monthly Samaj newsletter. The letter (written in Marathi) sought permission to work on the Samaj archives and clearly stated that if any member had objections to my research efforts, he/she/they should notify the board of trustees immediately. After three months had passed and no letter or call of objection was filed, the board of trustees drafted an official note of authorization on their letterhead, granting me permission to read, cite, and reprint any and all part of their archives. My letter of request and the Samaj's letter of permission acceding to my request are now both part of the extant Samaj archives.

54   Historians routinely and understandably expend much energy speaking to the torturous difficulties of accessing materials as they negotiate innumerable bureaucratic political and communal challenges to archival research, specifically in sites such as postcolonial South Asia. See, for instance, A. Burton, *Archive Stories*; and Blouin and Rosenberg, *Archives, Documentation, and Institutions of Social Memory*. In an effort to combat such difficulties, there has been an increasing push among scholars based in South Asia to encourage more open-access and digitalized archives. Such efforts purport to not just remedy questions of access but also endeavor to create an entire alternative imaginary for archival composition. The website *Archives and Access*, launched by scholars such

as Rochelle Pinto et al., is a wonderful example of such efforts: https://publicarchives.wordpress.com/.

55 Henry Scholberg's exhaustive and much-cited work *Bibliography of Goa and the Portuguese in India* lists Paigankar's text as the only available published biography on the social lives of devadasis in Goa (121, listing D148). However, even such an appearance in an erstwhile authoritative bibliography of Goan texts seems staged to garner attention (the entry occupies ten lines—more than any other entry), given the name of the Scholberg's research collaborator in Goa: Mrs. Archana Kakodkar. Kakodkar has spent many years as a senior librarian at the University of Goa and is herself a member of the Gomantak Maratha Samaj.

56 The bulk of the archives are housed at the Gomantak Maratha Samaj Society building in Mumbai, India. In 2004, the Samaj offices were moved from Gomantak Maratha Samaj Sadan, 345 V.P. Road, Bombay 400004 to Sitladevi Co-op. Housing Society Ltd., 7–16/B Wing, D. N. Nagar, New Link Road, Andheri (W), Mumbai 400053. A partial archive can be found at the Gomantak Maratha Samaj, Dayanand Smriti, Swami Vivekanand Marg, Panaji 403001, Goa.

57 Squires, "Roger Casement's Queer Archive," 596.

58 Moten, "Black Optimism / Black Operation." This talk contains many of the observations that were published later in the oft-cited essay "Black Operations."

59 Indrani Chatterjee, "Decolonizing the History of Slavery," work in progress.

60 Chatterjee has made this point repeatedly and poignantly in all her writings. Yet her challenges have not been sufficiently taken up. The sentence cited here is excerpted from a work in progress that provides an overview of slavery and its histories of difference in South Asia.

61 There are, of course, groups like the Dalit Panthers to highlight histories of the Black Panthers and histories of black resistance that draw from the struggles of "untouchables" in India. But as of now, there is no extant scholarship on the longer historical intersection of the two fields. See A. Arondekar, "What More Remains."

62 Wakankar, "The Question of a Prehistory." Kabir, the feisty progenitor of Dalit politics and protest, gifts a much-desired individuality to the non/human, untouchable Dalit subject through his singular achievements as bard and mystic.

63 For a defining account of the challenges posed by Dalit historiography, see Ilaiah, "Productive Labour, Consciousness, and History," 127–64.

64 Quoted in Chakrabarty, "The Public Life of History," 158.

65 Rawat and Satyanarayana, "Dalat Studies," 10.

66 For a broader review of the shifts in Dalit historiography, see also Jangam, "Dalit Paradigm"; Rege, "'Real Feminism' and Dalit Women"; Paik, "Am-

chya jalmachi chittarkatha (The Bioscope of Our Lives)"; and Pawar and Moon, *We Also Made History*.
67   Banerjee, "Writing the Adivasi," 132. See also Pandey, *Unarchived Histories*.
68   Barker, *Critically Sovereign*, 3.
69   Clifford, *Returns*, 15.
70   Clifford, *Returns*, 13.
71   Simpson, *Mohawk Interruptus*, 99. See also Rifkin's excellent study, *When Did Indians Become Straight*; and Byrd, "'In the City of Blinding Lights.'"
72   Helton et al., "The Question of Recovery," 1.
73   Saidiya Hartman and Tavia Nyong'o, for example, have brilliantly argued (albeit in different registers of fiction and performance) for the sustaining narrative of critical/Afro fabulation. For both, fabulation, in its multiple avatars, emulates, fashions, and enlivens lost "wayward" gendered and performing subjects. For both scholars, the historical inheritance of loss and absence remains the structural force behind any kind of rewriting. See Hartman, "The Anarchy of Colored Girls Assembled in a Riotous Manner"; and Nyong'o, *Afro Fabulations*.
74   Best, "On Failing to Make the Past Present."
75   Morgan, "Accounting for the 'Most Excruciating Torment,'" 188.
76   Morgan, "Accounting for the 'Most Excruciating Torment,'" 188–91. For further reading on the entanglements of archival hermeneutics, gender, and histories of slavery, see Fuentes, *Dispossessed Lives*.

CHAPTER ONE

In the Absence of Reliable Ghosts

Archives

> In the absence of reliable ghosts I made aria,
> Coughing into emptiness, and it came
> A west wind from the plains with its arbitrary arsenal:
> Torn sails from the Ganga river,
> Bits of spurned silk,
> Strips of jute to be fashioned into lines,
> What words stake—sentence and make believe
> A lyric summoning.
>
> —MEENA ALEXANDER, "Birthplace (with Buried Stones)"

One can no longer broach the idea of the archive without a few rehearsals of some settled axioms. We know altogether too well, for instance, that nowhere are the shifts in histories of sexuality, or in historiography writ large, more forcefully displayed than in the recent debates around archives. The archive is *the* value-form of our history of the present. No longer confined to brick-and-mortar state edifices, the revitalization of the archive or the archival turn has meant "more" materials and/or evidence, and a summoning of alternative archival imaginaries. For histories of sexuality of the global South, more significantly, the archive has become a figuration of such allure that it has produced an explosion of materials that roam over genres, geopolitics, histories, cultural experiences, and more. Archives are now collective ambitions, the primary placeholders of futurity and rights.[1]

This chapter arises from my commitment to, and frustration with, the current archival turn.[2] My commitment is to an archival hermeneutic that sutures histories of area to histories of sexuality, without recourse to analogy or structural affiliation. My frustration is that such an enterprise may well be seen as too ambitious, too geopolitically diffuse, to produce any practical method or theory. After all, loss, scarcity and erasure are still metonymically coupled with historical archives of sexuality in the global South—more specifically, in South Asia, as is the case here. Such a coupling has become, if anything, even more emphatic in the postcolonial/ decolonial moment. Even the recent efflorescence of scholarship around histories of sexualities in elsewhere geographies has done little to remedy such a coupling of archival loss with anachronistic geographies (Anne McClintock sharply reminded us of such formulations all those years ago).[3] As my coeditor Geeta Patel and I noted in our special issue for *GLQ: A Journal of Lesbian and Gay Studies*, histories of subaltern sexuality remain an "area impossible," worthy exemplars of itinerant archival forms but bereft of epistemological value.[4]

I have now spent over two decades deliberating on the continued recuperation of the historical archive, grappling throughout with the heightened hermeneutical demands placed on conjoined histories of sexuality and region. It is not just that we read for the lost and devalued archives of sexuality in the global South but that, in the very act of reading, we continue to keep them as such. As I noted in my introduction, if, in my previous work, I focused more on the seductions and occlusions of lost and found archives within subaltern geographies such as South Asia, I am drawn here more to the persistence of archival loss as an origin story for histories of sexuality.[5] Indeed, much of what I will argue invites a movement away from the recursive archival dialectic of fulfillment and impoverishment as the pathway to historical futurity. Two questions are at stake: What happens if minoritized collectivities anticipate such accretions of loss and therefore curate archives that activate the profits that such losses should or will produce? What archives do we summon, I want to ask, "in the absence of (such) reliable ghosts?" Rather than dismiss the pull of loss within sexuality studies, I am pushing for a more strategic and subaltern archival pragmatism, one where we extract value from the hegemonic historical form (lost archives must be resurrected, found, produced for future gains) precisely as we attenuate the very modes of its re/production.

To be sure, such an interest in alternative archival modes of re/production can be seen most vividly within scholarship that mediates histories of slavery and colonialism, and not as much within histories of sexuality. From the re/possession of archives of the enslaved,[6] to archiving the unspeakable, and the dead,[7] to name a select few, there is a discernible shift in the ways we now recuperate and/or materialize minoritized archives of the historical past. The analytics of recursive diagnosis (we know why our histories are not visible) gives way to more generative histories of emergence, most notably within histories of regions and/or areas.[8] Even as Achille Mbembe's oft-cited "chronophagy of the state" (i.e., the state both destroys and creates selective archives of colonial/postcolonial memorialization) continues to hold sway, there is now a more concerted effort to think beyond the damning circularity of that diagnosis.[9] If the colonial state (in all its varied geopolitical and temporal forms) was marked by forms of archival destruction, then one is urged to think post/decoloniality as the promise of reconstruction and reparation. The question of the archive continues to serve as a paradigmatic exemplar both of the abuses of the colonial rule and of the promise of reform its abolition offers.

That archives of minoritized collectivities are often called on to materialize histories of difference in preselected genres and lineages of evidence, in the language of "reliable ghosts," is made even clearer when it comes to "vexed" geopolitical markers such as the Middle East. For historians, such as Omnia El Shakry, the perils of such a colonial "history without documents" in decimated geographies such as the broader Middle East require a closer look at the "compositional logics" of the idea of the archive itself. To script histories of the Middle East is to script histories of archival destruction. Decolonizing such archival imaginaries of perpetual destruction, El Shakry writes, requires that we reassemble and refute the very logics that found an archive's intelligibility to historical analysis. Within "vexed" geographies, such as the Middle East, El Shakry argues, secular nationalism and radical Islamism equally partake of and produce decolonial archival imaginaries. To refuse the centrality of Islamist writing and thought, and/or to imagine the process of decolonizing archives as a purely "secular" project, is to literalize the very logics of Mbembe's "chronophagy." In other words, even as we attempt to reconstruct histories of colonized pasts, it is equally urgent that such efforts fully and inventively incorporate nonsecular (in this case, Islamist) writings about subjecthood and freedom. Such writings, as El Shakry reminds us, were never quite lost or disappeared; more precisely, they were routinely written out of a more conventional and secular history of the Middle East.[10] Here the destruction of archives is less about the absence of historical evidence and more about the strategic devaluation of one set of materials over the other. As Ariella Azoulay writes (when speaking specifically on histories of Palestine), one must precisely unlearn such habits of the imperial archive to make room for more radical and potential histories.[11]

In what follows, I will turn to an archive of sexuality where the language of loss has slipped into the granular smoothness of the everyday, breaking with its centrality as heuristic origin story. If, at first glance, the ethical responsibility of an archive is to host wor(l)ds that may otherwise be lost, in the end its central obligation may be to provide wor(l)ds that may never have left. What to make, then, of an archive that resists recuperative historiography's most cherished mantra: recover, restore, redress? Rather, the archive I will proffer here is an abundant ecosystem, at once imaginative and real, less a recordkeeper of lost lives, more a potential epistemology for how we know, translate, and amplify our relationship to the past.

THAT THRILLING DARK NIGHT

"*Bundachi tee romanchkari kaari raatr* (A thrilling dark night of insurrection). May 25, 1921. It is 10 p.m., and we are under attack. Our house has been surrounded on all four sides, and I can hear loud cries and whistles as stones and rocks pummel our doors and rooftop. I run to the courtyard to see all the women and children huddled together in fear. As the attack escalates, the children begin to lose control and defecate on themselves in fear. The women scream till their throats run dry, only to realize that there is no water left in the house. My wife, who is very ill, unable to bear the stress, falls to the ground in shock. I run to the rooftop, with my gun in hand, and shoot aimlessly into the darkness of the night, unsure whether I am killing or will be killed. I scream out into the night, and suddenly the attackers retreat, and an eerie calm returns."

Thus goes my translated summary of an account written by Rajaram Rangoji Paigankar, the son of a *kalavantin*—literally, a term used for women with kala (art), a subgrouping within the Goan devadasi structure—in the first volume of his much-heralded autobiography, *Mee kon* (*Who Am I?*).[12] The attack takes place in Paigin, a small village in the *taluka* (area) of Cancona, southern Goa, a key stronghold of the Goan devadasi community. Once morning breaks, Paigankar recounts the events to the village headman, who accompanies him back home to inspect and corroborate the damage done to his household. In due course, Paigankar and his extended family of twenty-five women and children abandon their home and seek shelter in a neighboring village.

There is, of course, as is to be expected in any narrative retelling, a prehistory to the *halla* (attack). Four days earlier, on May 21, 1921, Paigankar and his comrades hold a general *Satyanarayan pooja* (a religious ritual that celebrates Lord Satyanarayana, an avatar of Lord Vishnu, and is often held to commemorate an auspicious occasion or to ward off impending evil), calling for a refusal of caste hierarchies and religious differences. An enthusiastic crowd of over a thousand people from five neighboring villages gathers, composed primarily of the Deuli and Bande castes (the lowest subgroupings of the Devadasi community), a smattering of curious Portuguese officials, and a few breakaway Saraswat Brahmins. Enraged by the repeated caste humiliation and sexual exploitation suffered by the Devadasi families at the hands of the Saraswat Brahmins, Paigankar demands an end to Brahmin hegemony and speaks passionately at the pooja about the need for education and reform. Yet despite all the excitement and support of the gathered crowd, the pooja remains unfinished. No *purohit* (priest) is willing to step forward to complete the rites, fearful of incurring the wrath of the powerful Saraswats. And the wrath of the Brahmins does follow. Paigankar and the larger Devadasi community in Paigin are immediately banned from all social functions, their lands confiscated, their businesses shut down, and a general sanction is imposed against all of their interactions. Paigankar is seen as the key protagonist in an escalating drama of anti-Brahmin sentiment and is asked to appear before the ruling Brahmin council. Even worse, hundreds of Brahmin youth are rumored to have taken up arms in retaliation and threaten to attack and destroy Paigankar and his followers. There are signs that such anti-Brahmin activities are spreading apace in southern Goa: similar poojas are said to be taking place in nearby Lolegaon, a second stronghold of Saraswat Brahmin hegemony. The scene is set for the inevitable events of that thrilling dark night.[13]

After the attack, another extraordinary set of events follows. Paigankar and twenty-five kalavantins from his village travel to Panjim, acquire legal representation, and submit a writ appeal to the *governador-general* (governor general) of Portuguese Goa, Jaime Alberto de Castro Morais (1920–25). In the appeal, Paigankar et al. write,

> We, a Gayak Kalavant Samaj [community of singers and artists], based in Paigin, are endeavoring to free ourselves. We aspire to be worthy citizens of Portugal by emancipating our women from prostitution and by advocating education and marriage. The Saraswat Brahmins find our goals objectionable and have attempted to punish us by confiscating our lands, levying fines, refusing us access to all basic services, and by attacking the houses we live in. They have done so in the name of the Portuguese state. If this is indeed your law, then we wish to leave our village and ask permission to migrate to British India. If we are asked to stay, we would like to petition the Saraswat Brahmins for damages and compensation.[14]

In many ways, such a strategic appeal to the patronage of the Portuguese state is hardly surprising given the progressive political climate of the pre-Salazar era in Goa, and the protracted geopolitical claims of the so-called *Velhas* and *Novas Conquistas* (Old and New Conquests) in Portuguese Goa. Often referred to as the Republican period in Goan history, the period between 1900 and 1926 has been heralded as a time of renaissance for Goan arts, culture, and politics.[15] Such a renaissance, however, must be understood within the economic, social, and political demarcations of the more developed coastal talukas of the "Old Conquests": Ilhas, Bardez, Salcete, and Mormugao, conquered first by the Portuguese in the sixteenth century, and impacted more directly by the advent of Portuguese colonialism. The "New Conquests," acquired from the Marathas in the eighteenth century, included the talukas not directly along the coast, namely, Pernem, Bicholim, Satari, Ponda, Sanguem, Quepem, and Paigankar's taluka, Cancona. These talukas lacked the density of population and economic heft of the areas under the Old Conquest. One positive by-product of such geopolitical demarcations, some scholars argue, was that the New Conquests were less affected by the brutal project of Portuguese conversion (1560–1812) and were, by and large, left alone to flourish or perish at their own peril, at least till the discovery of raw materials and the rise of the mining industry. This difference in rule also translated to language acquisition, as the New Conquests had more Marathi speakers, while the Old Conquests had the monopoly on Portuguese and English speakers.[16] Goan devadasis were to be found more predominantly in the New Conquests, where Hinduism (allegedly) thrived with less persecution and where temples remained relatively unscathed.[17] The census of 1920, for example, the year before this halla (attack) takes place, notes that Goa officially had 405 bailadeiras (dancing girls), mostly located within the talukas of the New Conquests.[18]

Thus, it would come as less of a surprise that Governor Morais responds positively and in an unprecedented fashion to the submitted appeal. So moved is Morais by the plight of the distraught women accompanying Paigankar that he immediately censures the Saraswat Brahmin community of Paigin and orders official protection for the kalavants. News of the appeal and its aftermath spread like wildfire all across Goa, and editorials appear in both the Portuguese and the vernacular press, as the kalavantins appear to have incited the beginning of a grassroots resistance against Brahmin hegemony. And last but not least, the governor's judgment founds the basis of the first alleged legal case filed against Brahmins by a lower-caste community in Portuguese Goa. I say "alleged" here because there are no available archival records of the case, either in the Goa state archives or in the Portuguese colonial archives in Lisbon. However, the case, *Kalavantin Bhima versus the Saraswat Council of Paigin*, is repeatedly referenced in Paigankar's biography as a mark of the community's successful campaign for reform. The Brahmins, we are told, are asked to return the seized lands and monetarily compensate the kalavants for lost revenue and damaged property.[19]

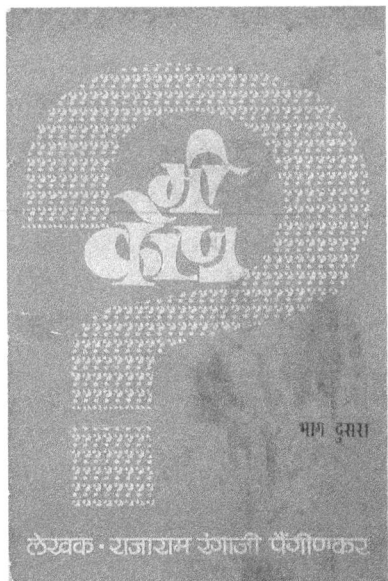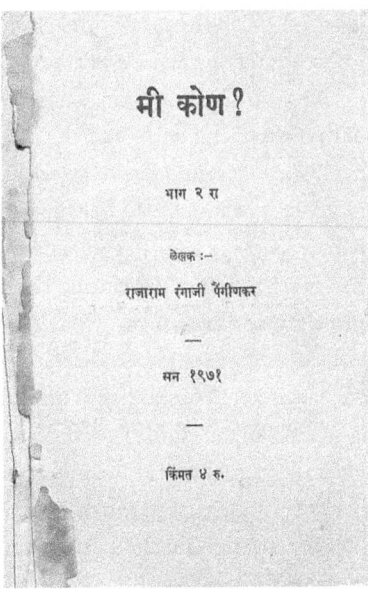

1.1 AND 1.2 Front cover and title page of Rajaram Rangoji Paigankar's *Mee kon*, vol. 2 (1971). A signed copy of the text is archived in the Gomantak Maratha Samaj, Mumbai, India. Courtesy of the samaj

IN THE ABSENCE OF RELIABLE GHOSTS · 39

But just as his readers are ready to settle into this rousing account of brave resistance, Paigankar reveals an even more thrilling twist to the tale. In the opening gambit of the *second* volume of his autobiography, titled "Mee gharavar halla ka ghadvoon aanla?" ("Why Did I Stage the Attack on My House?"), Paigankar explains that the attack was in fact *"ek saubhadr natak"* (a strategic drama), directed precisely to protect and advance the interests of kalavantins. Recall here that the description of the attack appears in the *first* volume of Paigankar's biography. His words underscore the constant humiliation experienced by the male and female members of his community, a humiliation that precipitates the ritual of the reformist Satyanarayan pooja. For example, Paigankar recounts his degrading experiences at the residence of a local Saraswat Brahmin where he is invited for a meal, only to then be asked to partake of the food on a soiled plate used to feed animals.[20] Such experiences are compounded by the fact that the yajemans (patrons) who frequent kalavantin houses are themselves Saraswat Brahmins. Paigankar's own bio-father, a well-known Saraswat businessman in the village, aggravates the situation further by urging Paigankar to appear before a Brahmin village council and pledge contrition for his actions. Paigankar even attempts to contest a legal claim against the seizure of kalavantin lands by the Brahmins, but his efforts are thwarted by a lack of funds and a general fear of Brahmin reprisal. With the sanctions against the kalavantins worsening each day, a sense of urgency and desperation defines their every word and action.

It is at this point in the drama, we are told, that Paigankar, at the behest of his best friend and lover, the kalavantin Bhima, and in complete secrecy, persuades six comrades to attack his home on that fateful night. The comrades are given detailed instructions about when they should attack, from which vantage point, and for how long. Each individual is asked to recite prepared lines explaining their whereabouts at a neighbor's residence, should any of them be questioned after the attack. Not a soul is told of the carefully orchestrated attack, except those directly involved, and (as we have seen through the extreme physical discomfort experienced by all) even Paigankar's family members remain in the dark. Such secrecy, writes Paigankar, guarantees the narrative heft of the attack as the heinous work of frenzied Saraswat youth. Bhima, the young kalavantin, who serves as the director behind the scenes, sets the stage perfectly for that fateful night of insurrection. Mobilizing established economies of rumor, fear, and humiliation, Bhima, along with her sister kalavantins, ensures that the larger village community truly embraces and anticipates the fiction of the attack. Guns are mysteriously set off around kalavantin homes previous to the night of the attack, and a general fear of Saraswat retaliation suffuses all conversation.[21] An attack on Paigankar's home thus provides the necessary climax to such calculated and frenzied fear, so perfectly scripted are the conditions of its production. And the staging, as we already know, does produce its desired effects. In addition to the alleged case against the Saraswats, a school is also established for the kalavantin community in Paigin (through the support of the Portuguese state) that exists to this day.[22]

THE KALA OF THE ARCHIVE

Does the revelation that the halla (attack) was so deftly staged denude it of salvific historical value, or does its narrative veracity (but, in fact, an event was being staged . . .) inaugurate a different orientation to archival production? Let me explain what I mean. This staged event provides an alternate historiographical model that refuses the stability of a spectacle, to hold or destroy, and focuses more on the salvific forms archives are asked to assume. That is, the halla opens up an archival space of *radical representability*, self-consciously replete with the figurations necessary to event-making and loss. For if a minoritized collectivity aspires to a memorable and memorializable history, the best qualification that it can acquire is an event of native resistance. In the case of the staged attack, Paigankar himself exhibits a keen understanding of such expectations as he situates his representational tactics within a longer, routinized, and mythical/political demand for salvific forms. Comparing himself to Subhadra (in the famous staged kidnapping of Arjun by Subhadra), Shivaji, and a long line of historical dupers within received Indian (read Hinducentric) history, Paigankar asks his readers to recapitalize our political commitment to compensation through an understanding of the staging of archives. The architecture of the mob halla, too, reprises a set of representations that are central to any subaltern history of opposition or resistance.[23] Turning to canny mimicry, Paigankar's staged halla brings with it a growing recognition that signature events may have been much less monumental than imagined. Within the lineaments of the story, Paigankar accesses earlier, stylized repertoires of representation that render the languages of empire through the revered architecture of Hindu mythologies. Thus, there can be no refusal of Paigankar's archive, nestled, as it is, within established histories of *méconnaissance* and hoax. These archival repertoires (to play with Diana Taylor's formulation) disinvest from the plots of social realism's truth telling, instead inviting us to reenact the archival event through the craft and craftiness of survival—this is the kala (the art, the aesthetics) of the archive.

In so doing, Paigankar subjects the veracity archive of sexuality to a crucial modification; he produces repeated evidence of the staging of the halla (in the second volume, as noted above) such that we are, as readers, asked to retool our foundational epistemologies undergirding historical recuperation. Much as it may resemble a refusal of the archive, and of history's investment in it, Paigankar's revelation ("Why did I stage this attack?") may be extending a more strategic attachment. Far from signaling the death of the archive, Paigankar's revelation may represent instead a much more ingenious archival ruse: we are asked to negotiate the modalities of archival representation and recognition, to document, as it were, the staging of a record. The ethical burden shifts away from the literal translation of the historical record to thinking more of its literariness, its kala in making a history possible. Here the archive defines itself through a deliberate hermeneutics of perfidiousness, through what Rey Chow has called a "situation, dramatization, staging, picture frame, window, and above all as the assemblage, or installation of a critical aperture, a supplemental time space."[24] Cautioning his readers against the seductions of a memorable archival event (the orchestrated attack with a full cast of characters), Paigankar intimates instead that the caste humiliations of the Samaj gesture toward a more ordinary, relentless, and brutal ecosystem—the very opposite of a dramatic, scripted, and highly visible attack.

Such a supplementary archive equally draws attention to the weight of origins as places of commencement within liberationist histories of sexuality (individual and/or collective). The challenge here is to not suture the place of origins to a landscape of repetitive loss, to a set of recursive displacements or suspended beginnings. Rather, as Elspeth Probyn writes (quoting Foucault), what would it mean to play with the "solemnities of origin," particularly when it comes to the histories of sexuality?[25] After all, Paigankar's ultimate disclosure of the fake halla, and the ease with which he provides details of the staging, deploys the very weight of the origin it undoes, and attests to the tenacity of such representational conventions. Paigankar's revelation ("Why did I stage this attack?") is meant to ward off the debunking of an archive that he at once promotes and resists. His disclosure deftly stops short of impugning the form from which it draws its historical authority; rather, Paigankar's belated "veracity" expands the idea of an archive by anticipating its compensations. Even as we examine the epistemological techniques that transform Paigankar's halla into an apocryphal event (how do we know something is an event?), its archival status as resistive event shifts focus away from broader structures of caste oppression onto those who suffer within it.

Any concerns about the success of Paigankar's archival kala are easily diffused through the lavish praise his biography garners from reviewers within the Samaj. In place of consternation or even outrage at Paigankar's revelation, the reviews express gratitude for Paigankar's strategic historical sense, urging their readers to learn from Paigankar's craft and commitment to the betterment of the Samaj. One reviewer, Sushil Kavlekar, writes passionately that Paigankar's staging of the halla provides an exemplary model for future action. For Kavlekar, Paigankar's success at promoting the Samaj's goals "without recourse to violence, hate-spewing" is to be lauded rather than lambasted, reproduced rather than repudiated. Indeed, if anything, the (non–)origin story of the Samaj's history expands its kala, its mastery, from the regimes of music and dance to the workings of historical drama.[26]

As we have already seen, initial efforts to organize the community were primarily led by Rajaram Rangoji Paigankar as early as 1902. Paigankar particularly rallied youth members of the community and staged multiple successful conferences all over Goa and Maharashtra. Based primarily in Panaji, Shiroda, Malvan, and Bombay, the Samaj championed itself as caste reformist (if you will), describing its shift in name—from Gomantak Kalavant Samaj (Goan Artist collectivity/group) to Gomantak Maratha Samaj (Goan Maratha collectivity/group)—as a primary indication of its commitment to a progressive pan-caste politics. The term *Kalavant* privileged a specific professional identity (linked to the arts), whereas *Maratha* engaged a field of membership that encompassed all subcastes of devadasi labor, emphasizing more affiliations of language and culture (Marathi). The shift in name occurred in 1927 after much heated debate over other possible names, such as Neethivardhak Samaj, Gayak Samaj, and Pragati Samaj, all of which focused solely on the project of reform rather than caste and region.[27] For example, the name Neethivardhak Samaj called forth the idea of truth (*neethi*) as the guiding principle behind the Samaj's emergence, eschewing any reference to the Samaj's attachments to sexuality and/or to Portuguese India, evident in "Gomantak" (from Goa). In many ways, the Samaj's early struggles around self-nominalization anticipate many of the paradoxes that have now become the mainstay in discussions of rights and representation. At issue here is the reification of a name such as Gayak (Singer) that at once secures visibility even as it strengthens the very category that founds its marginalization.[28]

In the first official conference, held on May 5, 1929, in Shiroda, a small village in central Goa, 750 delegates from all over Goa, Maharashtra, and Karnataka gathered to discuss the future of the Samaj—an extraordinary event given the difficulties of traveling between the borders of Portuguese and British India. Speech after speech made at the conference highlighted a commitment to education, caste reform, and the abolition of the sexual exploitation of the Samaj women. Sexuality featured heavily in all discussions of reform as the structuring mode through which to forge futures, as a space of radical possibility for opening up larger avenues for the Samaj's development. Members were urged to strategically mobilize their devadasi histories as pedagogical tools, to create much-needed societal discussions on sexuality and morality, and, in so doing, to *sudhaar* (improve) not just themselves but society at large. Despite such expressed zeal for large-scale social change, no salutary reference or connection was made to the ongoing liberation struggles, either in British or Portuguese India.[29] Indeed, the early absence of any collective involvement by the Samaj in the resistance movements outside of their local interests speaks to yet another twist in the tale of the Samaj. For a large part of their emergence in Portuguese India, the Samaj relied on the benevolence of the Portuguese state for a wide array of causes, from the building of schools and libraries to the funding of small businesses. But given that this chapter is also a rumination on the unmooring of attachments to revered lineages (whether of loss, opposition, or resistance) within histories of sexuality, the Samaj's refusal to join liberation struggles—a refusal that frustrates contemporary expectations of subaltern oppositionality—is hardly surprising. The Samaj, for example, had and still continues to have no interest in aligning with any other project of social reform. Its members are now largely and resolutely middle class, with the Samaj offices in Bombay and Panaji now being used to host monthly meetings as well as accrue revenue through wedding celebrations. In fact, one of the recursive and fascinating features of this Samaj's story is its refusal or, rather, sidelining of any social project outside of its own historicity.

RADICAL ABUNDANCE

At this point, one may well ask: How does an archival story of a staged halla in a remote part of colonial Portuguese India provide both the mass and the patina for a nonmelancholic historiography of sexuality? Those readers wishing to find queerness in this chapter through the materiality of lost subjects aspiring to gay, lesbian, bisexual, or transgender identity forms, or even through archives that might somehow fold back into an identitarian form, will find few treasures here. Rather, the Samaj archives offer a challenge to the lineages through which reproductive futurities constitute their authority, attending more to what those instances of becoming entail. Here the return to a history of sexuality is not through a call to loss (of object and/or materials) but, rather, through radical abundance, through an archive that is incommensurable and quotidian, imaginative and ordinary. Far from coupling archival accumulation with straightforward historical visibility, the Samaj's story challenges and indeed undermines the very idea and entelechy of an archive.

Bypassing the hermeneutical demands for recuperation, reproduction, revision, and reparation, the Samaj's archives stubbornly enact queer readings that unsettle the foundational link between historical reproduction and archival preservation. Radical abundance here is presence without return, without the fear of loss. Keenly aware of what archives "cannot not" deliver, what their evidentiary forms foreclose in their celebrated endorsement of rights and representation, the plenitude of the Samaj archives opens up the question of how we record histories of sexualities in many different keys.[30] The archive remains the aspirational value-form, even as its cherished representational forms are retooled. Composed at a strategic remove from the affective maelstrom of lost and erased histories, as I noted in the introduction, the Samaj archives are instead abundant, accessible, and continuous to this day. They grow and add to their content, even as I put pen to paper. The sheer proliferation of the Samaj archives, in contradistinction to their absence in official colonial and/or postcolonial state archives, stages the central problematic at play here: After all, if minoritized subjects craft their own scenes of representation (the speaking for, and the speaking about), then what exactly is subaltern or oppositional about them?[31]

An examination of the Samaj's massive, self-fashioned archives (housed in Panaji and Mumbai) reveals a wide range of archival genres—novels, short stories, minutes, property deeds, flyers, legal case records, programs, membership lists, and annual reviews, to name a select few. Any visitor walking into these archives will find no semblance of order or design in the placement of materials, which are strewn haphazardly across multiple rooms within the Samaj buildings. There is no central gathering space for reading or study. Instead, one is invited to wander and peruse the materials, and even "discover" some gems tucked away in unmarked boxes, cupboards, shelves, trunks, or dusty attics. Indeed, in every visit to these archives, I have been introduced to materials that I have not seen or known about in the past. The staff and trustees of the Samaj regard my efforts to organize or, more precisely, to discipline the materials as amusing, denuded of particularity and distinction, redolent more of elitist concerns with preservation and access. Instead, the spatial logic of the archive is much more renegade: materials are never lost because they are paradoxically never found. Through constant rediscovery (as it were), the archive lives on, conferring compositional responsibility and authority on anyone who accesses the materials.[32]

Perhaps the greatest sign of the Samaj's remaking of evidentiary forms is its persistent recourse to fiction, spread across hundreds of short stories and serialized novellas within its archives. As deliberately imaginative modes of representation, these archives of fiction operate less as testimonials to the enduring past of the Samaj than as circulating tales that live to tell. The absence of veracity genres such as testimonials, biographies, and memoirs is even more telling; when a rare biography does appear, as with Paigankar's biography, *Mee kon* (1969), it unfolds more as archival hoax, flipping the script of minoritized subjects who emerge into historical view through the legitimizing arc of subaltern resistance.[33] Paigankar's two-volume biography, as we have already seen, strives to refurbish the tropes and allusions of the archive into a new evidentiary avatar. In so doing, it provides an occasion to rethink the value of the archive itself: its elasticity and its status as a record of constant demystification. Much of the writing (mostly anonymous) appears in the monthly journal *Samaj Sudharak* (1929 to this day) and covers a startlingly wide range of issues, from education and marriage to devadasi reform, the perils of prostitution, caste shame, travel, contraception, sports, and even the evils of gossip. Bearing morally charged titles such as the serialized novella *She Had Her Mother's Heart* (January 1947–June 1949), or short stories such as "A Letter from God" (November 1943) and "Justice" (June 1941), these fictional modes exhort their readers to take action and self-reform through a language of sexuality. Readers are asked, for example, to set aside their moral discomfort with their mothers' professions (as devadasis) and embrace instead the legacies of art and affect that found such lineages of sexuality.[34]

It is of course impossible to do justice to the sheer volume and complexity of issues covered within the pages of the *Samaj Sudharak*. Given the limited scope of this chapter, I have chosen to focus more on the early issues of the *Samaj Sudharak* (1929–61), where the challenges of self-fashioning

1.3 Cover page of the *Samaj Sudharak*, January 1933. Gomantak Maratha Samaj Archives, Mumbai, India

and self-archiving are more pressingly articulated. One arresting example of such exhortations is a short story, "Kala-Sangeet" ("Kala of Music") (June 1937, 99–101), that deftly mobilizes allegory, irony, and a good dose of humor to capture the Samaj's variegated history. The story (written by Y. N. Tipnis) carefully assembles a recognizable collection of characters who effectively allegorize the different stages in the Samaj's history. They include Miss Kala (a word that, as we have already seen, literally means "art"), a gifted singer, accompanied by her friends, Miss Veena (also the name of a plucked stringed instrument) and Miss Nanda (meaning "joy" or "joyful"). The story opens with a heated discussion between Kala and Veena, airing their divergent views on the value of music. For Kala, music is a pursuit worthy of all sacrifice, a divine gift; for Veena, the pursuit of music promises no rewards, only exhausting hours of rehearsals that can be easily avoided through the simple purchase of a "Columbia record and a gramophone!" For Nanda, who arrives later in the story, the seduction of music looms as a cautionary tale; as she laments, "What use is the kala of sangeet if we remain degraded Kalavantins or Devadasis, or move to Bombay, and become actresses and singers in the film industry?"[35] The story ends with Kala sternly reminding her friends that it is kala that has funded their lives and afforded them the daily comforts they now take for granted. In fact, the kala of their Samaj is so sought after, she adds, that even Lokmanya Tilak, the great freedom fighter, has publicly praised their talents, tethering their history of sexuality to the history of a nation's emergence. Chastened by Kala's words, Veena and Nanda agree to continue their singing lessons and head to their respective homes.[36] Strategically and playfully mixing past and present readings of the Samaj's kala, the story argues for a protean understanding of the Samaj that resists any stable or purely positive form. The images and advertisements accompanying the text of such stories further open out into a different register of kala; even as Samaj actresses are celebrated for their roles as unwed mothers, prostitutes, and mistresses in Hindi and Marathi theater and cinema, it is their paid labor that guarantees the respectability and growth of the Samaj. In fact, almost every issue of the *Samaj Sudharak* between 1932 and 1949 carries an homage to the labors of such actresses by carefully listing their philanthropic contributions toward reform efforts within the Samaj.

Many covers of the *Samaj Sudharak* also carry lively, bold images of Samaj women. Far from courting aesthetic innovation, these images partake of a well-established, even hackneyed representational protocol. Take, for example, this series of cover images from issues in 1940 (see figure 1.4). Some are clearly professional headshots of Samaj women; others are suffused more with the informal intimacies of private pictures. These are recognizably studio portraits, their aesthetic textures clearly composed: studied makeup; clothes, poses, gazes askance. Even the most demure image is made up carefully, with touches that were recognizable enhancements (the eyelashes in figure 1.6, for example). Each portrait is cued to proclaim its repertoire of visual references, sometimes overtly, sometimes more subtly. Some references are lineages of ethnographic representation, translated through legacies in South Asian photo studios used for family portraits, meant to grace a wall in a home. But they equally draw on contemporary film magazine portfolios for female stars, or headshots from fashion magazines that invite aspirational forms of identification.[37] Each of them is not merely a representation but perhaps also proffers a template into which a viewer can be hailed. None of them are action shots; each is deliberately still, carrying within them, such as the tennis shot, a promise of future action. None of them are particularly nationalist; rather, they suggest sight lines, shorn of any discernible politics.[38]

Akin to most of the Samaj's archival content, these images too refuse to follow the script—they neither reject the animating properties of the colonial image nor surrender to it. Colonial photography, as Zahid Chaudhary and Malek Alloula have argued, is structured around the exhibitionism of the image and the voyeurism of the spectator.[39] Here there is a shift in spectatorial address, as the photographs solicit new orders of meaning, for a new kind of gaze in which looking as pleasure may be the only pathway into archival presence. Even as we shift from the scopic register of colonial (and upper-caste) representation to these images of lower-caste self-representation, we continue to know very little about the women moving through these images. No attribution accompanies the images, and their presence is left untouched in the contents of the issues. Unlike portrayals produced under colonial auspices, for whom recognition was unimportant and in fact had to be shed, such as Herbert Risley's infamous representative typologies, these images from the *Samaj Sudharak* moved among an audience of familiars.[40] As Bishnupriya Ghosh observes, to focus primarily on the truth value of the biography behind an iconic image is to bring it into equivalence within a standardized mode of view, almost didactic in purpose. To refuse this iconic message, to refuse to tell the story of a singular life, Ghosh writes, requires us to attend to the "creative force of figuration" that volatizes the image and puts it "up for grabs."[41] A call to such figuration generates the epistemological frisson: we move away from

समाज सुधारक
वर्ष १२ वें — फेब्रुवारी १९५०
क्रमांक ११४

समाज सुधारक
वर्ष १२ वें — मार्च १९५०
क्रमांक ११५

समाजसुधारक
वर्ष १२ वें — मे १९५०
क्रमांक ११७

समाजसुधारक
वर्ष १२ वें — जुले १९५०
क्रमांक ११९

1.4 Cover page of the *Samaj Sudharak*, February 1940. Gomantak Maratha Samaj Archives, Mumbai, India

1.5 Cover page of the *Samaj Sudharak*, March 1940. Gomantak Maratha Samaj Archives, Mumbai, India

1.6 Cover page of the *Samaj Sudharak*, May 1940. Gomantak Maratha Samaj Archives, Mumbai, India

1.7 Cover page of the *Samaj Sudharak*, July 1940. Gomantak Maratha Samaj Archives, Mumbai, India

1.8 Cover page of the *Samaj Sudharak*, August 1940. Gomantak Maratha Samaj Archives, Mumbai, India

1.9 Cover page of the *Samaj Sudharak*, September 1940. Gomantak Maratha Samaj Archives, Mumbai, India

1.10 Cover page of the *Samaj Sudharak*, November 1940. Gomantak Maratha Samaj Archives, Mumbai, India

the mandates of biographical certainty (tell us who these women are) to the invitation of an archival form that nudges image and meaning into a different order of liveness.[42] Their stories are literally left to one's imagination, as histories that are at once singular and unverifiable, the marker, as Gayatri Spivak reminds us, of the literary and the figurative.[43]

My meditations on the Samaj archives have thus far sought to draw attention to evidentiary forms (like the origin story, the attack) that offer an alternative political or historical response, even—or especially—in the face of their persistent invocation. Far from constituting an unethical response (we make, you believe) to the demand for historical evidence, the Samaj archives perform a more vital function: reconstructing and reinventing sundered lineages of history and sexuality. An archival genre that continues to garner heightened attention within histories of sexuality is of course the lost letter. Across a range of queer histories, lost letters (and diaries) invariably incorporate the central distinguishing genre of evidence: a personal account, borne with great fortitude and equanimity, meaningful words where one last expects to find them.[44] For readers of the *Samaj Sudharak*, especially in early to mid-twentieth-century India, lost letters were also the recognizable genre for extended musings on sexuality and gender roles, as well as caste and class formations. After all, the *Samaj Sudharak* was published alongside the increasing popularity of the Indian sexologist, novelist, reformer, and eugenicist Narayan Sitaram Phadke.

Phadke's novels (especially from 1920–50, the period often known as "the Phadke era" in Marathi literary-cultural history) were mostly sexological treatises garbed in the realist aesthetics of the new Marathi novel.[45] Each novel—and he wrote more than seventy formulaic novels by the end of his career!—circled around the romantic trials and tribulations of the modern Indian couple. Most novels featured elaborate correspondences between the hero and the heroine, or between the hero and his family, where the virtues of chastity, sexuality, and gender formations were avidly discussed.[46] For example, Phadke's first and most popular modern romance, *Kulabyachi dandi* (*The Lighthouse at Colaba*), the founding "love story" in Marathi fiction, features a young male protagonist, Jagdish, and his ill-fated romantic interest and "new woman," Manik. It is Jagdish's overblown letter-writing (*patra-vyavahar*), his repeated efforts to send love letters that remain unanswered or lost, that characterizes the novel's most effective pedagogical tool. Jagdish writes and rewrites several drafts of passionate letters to Manik, and in each letter sent or refused, we are schooled in the appropriate languages of sexual intimacy.⁴⁷ Even as Manik is eventually jettisoned from the marriage plot (she is too sexual, too bold, too nonconforming), the letters in abeyance (what if she had read the letters?) hint at sexual knowledge that the novel must eventually forgo. The letters (not sent) are printed verbatim in the novel, cautionary blueprints for sexuality's maligned forms.⁴⁸ Such a turn to letters as sexuality's confessional elsewhere appears with equal frequency in the popular Marathi-language journal *Samaj Swasthya* (1927–53). Douglas Haynes and Shrikant Botre argue that the letters written to the journal's editor, R. D. Karve, a major advocate of birth control and sex education in western India, "constitute perhaps the earliest sex-advice column in Indian print media." Written primarily by middle-class males in mid-twentieth-century India, the letters address anxieties around "masturbation and seminal emissions, the nature of the female body and processes of conception, birth control and same-sex sexual practices."⁴⁹

It would seem no wonder, then, that the genre of "lost letters" appears with some frequency within multiple issues of the *Samaj Sudharak*. The lost letter's always ambiguous epistemological enticements, its infinitely malleable features, appears ideal for the Samaj's archival project.⁵⁰ Like Paigankar's biography of a fiction, these letters too reiterate a singularly nonrecuperative relationship to the archive. To be found is not to be restored to value but, rather, to be set adrift on more inventive economies of meaning. From August 1940 to December 1940, a curated five-part series titled "Harvelele patr" ("Lost Letters") appears with great fanfare in the monthly *Samaj Sudharak*. The collector of the letters, Shashishekhar, appends a long introductory paragraph to the letters, situating their discovery and publication within a broader mandate of historiographical responsibility. To explain his publication of the letters, Shashishekhar asks, "What if you run into letters that are lost but call out to be read and received?"⁵¹ The temptation of looking, he adds, far exceeds the *gunha* (crime) of intrusion and any claims to ownership. We are told the package of letters is found abandoned in Victoria Gardens, near the Samaj buildings in Bombay, carefully tied together with string, and all addressed to a young man named Anil. The letters appear to be a correspondence between Dada (older brother) and his younger brother, Anil, even as we only have Dada's letters, with Anil left to the reader's imagination. Preserved and published without revision or censorship, the letters are reproduced with the hope of finding the elusive Anil, and for the edification and learning of the readers. After all, writes Shashishekhar excitedly, we have been fortuitously gifted an "amrutacha pela [cup of ambrosia], and it would be foolish not to drink its contents and learn how to produce our own."[52]

And the letters do manifest much of the promise of Shashishekhar's opening gambit. Each of the published letters exhorts its addressee, Anil, a university student, to reflect on the temptations and possibilities of upward mobility, in terms of both class and gender. Dada, the voice of the letters, cajoles Anil and cautions him against the perils of too much sex, too many distractions, and ultimately the enticements of urban life in Bombay. Dada casts himself as uneducated, poor, and lower caste, yet his prose exceeds the limitations of his self-production. Using a mixture of Portuguese, Marathi, and some misplaced English phrases, Dada uses the letters to reiterate conventional and heavily Brahminical storylines of female chastity and sexuality. By the time we get to the third installation of the lost letter series, a short editorial note is appended to the letters: "We know that many women will not agree with the content of the letters. But we are committed to publishing them in their original found form. If you are angry with what these letters say, use this opportunity to write and send us letters of your own."[53] Here the incitement to formulate "letters of your own" is not a call to excavate, detect, or unearth a corrective truth. Rather, the editorial note exhorts its female readers to give life to more telling and fictionalized ripostes.

Another extraordinary feature of the *Samaj Sudharak*'s early writings is its concerted effort to refuse reproductive futurity through proprietary kinship structures. After all, as we have seen through the evidence of Paigankar's biography and other available historical records, the kalavantins were seen as distinct from the category of "prostitute" by the Portuguese colonial state primarily because these women maintained coercive and noncoercive monogamous relationships with Saraswat Brahmin men (and occasionally women). As the children of such unions were rarely recognized as legitimate heirs to their fathers' caste status and/or properties, various creative forms of kinship were developed to survive and prosper. In some cases, the children took on their fathers' Saraswat Brahmin surnames (without consent), such that there are now Samaj members in both Goa and Maharashtra with deceptively upper-caste surnames such as Kakodkar, Shirodkar, and Welingkar. While these members are clearly not received as Brahmins in larger society, their acquisition of Brahmin surnames has created sufficient confusion within normative kinship structures. Given the primacy of blood and laws of primogeniture within Hindu legal and religious formations, such sleights of caste (if you will) are more than efforts at upward mobility.⁵⁴ Rather, they gesture toward an astute anticipation of sexuality's compensatory economies, entangled as they are with regimes of profit and pleasure.

A similar discomfort with the compulsory script of kinship can be seen in the poignant writings of a sixteen-year-old Samaj member, Ramakant Arondekar. Published in the July 1949 issue of the *Samaj Sudharak*, almost two years after the liberation of British India, Arondekar's short opinion piece is intriguingly titled "Matrudevata aani matruprem" ("Mother as God and Love for One's Mother"). The text opens with an elder, Rambhau, commanding the author to love and worship his mother. Finding such a proposition troublesome, Arondekar argues that it is irresponsible and unethical to follow such a dictum, given its flawed and unrealistic logic. Surely, Arondekar writes, one must be able to choose whom one worships and whom one loves, especially given the murky genealogies of the Samaj's own family histories. Refuting the claim that to love one's mother is "natural" and divinely ordained, Arondekar proposes that the Samaj advocate for families forged through choice rather than mere blood relations. Nestled within the laments of this short piece is a startlingly radical script of kinship: even as the authority of bio-fathers (read: Saraswat Brahmins) is challenged, one must extend the same ambiguity of affect to the authority of one's bio-mother (read: kalavantins). Within such a refusal of normative kinship structures, no biological determinism can prevail, even if it means decentering the presence of the very women the Samaj seeks to valorize. While it may be possible to dismiss Arondekar's young voice as overly speculative and inexperienced (or even ashamed of his bio-mother's profession as a devadasi), his questions still echo the extant kinship structures within the Samaj. Available records of kalavantin families from Paigin, for example, clearly point to children (both male and female) being raised and/or adopted by a diffuse set of relatives, with bio-mothers rarely occupying central parenting roles. In fact, the thread of straight kinship is so undone that few children of Arondekar's generation were fully aware of their bio-parentage. Of equal import is that Samaj members continue to express little or no interest in tracking or privileging the origin stories of their birth.⁵⁵ It may thus come as little surprise that when Arondekar himself becomes editor of the *Samaj Sudharak* in 1969 (twenty years later), he reiterates his difficulty with any efforts to smooth Samaj kinship structures into normative kin formations. In a biting editorial titled "Lagn zurvene: Ek manastap" ("Arranging Marriages: An Irritation") (November 1970), he speaks to the contradictions inherent in the efforts of the Samaj to arrange marriages within its own ranks. Even as marriage provides the sanitized resolution to the Samaj's checkered history of sexuality, Arondekar questions the need for such conventional arrangements.[56]

WHAT MORE REMAINS

I have thus far elaborated on the textual nature of the Samaj archive—its overflow of writing, if you will—as a supplement (in the Derridean sense) to the overprivileging of the visual or the acoustic when it comes to the consumption of kalavantin bodies such as those of the Goan devadasis.[57] My emphasis here on the multiple genres of written materials housed within the Samaj highlights the difficulty of narrating a history drawn from such different, incommensurate, and textured archives. My reading centers, instead, the dialectic between the banality of the written form (here the copious content of the *Samaj Sudharak*) and the recourse to the hagiographical (something transformative is happening in the pages). I have struggled to read the history of the Samaj neither as a seductive exemplar nor as an exceptional case study that needs decoding (which is, of course, the preferred form). After all, there remains the enduring allure of a virtuoso reading (in which I too am mired) that will somehow unravel the secrets of sexuality. Rather, the Samaj archives speak more to a history of sexuality that is unfinished, messy, upending sedimented genealogies of recuperation and representation.

I began this chapter with a summoning of a historiography of sexuality that eschews the language of loss as the structuring mode of its narration. What we have here in the archives of the Samaj is a story that stubbornly refuses to move on from the ordinary plenitude of sexuality. Here the story of sexuality estranges settled readings of recuperative scrutiny, drawing us more into the queer forms of an archive's becoming, angled through lineages of the nonreproductive and the unfinished. Almost from their inception, the Samaj archives thus embrace the fully contradictory status of any archive: whole enough, on the one hand, to cohere to a set of identifiable concerns, yet partial enough to frustrate and unmoor the form itself. As such, these archives succeed precisely by habituating their readers to displacements, fictions, reinvestments in a historical script that works all the more effectively at the very moment of its undoing. Taken together, these archives constitute a kind of lyrical abundance that comes fully to life through genres of critical and rhetorical invention.

NOTES

1. Instead of providing a more conventional listing of the many excellent monographs and special issues published in the past decade on new/found archives of sexuality in Asia, Latin America, Africa, and the Middle East (which will feature later in the bibliography of this book), I want to turn to a slightly different exemplar of the explosion of such archives. I recently served as a regional editor for Asia for a new encyclopedia on LGBQTI histories of sexuality. Together, the six editors of the encyclopedia reviewed over six hundred entries on new archival research on queer history across the world, with topics ranging from more familiar topics such as sodomy and human rights, to more unfamiliar ones on issues such as queer working-class bars and homosexual blackmail. See Arondekar and Chiang, *Global Encyclopedia of Lesbian, Gay, Bisexual, Transgender, and Queer (LGBTQ) History*.

2. "Archival turn" is a term first coined by the anthropologist Ann Stoler to foreground the shift to archive as subject, over a repository for research, especially in the 1990s. See Stoler, "Colonial Archives and the Arts of Governance." See also Eichorn, *The Archival Turn in Feminism*. Of note here, however, is that scholars within archival studies, such as Michelle Caswell, have been quite critical about the embrace of the archival turn, especially within the disciplines of history, literature, and anthropology. In a biting and insightful essay, "'The Archive' Is Not an Archives," Caswell rebukes historians in particular for their complete erasure of the epistemological and material labors of fields such as archival studies. For Caswell, archival studies (at least in its postcolonial and decolonial avatars) has continually decentered and decomposed the imperial archive well before the current enthusiasm around the innovations of the archival turn.

3. McClintock, *Imperial Leather*, 40.

4. Arondekar and Patel, "Area Impossible." I will take up the conceptual quagmire of "geopolitics" in more detail in my last chapter.

5. Vilashini Cooppan astutely cautions against set temporalities of origin stories and loss. As she writes: "Which is worst? Slavery, colonialism, apartheid, the Holocaust? Which is first? To avoid the fatal logic of origin and priority, a logic through which Eurochronology can never be dismantled, I have found it instructive to think these things together." See Cooppan, "Time-Maps," 412.

6. Fuentes, *Dispossessed Lives*.

7. Caswell, *Archiving the Unspeakable*; Weld, *Paper Cadavers*. For other critics, such as Jenny Sharpe, the "poetics of loss" has not meant an absence of archives; rather, Sharpe argues for an ethos of "immateriality." See Sharpe, *Immaterial Archives*.

8   Some provocative pushback against such an extractive analysis can be seen in Barak, "Archives and/as Battlefields"; Bsheer, *Archive Wars*; and Seikaly, "How I Met My Great-Grandfather."
9   See Mbembe, "The Power of the Archive and Its Limits," on the archive as a materialization of power and imagination.
10 El Shakry is referring here specifically to the work of Sayyid Qutb (1906–66), who has often been reductively viewed primarily through the lens of Islamism and not as the central figure of Egyptian radical and decolonial thought. El Shakry is clearly also drawing from the pioneering work of Saba Mahmood, who cautions against the reductive and imperial ambitions of a Western secular historicism. See El Shakry, "History without Documents." See also Mahmood, *Politics of Piety*.
11 Azoulay, *Potential History*. Of note is the chapter "Archives." See also Stoler, "On Archiving as Dissensus."
12 Paigankar, *Mee kon*. The translated summary I provide here covers over eight pages of text in Marathi. Part of the challenge here is to render the affective tone of the description of the attack within the limitations of translation.
13 Paigankar, *Mee kon*, 1:73–80.
14 Paigankar, *Mee kon*, 1:84–87.
15 R. Pinto, *Between Empires*.
16 De Mendonça-Noronha, "The Economic Scene in Goa, 1926–1961." See also Ferreiro-Martins, *Historia da misericordia de Goa*.
17 Newman, *Of Umbrellas, Goddesses, and Dreams*; Axelrod and Fuerch, "Flight of the Deities."
18 *Censo da populaçao do estado da India*, 1920. See also Boxer, "Fidalgos portugueses e bailadeiras indianas (seculos XVII e XVIII)."
19 In addition to multiple references in Paigankar's *Mee kon*, the case is also mentioned in Radhakrishnan, *Purushatra* (55, 63, 79). Radhakrishnan was a reputed Brahmin journalist who took it upon himself to write what he saw as one of the most revolutionary histories of Goan society.
20 Such invocations of caste shame and humiliation routinely appear in available biographies and life histories of lower-caste subjects in South Asia. There is much work still to be done in the continuities of content within the writings of Other Backward Caste (OBC) communities such as the Samaj and Dalit communities. See Guru, *Humiliation*.
21 Paigankar, *Mee kon*, 2:43–56.
22 References to the land awarded for the establishment of the school can be found in "Matriz Poinguinim," unpublished land documents at the Sub-Treasury Office, Chauri, Canacona, Goa, and Paigini Temple Documents (in Marathi, Modi, and Portuguese) located at the Parashuram Temple, Paigini, Goa.
23 R. Guha, *Elementary Aspects of Peasant Insurgency in India Colonial India*.

24 Chow, *Entanglements*, 12.
25 Probyn, "Suspended Beginnings of Childhood and Nostalgia." See also Morris, *In the Place of Origins*. For more on biography as a genre within South Asia, see Arnold and Blackburn, *Telling Lives in India*.
26 Paigankar, *Mee kon*, 2:13.
27 The term *Marathas* denotes a collective (and heavily debated) reference to Indo-Aryan groups of Hindu, Marathi-speaking castes of warriors and peasants hailing largely from the present-day state of Maharashtra. Through their creation of a substantial empire in the late seventeenth and eighteenth centuries, the Marathas occupied a major part of India. Of note here is that the "Marathas" were known by the term primarily because their native tongue was mostly (though not always) Marathi. Thus, the terms *Marathi people* and *Maratha people* are not interchangeable and should not be confused for each other. See Deshpande, *Creative Pasts*. Marathas as a caste in contemporary India have now become part of the problem of caste oppression. As Suryakant Waghmore notes, Marathas are the new "oppressors," the new landowners/*zamindars*, who claim victimhood and class poverty despite their obvious capital gains and wealth. While such characterizations are indeed accurate, they apply unevenly to the Samaj and its collectivities across Maharashtra, Goa, and Karnataka. Samaj members are rarely landowners, and their caste status (as will be discussed in later chapters) remains malleable and divergently precarious. See Waghmore, "The Dominant Victim?"
28 In many ways, the Samaj's debates around self-naming anticipate the paradoxes that Wendy Brown invokes around the limitations of rights discourses for minoritized communities (in her case, women and/or queers). See Brown, "Suffering Rights as Paradoxes."
29 See Kamat, *Farar Far*.
30 I am of course referring here to Spivak's attentiveness to the perilous demands of a liberal project as "that which we cannot not want." See Spivak, *Outside in the Teaching Machine*, 44.
31 Pandey, "Can There Be a Subaltern Middle Class?" Pandey focuses "on specific assemblages that have historically been seen as communities of lower-class and underclass individuals and families. His essay examines the history of members of these 'communities' who come to inhabit not the positions of the down-and-out, where they allegedly belong, but those of the more comfortable, educated, professional middle classes. Thus it asks what the history of the struggles of these subaltern middle classes tells us about the limits of the middle-class idea and about the conditions necessary for the consolidation of particular groups as middle-class, modern, and unmarked" (322–23).
32 In an early talk I gave on this project to a group of archivists and librarians at UCLA in 2006, I was asked a question about the arrangement of the

materials in the archives. For many in the room, committed as they were to preserving minoritized histories, one of the major concerns was what one did with the materials after one had a chance to look at them. I was pressed to explain if I put the materials back where I found them, so as to preserve the "originary" order of the materials, instead of displacing them into new arrangements. At that time, I was flummoxed by the question, as such concerns were not part of my relationship to these archives. Since then, I have had time to return to that question and speak more directly to its extraordinary potential.

33 Miller's *Impostors* may be of interest here. Miller speaks to the rise of literary hoaxes, specifically within intercultural communities in France, as modes of minority representation. For Miller, literary hoaxes call attention to the paucity of minority voices and the ease with which they can be ventriloquized into presence (1–6).

34 All issues of the *Samaj Sudharak* are currently housed in the Mumbai branch of the Samaj. The publication continues to appear on a monthly basis to this day but is now called *Gomant Shardha*.

35 Tipnis, "Kala-Sangeet" [Kala of music], 100.

36 Tipnis, "Kala-Sangeet," 101; Balachandran, "Documents, Digitisation and History."

37 There is a robust corpus of scholarship that speaks to the stylizations of gender and visuality in colonial and postcolonial South Asia. I am grateful to Geeta Patel and Benedito Ferrao for alerting me to these genealogies of representation. See specifically these texts: Pinney, *The Coming of Photography in India*; Thapan, "Embodiment and Identity in Contemporary Society"; Rizzo, "Gender and Visuality"; N. Majumdar, *Wanted Cultured Ladies Only!* See also Masood, "Catering to Indian and British Tastes"; Gadihoke, "Selling Soap and Stardom"; Freitag, "Consumption and Identity"; and McGowan, "Modernity at Home."

38 Tambe, "From Romance to Reproduction."

39 Chaudhury, *Afterimage of Empire*; Alloula, *The Colonial Harem*. See also Rice-Sayre, "Veiled Threats."

40 Sir Herbert Hope Risley was the infamous British civil servant, anthropologist, and linguist who published widely on the customs and social structures of India. Risley is arguably most heralded as the architect of the 1901 census of India and his subsequent publication *The People of India* (1908), based on the survey information gathered for the census. Following in the footsteps of his predecessors, John Forbes Watson and John William Kaye's photographic collections, Risley's book similarly contained illustrations of tribes and peoples and an ethnological map of India, all of which became prototypes for taxonomical representations of "the people of India." See Risley, *The People of India*. For further read-

41 ing and the continued force of such taxonomical practices in postcolonial India, see Jenkins, "Another 'People of India' Project."

41 For more on the relationship between biographies, images/icons, and figuration, see B. Ghosh, *Global Icons*, 183. I am indebted to Bishnu for her timely reminders of the gendered intercalations of iconicity and the popular in South Asia.

42 When I first encountered these images, I spent many hours in the Samaj archives, looking for any biographical records that would help me "identify" these women, but to no avail. I also spoke to many living elders (the images were taken circa 1939–40, as far we can tell) to see if anyone remembered the women featured in the images. Almost everyone I spoke to (and I spoke to over fifty Samaj members between the ages of seventy and eighty-seven) had no specific recollection of any of the images. Instead, they all claimed a kind of general kinship with the figures; some said one or more of the women reminded them of an aunt, or a distant cousin, or a relative they could not quite put their finger on. As Adhik Shirodkar, one of the more prominent figures in the group I spoke to, quizzically said to me: "They all look familiar. But then wasn't that the point?"

43 Spivak: "Notwithstanding all the legalistic efforts of literary criticism, literature remains singular and unverifiable." Spivak, *Critique of Postcolonial Reason*, 174–75.

44 There is, as has been much discussed, a much-revered place for lost-and-found letters within queer histories as pathways into the private lives of figures written out of history's front page. More recently, the discovery of the private letters and diary of a working-class farmer in England has finally confirmed what historians of sexuality have always believed: that ordinary people did not reject alternative sexualities, and all we had to do was find evidence to prove that was just the case. The historical challenge here was that ordinary folks were largely illiterate and did not keep collections and private cases of letters and memorabilia. As such, this discovery is deemed even more "authentic" and valuable. See Coughlan, "The 200-Year-Old Diary That's Rewriting Gay History." For a broader sampling of texts within queer history that speak to the pivotal evidentiary value of lost-and-found queer letters, read Garlinger, *Confessions of the Letter Closet*; Dever, "Greta Garbo's Foot"; and Clarke, "'I Am Your Loving Boy-Wife.'"

45 See Kosambi, *Women Writing Gender*.

46 See Phadke, *Kulabyachi dandi* [The lighthouse at Colaba]; Phadke, *Sex Problem in India*; Phadke, *Jadugaar* [The magician]; Phadke, *Sex Problems in India*; Phadke, *Ajace tarun stree-purush va tyanpudhil prasna* [Contemporary youth and the problems before them]; and Phadke, *Manas-mandir* [The temple of the mind].

47 Phadke, *Kulabyachi dandi*, 51.

48 Phadke, *Kulabyachi dandi*, 22. Of note here is how Jagdish, in one of his letters, collapses Manik with an image of a "dark-skinned dancing girl with a shriveled face" (ek kaali kulkuleet khappad tondachi natvi bai) when he is describing her sexuality, and then writes how he is embarrassed to have had such vile thoughts.

49 Botre and Haynes, "Sexual Knowledge, Sexual Anxieties." For more on the relationship between caste and sexual politics and their effect on theories of self, see Omvedt, *Cultural Revolt in a Colonial Society*; and Mitra, *Indian Sex Life*: see particularly the chapter "Veracity" (176–202).

50 For more on letters as malleable and epistemologically ambiguous genres, see Jolly and Stanley, "Letters as/Not a Genre."

51 Shashishekhar, "Harvelele patr" [Lost letters] (August 1940), 151.

52 Shashishekhar, "Harvelele patr" (August 1940), 151.

53 Shashishekhar, "Harvelele patr" (October 1940), 198.

54 Kakodkar, "The Portuguese and the Kalavants." I am grateful to Dr. Kakodkar, senior librarian (retired) at Goa University, for her invaluable help. See also C. Pinto, "Women's Inheritance Rights."

55 See chaps. 2–4 in Prakash, "The Social and Cultural Dimensions of Migration." Prakash's study continues to be the only available sociological study of the Gomantak Maratha Samaj.

56 There is a robust set of literatures in kinship studies that explores more substantively the questions Arondekar stages around collectivity, belonging, and affect. Some representative texts include Carsten, *Cultures of Relatedness*; Strathern, *Relations*; McKinnon, *Vital Relations*; and Garroutte, *Real Indians*.

57 To recapitulate the well-rehearsed Derridean argument here in a slightly different tenor: supplementarity performs multiple functions of plenitude. On the one hand, the supplement cumulatively "adds itself, it is a surplus, a plenitude enriching another plenitude, the fullest measure of presence." As such, "it is thus that art, techne, image, representation, convention, etc. come as supplements to nature and are rich with the entire cumulating function." But the supplement also "adds only to replace . . . as if one fills a void [so that] . . . something can be filled up of itself, can accomplish itself, only by allowing itself through sign and proxy." Derrida, *Of Grammatology*, 144–45.

CHAPTER TWO

A History I Am Not Writing

Sexuality's Exemplarity

If my previous chapter introduced us to an archive of sexuality, so widely calibrated in tone and content that any number of readings could be woven out of the sheer diversity of its subject matter, this chapter is about the errant tales, the historical lessons, and the possibilities of amplification afforded by such archival materials.[1] While the pursuit of alternatives to Euro-American histories has certainly reoriented the critical priorities and geopolitical stakes of sexuality studies, we continue to want histories whose anticipated recuperation bypasses the narrative-stopping doom of an always impending loss. Such attempts to diversify histories of sexuality have now engaged me for almost two decades, and I have returned over and over again to the modes by which we gather archival evidence and the fault lines on which we produce queer readings.[2] Inseparable from these preoccupations is an awareness that histories (including of sexuality) are an always imploding narrative genre, only ever a reading and/or archival "find" away from dissolution.

Perhaps this awareness may in part explain why so much ink (toxic and otherwise) has been expended over the past few years on how to read and extract meaning from historical archives. Diatribes against the hermeneutics of suspicion or reading against the grain (where all readings are necessarily symptomatic readings of something that is missing and/or erased) have become the new hegemony, leading to a rallying call for surface readings and/or readings along the archival grain (where the surface of the texts bears witness to the violence of the moment). There is now a shared sense that how and why we make meanings out of the past must constantly be debated.[3] Yet for all the exegetical flair around the practice of reading and its concomitant revelations, less has been said about how we read historical archives of "distant" elsewheres and/or literatures. As Nirvana Tanoukhi pointedly avers, such diagnostic, prescriptive, and even reparative (pace Eve Kosofsky Sedgwick) forms of reading rarely engage with the challenges of geopolitics, relegating such reading more to a citation of cultural and historical exemplars than to a live space of hermeneutical transformation.[4] Through his work on colonial Egypt and world literatures, Michael Allan expands further on the limits of such extant reading practices. He trenchantly reminds us that there is always a *history of reading*, an entire way of being in language that undergirds any encounter with archives and literatures. To enter into a history of reading is to enter into a relationship with words and worlds. What would it mean, Allan asks, for example, if we were to refuse the opposition between "a practice of reading based on memorization, embodiment and recitation in Qur'anic schools, and another practice based on reflection, critique, and judgment, increasingly central to what gets defined as literacy in the modern Egyptian state?"[5] What worlds do we devalue through the absence of such histories of reading?[6] Allan's embrace of the simultaneous primacy of multiple practices of reading is what interests me here. To seek such equivalence, to value worlds within words, is a kind of unlearning, a way of reading with "distant" archives and not just about them.

It is thus hardly surprising that the most trenchant challenges to our readings of times past and spaces distant have overwhelmingly come from scholars working on histories of slavery, sexuality, and colonialism, acutely critical of archival economies of loss, paucity, and/or devaluation. Scholars such as Jennifer Morgan, Indrani Chatterjee, and Elizabeth Povinelli, to name a select few, have foregrounded the fervent born-again historical materialism (if you will) that has plagued, indeed haunted, the recuperation of histories of slavery and colonialism, contrasting it with more robust informal and imaginative economies of survival that are often ignored or elided in such readings. For these scholars, the past has become the propertied subject of critique, gathering value through triumphant readings of conventional economic histories (even if they are directed to emancipatory ends) that preserve rather than trouble the vexed calculus of gender, labor, and capital.[7] But I am getting ahead of myself here, proffering critical claims without first hailing the worlds and words from within which I begin. Let me turn to my history of reading here.

Even as I write, historical vernaculars of reading feature prominently within contemporary South Asian history. State-sponsored campaigns to purify South Asia, more specifically India, of *sanskritik pradushan* (cultural pollution) have become the mainstay of a Hindutva-fueled polity. Within such state formulations, the pollution of the Indian populace derives from its historical amnesia, from its refusal and/or erasure of proper historical readings, cast in the loss of Sanskrit as mother tongue, or in the aspiration of a *swachh bharat* (pure/clean India), emptied of the corrupting forces of minority lives (read Muslim, Dalit, queer, and more). The historical past, now more than ever, founds the moral authority of the Indian nation-state where all forms of difference are coercively shunted aside to make way for a new "India shining." When it comes to historical evidence, any shoddy travesty of research appears to pass muster, as the recent appointment of Professor Y. Sudershan Rao as chairperson of the Indian Council for Historical Research (ICHR) so clearly demonstrates.[8] For Rao and his ilk, Indian historians need to abandon their Marxist and Western historiographical ways, to make way for a Hindutva-infused empiricism that would eschew archival ambivalences and establish historical dates for the "factual" events of the Ramayana and Mahabharata.[9] Aiding and abetting such twists of historical knowledge are strategic claims to "decolonization and democratization," whereby the glories of ancient India are rescued from the denigrations of a blinkered and dominant academic left. To "decolonize" Indian history, Vikram Sampath (the author of a two-volume biography of V. D. Savarkar) argues, is to rediscover an impressive Indic past and, at the same time, to confront the trauma of the so-called Islamic conquest.[10]

Such concerns with the manipulation, erasure, and/or refusal of diverse pasts are especially pressing for the lives of sexual minorities, as the legal and economic right to be here and now is often authorized by the evidence of histories past. One only has to recall the past legal challenges around the repeal of the so-called antisodomy statute, Section 377, which remained embroiled in debates around the presence/absence of alternative sexualities in India's past.[11] As scholars of sexuality and South Asia, we are thus called on to insist on a protean and diverse past that rejects an instrumentalist and triumphalist Hindutva worldview.[12] To put it more bluntly, the reading of sexuality's past(s) (in South Asia and elsewhere) has now clearly become a complicated affair: a balancing act between an embrace of sexuality's munificent diversity (divergent temporalities and spaces are fodder for theories of difference) and a capture of its genealogical sameness (the past surrenders lineages of our queer presents). The cornerstone of such efforts is of course the archival exemplar, the preferred critical object, through which we accrue and restore meaning to lost pasts. Even as it is almost commonplace, particularly for those of us who work within colonial archives, to argue that historical archives must be read as registers more of selection than of empiricism, there is less debate around forms of archival consumption and dissemination, particularly as they unfold in minoritized historiographies.[13] To write good histories of sexuality is to seek out that perfect, elusive archival trace, the vastness of a history glimpsed and compacted in an enticing, fragmentary form. Most times, such an archival trace coheres as a narrative form precisely when it contains the stories we want to hear, stories that restore presence and vitality to an often-diminished past.

I want to begin, then, with one such critical object that continues to inaugurate most historiographical and/or ethnographic projects: the problem event, the detail, the legal case, the anecdote—in other words, an archival trace that is often a tantalizing obstacle to clarity, which then comes alive through our reconstructive hermeneutics.[14] In these history-swamped times, the archival trace appears to be working overtime, as an infinitely malleable tool for scripting dramatic and heroic readings. Most often than not, the turn to such an inaugural problem event becomes a story of exemplarity, where the critical encounter opens up potentialities that we as scholars want to and usually do figure out. A history worth telling, one might even insist, depends on exemplary and representative readings of such archival traces: narrative weavings of particularity and wholeness, of details erupting into insights, insights into veracity. For scholars working at the interstices of multiple minoritized historiographies, such as myself, the problem event often becomes a crucial way of resolving the crisis of marginality, where the scarcity of historical evidence is refused by the hermeneutical performance of plenitude—where you recover the archival trace for the promise of historical precedence and futurity. The ineluctable feature of a good archival exemplar is that it will tell us a story, preferably a compelling story, a story worthy of repetition and citation. To imagine otherwise is to strip the exemplar bare.

In what follows, I want to meditate on what exemplifying readings of problem events means for the way in which we encounter archives—particularly, as is the case here, archives of sexuality. Simply put, what makes something an archival exemplar and not merely a gesture, illustration, or historical footnote? That is, why does the writing of a history of sexuality take a particular exemplary form, and what creates obstacles to its lithesome storytelling? What are the hermeneutic demands placed on its revelations? As Lauren Berlant so sagaciously asks in her work on the idea of the case/event, how do we decide which critical objects are worthy of, and adequate to, the weight of representation? And how do such selections sustain and even vitalize our sedimented habits of reading?[15] As she notes in a second brilliant essay, aptly called "Genre Flailing," is it even possible to "control the object enough to say a thing about it and to change it enough that it comes to organize surprising kinds of exemplary association"?[16] Are historical exemplars of sexuality preselected, an effect of what Kadji Amin has called "attachment genealogy," where inconvenient histories (like pederasty) fall away?[17] Or, alternatively, are sexuality's exemplars more "aleatory conjunctures," as Jonathan Goldberg noted all those years ago, chance seeds of an analysis that extends indefinitely and infinitely?[18]

The provocation of my title, "A History I Am Not Writing," is an invitation to move with these rich deliberations on the archival exemplar, without presuming it as a mode of historical stabilization or recuperation. When I first started research on the Gomantak Maratha Samaj (the intellectual archive that founds this book), I was routinely pressed on the message and use of my work, as it engaged a collectivity whose history was mired in the messy discomforts of sexuality, caste, and region.[19] For an archive as unexamined as the one I am writing about, the exemplar becomes even more key, freighted as it is with the weight of an allegedly erased history. Exemplars materialize the variegated patinas of loss; we excavate facts that allow us to participate in what Alisa Lebow (in the context of documentary realism) terms a recursive "epistephilia," an excessive, relentless preoccupation with veracity that becomes the only value invested in an archive.[20] Bothered by what was then, and what remains, the persistent demand for a historical value-in-the-making (which would leverage the elusive archival detail to memorializing and/or truth effect), I wanted to make room for a more paradoxical possibility: to read the archival exemplar precisely for what it cannot hold. To find a way to craft a history that would speak to the conundrum of the archival trace, not to decode it (because we cannot) but more to embrace its roving and fractal complexity. Let me reiterate here (as I noted in my introduction) that this is not a call to the ungraspability or incommensurability of the critical object, too routinized a claim in encounters with geopolitical elsewheres.[21] There is, as I will demonstrate in the second half of the chapter, plenty to learn, know, and let go. Bear in mind also that the Samaj archives (with their attachments to Portuguese India) are as foreign to South Asianists as they would be to anyone within Euro-American circles of reference.[22]

What I want to do instead is to proffer a different sight line for the consumption of archives, of times past. I want to think of a way to read archives that bypasses lineages of reproduction or value, of loss or absence. I want to imagine a relationship to archives that is about loitering, stalling, digressing, and defamiliarizing the very process of writing history. What I want to think about, tout court, is "timepass." Belonging to the postcolonial vernacular of Hinglish (a potent cocktail of the queen's and the people's English), timepass is a concept peculiar to the natives of South Asia. It encompasses a range of meanings, from killing time to engaging in casual (often sexual) activities that defy time's value.[23] To do or invite timepass is to unmoor oneself from the value chain, from the weight of time, to surrender (for better or worse) to the process; all that matters is that time passes and we along with it. Even the etymological mappings of the *Oxford English Dictionary* (OED) catalogue the promiscuous leanings of the concept, dating back to its official print appearance in the 1980s and 1990s.[24] "Timepass" designates, on the one hand, an activity of mindless distraction, chosen by illiterate masses, and, on the other, a more general assessment of taste and value, crossing class and linguistic divides.[25] What is clear is that it is a term whose meanings routinely elude textual capture. Scant scholarly research can be found on the topic, beyond a few socially responsible studies that point to the concept's presence in disgruntled, bored youth (who are unemployed and have too much time on their hands), or in urban collectivities where the inclination to timepass has led to an increased proclivity for casual sex. I am of course being ironic here.[26]

For the purposes of this chapter, I am interested more in thinking of timepass as an epistemology for queer historiographical work that reroutes our orientation to the past.[27] How might we approach the issue of sexuality and exemplar askance, without revisiting routinized habits of analysis, even as we attend to the generation of value that is implicit in the act of reading itself? What would it mean to think of our encounters with times past as timepass, as spaces of delight, boredom, distraction, dynamism, and even nothing?[28] Timepass here is immanent to history's becoming: it contains, akin to Vinay Gidwani's theses on capital and waste, both historical "value-in-waiting" and "an omnipresent logic of dissipation" that attenuates the legitimacy and exercise of history-writing.[29] Timepass incorporates and implicates the labor of time into its referent, even as it remains disorderly and distinct from it. To do timepass history is not to devalue the critical object (as one of the definitions in the OED would have us believe!); rather, it is to access archival moments where the demands of representation are outlived, canceled, evaded, and reanimated.[30] If you recall, I began this book by asking us to consider why the history of the Samaj has not been written, despite the overwhelming availability and accessibility of its archives. Was it, I asked, because the Samaj archive did not summon the more reliable ghosts of an oppositional and lost history of sexuality and region?[31] As such, timepass as heuristic comports with the intimate and immanent logics of this archive's form, extricating our reading from the more burdensome reproductive protocols of message and use. We need not worry, then, about the hoary machinery of persuasion and purpose when we find ourselves doing timepass with this Samaj's archival exemplars. No peeling of critical layer upon layer here, but more an exhortation to think the archival exemplar as an absorbing and abundant discursive presence, reassembled through our every reading.[32]

MORE IMAGINED THAN REAL

Imagine, then, finding an archival exemplar that has all the elements needed to sustain clarifying historical reclamation. Now imagine that exemplar torquing away from the askesis of such readings. Let us begin our foray there. A public meeting of the residents and ratepayers (taxpayers) of Girgaum (in South Bombay) is hastily convened on July 16, 1911, with the express purpose of protesting "against the growing evil of women of bad repute coming to reside in increasing numbers in Girgaum." A petition is drafted, and four unanimous resolutions are passed (under the leadership of Sir Bhalchandra Krishna) and in turn forwarded to the secretary of government (Judicial Department papers), Bombay. The resolutions in the petition argue (1) that it is "highly objectionable that women of ill-fame should at all be allowed to occupy houses even on main roads and thoroughfares, and generally in quarters inhabited by respectable families and they emphatically deprecate the recent increase of this evil in Girgaum," (2) that "effective steps should be taken to induce house-owners to refuse to let their houses or premises be used for immoral purposes," (3) that the "Commissioner of Police should use all the powers given to him by law to reduce this evil" and "fresh legislation" should be passed to further "empower him," and (4), last but not least, that a committee consisting of the gentlemen from the association should be appointed to take any steps necessary to "carry out the object of the meeting."

Responding with some testiness, the secretary to the government, C. A. Kincaid, writes a long and disciplining letter (dated November 13, 1911) to the ratepayers of Girgaum. In the letter, Kincaid applauds the "spirit" of the petition against the "evil of prostitution" but cautions against the inflammatory rhetoric used by the ratepayers, arguing that "he has reason to believe that the growth of the evil is more apparent than real." He further adds that in the "absence of definite statistics," there is no indication that the evil of prostitution has in fact increased in Girgaum—the more obvious explanation for the threat being that "ill-houses of fame" had been shut down in North Girgaum and forced the "women to scatter and invade the southern part of the ward." In case the ratepayers still think it is incumbent on the commissioner of police to take action, the secretary further adds that the commissioner cannot use the "power invested in him by the law" to take action against the large proportion of these immoral women who are more "kept mistresses" (devadasis) than "common prostitutes." And further, even if the women are redistributed and moved to other parts of the city, it would interfere with the goals of the City Improvement Trust, which does not have a particular investment in providing "harlot's quarters." To do so would be to endorse such vice, and perhaps, the letter snidely questions, is that what the ratepayers want?

The letter ends with a final flourish, saying that "prostitution in Girgaum is a subject which usually comes in for publicity during the monsoon season when there is not much going on in Bombay and the Government are away in Poona." Castigating the ratepayers for their own involvement in the "apparent" evil of this vice, Kincaid adds that the houses where the women reside are owned and supported by the very ratepayers advocating these resolutions. And, moreover, in his own "experiences" of Bombay, "the very gentleman who presided over the meeting recommended to Government the other day for an honour an individual who counts among his nearest female relations three ladies who according to my Criminal Investigation Department must be classes among those who, in Census parlance, are following dishonourable professions." In a last note, he also reminds the ratepayers that the government must act "with great caution," especially as the commissioner of police is still recovering from "being hauled into court by a woman upon whom he has served a notice and be told that he had acted *ultra vives* and that the woman is not a common prostitute." And in an effort to erase any doubts on this question, Kincaid writes that he himself has visited similar houses accused of being "disorderly brothels" in response to like complaints, only to find that one of the members who visits the house is "a member of a Parsi Purity Brigade or Vigilance Committee."[33]

At the heart of the debate between the two sides is a rather peculiar crisis of reading, embedded in an even more fascinating and humorous palimpsest of arguments. There is always an uptick in petitions in the monsoon, the colonial official notes, a time of less "real" action and more "apparent" commotion. The hermeneutical demand on either side is to make visible and/or eradicate an object of sexuality that is for all considered "apparent"—a paradoxical term that traffics equally in the realm of the obvious and of the elusive (we know the "evil ladies" exist, but the force of their threat may or may not be real). For someone like myself who is writing a book on these "evil ladies of Girgaum,"[34] this exchange inevitably becomes an archival exemplar, laden with the challenges and possibilities of historical value. Surely, I must insist, fueled by a restorative historiographical impulse, that what is lost in the back-and-forth of this exchange is the material histories and contexts of the very object of knowledge under debate. The slipperiness of the arguments made on both sides (are they or are they not prostitutes, are they "kept mistresses" or devadasis?) could become the perfect foil for the "real" history of sexuality that needs telling: that to reduce these women to the confines of this debate is to limit our analytical horizons, to forget that these so-called evil ladies founded, in the decade or so after this event, one of the most successful devadasi collectivities in Bombay, the Gomantak Maratha Samaj, earning them the mighty moniker Bharatatil Ek Aggresor Samaj. As we have already seen in the previous chapters, the Samaj endures neither the pitfalls of archival loss nor the indignities of historical erasure.[35]

In what follows, I want to amplify the two registers of critical reading that lead us to the exemplar here: one that sees histories of sexuality as absent, lost, and miscast, and another that views them as abundant, vital, and available. Rather than emphasizing the disjuncture between the two registers, this juxtaposition means to highlight their differences with regard to inflection and epistemology. Indeed, any historical reading (of loss and/or abundance) oscillates between the conceit of recovery and the awareness of a history that punctures any such recuperative imperative.[36] What happens when we approach the archival exemplar through the history of make.believe I outlined in my introduction? What if our critical energies are directed not solely at explicating the historical trace (through historical context and more) but more at anchoring it in modes of "timepass" and the stories we cull? Even as sexuality's capital in the abovementioned exemplar takes shape through a dispute over legal authority, the force of the exemplar is organized more around the question of narrative ownership. That is, the evil ladies enter the archive as an exemplar of a dispute that addresses the threats of a nonmonogamous conjugal form. This epistemology of the narrative (how do we know what to know and circulate?) determines the means by which information about sexuality is simultaneously conveyed and held back—in short, the means by which it becomes an exemplar of sexuality's history.

My task in this chapter is thus twofold: First, I have furnished you with an archival trace that clearly has, as I will demonstrate, robust historical and genealogical content. The story of the evil ladies of Girgaum will inevitably deepen our attachment to past identities and histories, as there is much to learn and hold on to. Yet as we learned in the previous chapter, the Samaj's archive anticipates and indeed relies on these well-worn critical habits, leaning in to their prescribed purpose to fresh and surprising ends. As we have seen, the Samaj's archive accepts the imperative of exposure, staging scenes of recognition (as in the case of the "fake" halla) that deliberately allow it to be seen. The dynamism inside the archive—past, present, and in between—comes from observing seemingly staple archive genres (letters, biographies, photographs) rearranged and refurbished in myriad and unexpected ways. How, then, do we take these lessons in archival formation to the reading of an archival exemplar?

Second, how do we approach divergent historical readings of sexuality's exemplars as noncompetitive, not as exercises in exposure or critique but as an invitation to "timepass," to extend the complex encounter with the exemplar into a language of others? How do we activate a history that does not partake of the pendulum, of an oscillation between recovery and a punctuation of the recovery imperative? Even as the archival record of the evil ladies appears perfectly crafted for storytelling, with inbuilt elements of mystery and mayhem, how do we move away from the enticements of its exemplarity? As Carolyn Steedman cautioned many years ago, the constant reiteration and recuperation of "missing" exemplars in minoritized histories (in her case, labor history and women's history) does not necessarily intervene in the disciplinary and disciplining scripts of history-writing.[37] Rather, it creates a paradoxical sense that there must be little to recover if much discursive effort is needed to signal such historical absences. In what follows, I want us to think of the collective constitution of the archival exemplar, as other narratives are continuously added to a record always partially recoverable in itself, where meaning is generated not as much by singling out as by what Hortense Spillers calls "an opening in the chain of necessity."[38] Every reading of the exemplar's historical context, every rendition of its minutiae, demands a recalibration of its overall meaning. The force of the exemplar thus rests not in its revelation, which is so scripted as to be antidramatic (we must look for evil ladies!), but in the waywardness of its composition. In coming to such observations, I have also had to dissent from my earlier thinking on this subject, where I remained enamored of sexuality's archival trace as an agonistic space of absence and presence. I wanted to queer the historical record, even though the record was never stable to begin with.

THE PROPERTIES OF EVIL

Several historical accounts from the period set the stage for the recuperation of the evil ladies of Girgaum as the progenitors of the successful and celebrated Gomantak Maratha Samaj. From the outset, there is a concerted effort to fix their value as maligned subjects—unruly, corrupt, dangerous, sexual, or otherwise. And for the most part, those efforts remain thwarted as more and more conflicting information on these troublesome evil ladies continues to surface. Padma Anagol, for example, outlines early twentieth-century public reform initiatives to read the evil ladies as morally contagious within a larger respectability movement orchestrated by largely middle-class (and mostly upper-caste) women. Within such narratives of reform and progress (primarily in western India), the evil ladies become purveyors of a curiously fecund set of cultural threats. Here the evil of the ladies shifts from the corruptions of sex to the debasement of kala (art), a shift that needs to be rerouted (and stabilized) through a more heteronormative marriage economy. On the one hand, the evil ladies trouble cherished distinctions between kalavants/*naikins*/artists and prostitutes; after all, if they are primarily repositories of arts (kala), then their growing presence cannot be regulated within antiprostitution regulation, and the petition of the Girgaum ratepayers holds no ground. On the other hand, the rise of such evil ladies and their clientele demonstrates the need for a more robust cultivation of arts (kala) within middle-class women themselves. In this vein, middle-class men become clients of evil ladies in search of artistic enrichment, not sex, a turn that rouses middle-class women to claim the domain of the arts (kala) for themselves. For Anagol, groups such as the Maharashtra Mahila Mandal (Maharashtra Women's Association) (1902) embody the tensions of such concerns as they plot efforts to both train in the arts and organize against the presence of the evil ladies. Vernacular newspapers of the day, such as *Bodh Sudhakar* and *Subodh Patrika*, Anagol writes, equally register the scale of these efforts, carrying accounts of middle-class women trying to oust the evil ladies from their residences, even as others, such as *Indu Prakash* and *Dnyan Prakash*, run editorials extolling the naikins' bravery in resisting eviction.[39]

Lest we settle into these florid accounts of the evil ladies, their alleged moral turpitude and theft of native (middle-class arts/kala), there are other historical details that erupt onto and further muddle the historical plot. As Ashwini Tambe and Stephen Legg remind us, the social geography of the sex trade in colonial Bombay rarely conformed to any settled organization of race, class, or spatiality.[40] Simply put, there is no stable referent for the specter of evil ladies within archival records in terms of their racial, spatial, or class status. Tambe, for example, pointedly argues that the spatial stratifications of Bombay required white European prostitutes to live alongside and even economically align with native women, especially in dense areas of sex trade, such as Kamathipura, that were adjacent to Girgaum. Such racially complex urban geographies often meant that European prostitutes (of Polish, Italian, and German origins) were ironically depicted as more "evil" than Indian prostitutes: they were too "bold," "going about in a state of semi-nudity," and catering to mostly working-class men (of all races).[41] Indeed, petitions filed as early as 1871 by residents of Girgaum and its vicinity record similar calls as the 1911 petition, albeit for the removal of European prostitutes from congested thoroughfares in neighborhoods such as Girgaum.[42]

Ethnographic and travel accounts of colonial Bombay register other twists and turns in the vexing history of the evil ladies. Govind Narayan's *Mumbaiche varnan* (1863) documents the author's migration to Bombay from Madgaon through a series of lush accounts of the city's shifting urban landscape. In a chapter describing the rise of arts and theater in Bombay (circa 1861), Narayan writes with great disgust about the rise of "dancing girls" who appear to have garnered clientele across the city, their "numbers increasing daily." Of great concern to Narayan is the successful dancing girl's acquisition of properties and her vulgar display of wealth. As he writes, "She spent nearly four thousand rupees" on an initiation ceremony for her daughter to become a devadasi, reminding him of the "stories of the matriarchates [sic] mentioned in the Puranas."⁴³ K. Raghunathji expresses a similar articulation of shock and awe in his documentation of the rise of "Bombay Dancing Girls." Writing for the *Indian Antiquary* (1884), Raghunathji provides detailed descriptions of these dancing girls (who are "both Hindu and Musalman") and their practices, noting that a large percentage of the Hindu girls appear to have migrated "from Goa and the places around it."⁴⁴ He notes that the "Hindu dancing girls are of four sects, viz:—Naikins, Bhavins, Murlis and Kasbins. Of these the first two belong to Goa and villages round it, being natives of that district." Unlike Narayan, Raghunathji paints a more flattering picture of these women, extolling their beauty and their generally "intelligent pleasing appearance."⁴⁵ While they arrive in Bombay speaking "Goanese" (which we are mysteriously told differs from the "language of Bombay"), they quickly acclimatize and soon read, write, and even compose songs in Marathi. As in Narayan's account, Raghunathji too emphasizes the perplexingly "large sums of money" that the women appear to have access to, describing in excruciating detail the gold ornaments the women routinely wear.⁴⁶ Although such anthropological accounts are to be consumed with some trepidation (after all, we are rarely provided with any sources for the information that is provided!), references to the women's growing presence and appetite for wealth can also be found in other genres of archival records.⁴⁷

Of equal interest are several legal appeals filed on behalf of these evil ladies petitioning the state for support in their claims for maintenance from the families of dead patrons, or yajemans, residing in or around Girgaum.⁴⁸ As in the accounts discussed above, the focus continues to be on the acquisition of ill-gotten wealth by the evil ladies and the threat it poses to the sanctioned circulation of capital within family formations. One series of appeals, in particular, stand out in their detailed listing of monies acquired and requisitioned from the family of an upstanding member of society (a member of the Girgaum ratepayers association I began with) after his untimely death in 1919. In *Bai Monghibai v. Bai Nagubai* (August 11, 1922), Bai Monghibai (widow of the deceased Vasanji Madhavji Thakar, who died on November 21, 1919) appeals a previous judgment of Mr. Justice Kanga that awarded monthly maintenance of four hundred rupees to Bai Nagubai Manglorkar as "the permanent concubine of the deceased." According to the details of the previous judgment, the deceased, "possessed of moveable and immoveable property of a very large value," had abandoned his family domicile in Vadgadi and had come to reside with Bai Nagubai, a Goan naikin, "in her house in Girgaum and that he continued to reside there until the day prior to his death." Bai Nagubai claimed monthly maintenance and "alleged that a sum of Rs. 25,000 was specially promised by the deceased" for the benefit of her and her daughter after his death. In the series of legal skirmishes that followed the original judgment of Justice Kanga, much effort is made to determine whether Bai Nagubai was the "exclusive mistress" of the deceased and whether she maintained sexual chastity even after his death. Bai Monghibai, the deceased's widow, argues that the deceased merely visited Bai Nagubai in her Girgaum residence and was permanently domiciled elsewhere. Acting Judge Lallubhai Shah, who reviewed the widow's appeal, concurs with her claim, even as he is "willing to admit that Bai Nagubai used to live in a house near Kennedy Bridge at Girgaon where the deceased Vasanji used to visit her regularly ... prior to his death and used to pay her some monthly allowance."

The crux of the appeal relies on the status of Bai Nagubai's residence in Girgaon/Girgaum: Is it or is it not the primary residence of the deceased? For Shah, the true nature of the deceased's relationship with Bai Nagubai cannot be ascertained without "knowing the nature of his visits" to the Girgaum residence. True companionship, for Shah, can be determined only through open and continuous cohabitation with Bai Nagubai, something that the facts of the case do not appear to corroborate. Shah's judgment is appealed further by Bai Nagubai; she provides evidence that the deceased had rented the Girgaum residence "in her name ... and that he was nursed there during his last illness and only removed shortly before his death."[49]

As the story of these evil ladies unfolds in multiple historical accounts of the period, it becomes "apparent" that the "real" archival substance of their evil unfolds in variegated scenes of capital. From their ostentatious displays of wealth to their corruption of the family form as value, the evil ladies appear to play exemplary roles in what Mariam Dossal has called Bombay's "theatre of conflict."[50] At the time of the ratepayers' complaint against the evil ladies of Girgaum, the city of Bombay appears mired in various struggles around land expansion and reclamation, gentrification and the increasing demands of native franchise. Prashant Kidambi reminds us that this is also the period when the Bombay Improvement Trust (BIT) emerges as the central force in shaping the city's physical landscape. BIT was an ambitious colonial enterprise that was largely a response to the sanitation risks of overcrowding that had come to the forefront in the devastating aftermath of the Bombay plague. One of its key projects was the construction of thoroughfares such as the Princess Street Scheme II and the Sandhurst Road Scheme III that opened up a wide corridor in the otherwise crowded locality of Girgaum. But such efforts were continuously mired in multiple property disputes around land acquisitions as native landlords and homeowners rushed to capitalize on the increasing value of their assets.[51] Preeti Chopra, for instance, argues that the expansion debates pivot around the "joint public realm" where native elites collaborate with the colonial state (with varying degrees of success) to create public institutions of finance.[52] One key stage of these financial ventures circles precisely around the acquisition and control of lucrative land, such as the properties the evil ladies of Girgaum inhabit.[53]

For Kidambi, Bombay's transformation (from the 1890s onward) from a quiet coastal town to a bustling industrial colonial metropolis was accompanied by a rise in migrant collectivities, spanning diverse discursive, religious, and class/caste status. These migrant collectivities created more flexible and hybrid understandings of the category of native elites, evident from the motley collection of ratepayers in the Girgaum association. Such an ethos of urban transformation, Kidambi suggests, further paved the way for what he terms *petitioning culture*. The evidentiary genre of the petition (like the one that produces our critical object, the evil ladies of Girgaum) constitutes a resistive "event" in colonial Bombay, an interstitial space of opposition, complication, and even aporia. The petition, Kidambi argues, is more than a state regulatory practice that solidifies hierarchies of supplication between the native subject and colonial state. Rather, it becomes an arena of political, oppositional, and often transformative action within the confines of a state-sanctioned bureaucratic ritual. Other scholars too, including Bhavani Raman, note that while the petition is used as a state disciplining apparatus (in southern India) to model dissent into more state-sanctioned forms, it still gathers a diverse group of merchants, producing cross-communal and collective bargaining, often against the intrusive expansions of the colonial state. Hence, the petition that produces the archival record of the evil ladies is itself embroiled in a paradoxical narrative of refusal and compliance. No pabulum here![54]

Another factor elided in our focus on the evil ladies of Girgaum is their emergence in the context of a precarious and controversial period of property tax legislation in Bombay Presidency. The crux of the controversy revolved around the famous Girgaum Memorial Memorandum of 1870, which called for the abolition of occupier's and house taxes, and what more reformist newspapers at the time such as Native Opinion derisively called the "landlord's movement." The memorandum, as Christine Dobbin argues, principally involved the tax levied on house property by the colonial state and asked for a reduction of the taxes from 7 to 4 percent. The Bombay Municipal Act of 1872 further complicated matters by allowing the upper echelon of ratepayers (primarily landlords and businessmen) to be elected members of the Municipal Corporation.[55] S. M. Edwardes too, inveterate colonial chronicler and Special Collector for the BIT, attributes the boom in land values in areas such as Girgaum between 1904 and 1907 to efforts such as the "landlord's movement." For Edwardes, the expansion of the municipal membership, along with more native involvement in land acquisition and tax reform, also provided the catalyst for more large-scale investment after the years of the plague pandemic.[56]

Leading up to 1911, the year in which the Girgaum residents and ratepayers association files the public resolutions against the evil ladies of Girgaum, the tax rate legislation on property continued to be heavily disputed, with property values escalating (as mentioned above) thanks to the redistribution of lands due to the institution of the City Improvement Trust. In such a context, the evil ladies' occupation of homes in the main thoroughfares of Girgaum needs to be examined more carefully. According to the census of 1901, the number of prostitutes in Girgaum had significantly diminished in numbers (dropping from more than 1,200 or so in the late 1890s to about 235 in 1901—figures cum grano, of course, given the unreliability of census reports at the time).[57] So the secretary to the state is right in arguing that a statistical case cannot be made for the rise of evil ladies in Girgaum. Alternately, what the private archives of the Gomantak Maratha Samaj (which contain many property deeds and genealogies of inheritance and distribution) reveal is that the evil ladies of Girgaum occupied and then gradually took possession of the multiple residences they were inhabiting, thanks to their complex negotiation with their yajemans of a payment system that bypassed cash payments for property deeds.[58]

The association of the Girgaum residents and ratepayers lists as its members prominent Saraswat *shetias* (commercial elites), "Mohammedan" merchants, and a few converted Christians and Eurasians, a motley crew of caste and races that is reflected in the current geography of Girgaum.[59] In the back-and-forth between the members of the Girgaum association and the secretary to the government, no such skirmish over tax rates and property values is made visible.[60] The repeated and "apparent" invocation of "vice" and prostitution seamlessly covers over the economics and exigencies of the Samaj women's day-to-day survival. It is therefore with no small measure of historical irony that I note here that the economic success of the Samaj is also largely built on their acquisition in the early 1900s of prime property all over Bombay Presidency, particularly in the area of Girgaum, Gamdevi, and Chowpatty.[61]

As is "apparent" by now, all these readings of return clearly enjoy a wide disseminative force, more politically enabling than an accessible transparency or an uninterrupted linearity of action. The evil ladies emerge over and over again, albeit for a different vice of collective reform, within the Samaj archives. From 1910 to 1912, concerted efforts are afoot to provide access, education, and representation to the collectivities of evil ladies inhabiting Girgaum and its environs. In his history of the emergence of the Samaj and its activities in Goa and Bombay, N. A. Marathe writes of extended meetings organized by Rajaram Rangoji Paigankar (the author of *Mee kon*, and one of the principal forces behind the establishment of the Samaj, as we have already seen) along with multiple associates (Sudharamji Mandrekar, Tukaramji Kamulkar, et al.) from the area. Meetings were held at the residence of Mukundraj Engineer in Kandewadi, Girgaum, to garner support for an initial organization, Kalavant Samuh/Group/Collectivity, which also led to the establishment of circulating libraries and tutorial services for members of the kalavant community.[62]

More recent scholarly studies on the migration into Bombay of "prostitutes" (with a "reference to family background") and their rehabilitation, such as a key one published in 1962, applaud the positive efforts of the evil ladies of the Samaj and contrast them sharply with other organizations, such as the Association of Tawaifs and Deredars, that continue to use "singing girls" as a "shield" to propagate more "unscrupulous" and unlawful activity. The authors, Punekar and Rao, conducted extensive ethnographic research, as the long lists of tables, surveys, and data confirm. But the study notes (with some irony) that "the majority of their respondents" are migrants from Goa, whose mother tongue is Konkani, so their input is therefore to be taken with a grain of salt![63]

Even as I write this, I continue to "discover" new archival evidence that can further unpack the telling tales of this problem event. Generous colleagues working on histories of policing and surveillance in colonial Bombay reference (with great confidence, I would add) the presence of numerous classified files on these evil ladies of Girgaum that still lie outside the realm of public consumption. As of now, such files remain sequestered within the bureaucratic walls of police archives, though their content, like the material of this problem event, offers the promise of multiple readings.[64] We also know, from available archival records, that there exists correspondence between British and Portuguese police on the criminal activities of female migrants from Goa, resulting in a report that chronicles their political and entrepreneurial interests.[65] Such invocations of classified (and therefore potentially explosive) evidence further concatenate the value accrued around the problem event. After all, any new historical reading, especially of sexuality's pasts, surely benefits from the continued promise of archival evidence. To hold such evidence in narrative abeyance makes possible further heroic reconstructions of the event, bypassing any closure of an ever-possible "real" history.

In light of such concerns, the scandal now shifts from an evaluation or disputation of the "evil" of the ladies of Girgaum to the "apparent" entanglements behind their invocation. Let me be clear: to read sexuality here as a cover story is not merely to make the familiar but necessary argument for sexuality's material contexts. It is more an attempt to think of these contexts themselves as being equally locked in the dialectic of the apparent and the real. Within such imaginaries, the matter of the evil ladies of Girgaum works not as an exemplary case that resolves historical ambivalence or loss through its successful recognition and emergence but, rather, as a narrative that inserts epistemic discontinuity in how and why we write histories of sexuality.[66] The supplementarity of each reading (and we have many at play here) is the currency through which the archival exemplar accrues value. A problem event becomes a fiat of fictions, where each reading of its content becomes a form of currency, underwritten by what becomes necessary for the instance. There is no settled abundance of meaning; meaning accumulates in a multitude of keys, none of which hold more or less value than any other, except for their particular circulatory value at any one time.[67]

Even as the story of the evil ladies morphing into the successful emergence of the Gomantak Maratha Samaj is a crucial and inspiring one, it is more than just yet another exercise in recuperative and redemptive historiography. It pushes us to consider the archival trace, less as a marginalized, erased archival trace of sexuality, and more as a warehouse of the imaginaries of property, caste, and sexuality. The exemplar of the evil ladies does not affirm or erase their liminality as archival objects; rather, it simply presses against our desire for an archival hermeneutics that will recover to restore value to a lost form/collectivity. In this case, the collectivity, as I have noted, is never lost or erased or missing an archive. As is clear by now, these evil ladies not only exist in multiple archival forms; they also maintain and sustain an archive of their own making. The evil ladies of Girgaum function (then and now) as a scene of exemplarity whereby we return over and over again to the vice of sexuality as the familiar place of historical redress and reform. How can we fashion new habits of reading that disarticulate sexuality from its inevitably "evil" form, to move toward its ordinary plenitude within the conventions of capital, caste and, historiography? What would it mean to archive the "evil ladies" not as an alluring exemplar nor as an aspirational problem-event that will somehow unravel the secrets of sexuality? As we have seen, the exemplar of the "evil ladies" speaks more to a history of sexuality that is in defiance against over-zealous mandates of historical recuperation; as if to say, if you keep reading, there will be no end to representation. As readers of the exemplar, and of my multiple narrations of the exemplar, we are doing "timepass" as we move through cue and clues without falling prey to the so-called true value of the event. Bypassing the heroics of recuperative historiography, the exemplar here is less an exceptional record of lost lives than an open horizon for reading and gathering. Let us try to imagine that history together.

NOTES

1. These formulations of the Samaj's variegated archive are lessons learned in reading and writing from one of my earliest teachers of the English language at Cornell University: Lydia Fakundiny. Fakundiny's remarkable "On Approaching the Essay" (1991) remains to my mind one of the best mediations on the craft of writing and inhabiting the confines of an essay. I have turned to it often in my own deliberations on the contours of this archive. See Fakundiny, *The Art of the Essay*, 1–21.
2. I borrow the term *fault lines* from Alan Sinfield's provocative early work on dissident reading and literatures of sexuality. See Sinfield, *Faultlines*.
3. See Best and Marcus, "Surface Reading"; Ricoeur, *Freud and Philosophy*; Stewart, "The Hermeneutics of Suspicion." As Cannon Schmitt writes, "It is as though we are so accustomed to straining our ears for faint whispers of the *non-dit* beneath or behind the obvious, the loudly *dit*, that affirming that texts say what they mean and mean what they say takes on the force of a revelation." See Schmitt, "Interpret or Describe?"
4. Tanoukhi turns to a critique of the term *distant reading* to speak to the limitations of current approaches to world/comparative literatures (pace Franco Moretti et al.). See Tanoukhi, "Surprise Me If You Can." Tanoukhi's invocation of the term *distant reading* emerges from the critical lexicon of comparative literary studies and is not to be confused with work being done within digital humanities. The idea of "distant reading" in digital humanities uses natural language processing and artificial intelligence to "read" a corpus of European texts, across time and space, especially within medieval and early modern studies. For further reading,

here are some sample texts: Jänicke et al., "On Close and Distant Reading in Digital Humanities"; Underwood, "A Genealogy of Distant Reading"; and Bode, "The Equivalence of 'Close' and 'Distant' Reading." I thank Durba Mitra for alerting me to this set of literatures.

5   Allan, *In the Shadow of World Literature*, 3.
6   Allan, *In the Shadow of World Literature*, 2–21.
7   See Chatterjee, "When 'Sexualities' Floated Free of Histories in South Asia"; Povinelli, *Economies of Abandonment*; and Morgan, "Accounting for the 'Most Excruciating Torment.'" Within South Asian studies in particular, the early work of the Subaltern Studies Collective attended to the elitist compositional and distributive logics of archives in colonial and postcolonial India. Yet for the most part, the focus of the collective has still largely been recuperative and reparative, and only more recently supplemented by the work of feminist historians such as Indrani Chatterjee, Tanika Sarkar, Janaki Nair, and their emphasis on more discrepant and gendered histories of labor, governmentality, and affect.
8   For a prescient reading of this appointment, see Thapar, "The Appointment of a Historian Whose Work Is Unfamiliar to Most Historians Shows Scant Regard for the Impressive Scholarship That Now Characterises the Study of Indian History and This Disregard May Stultify Future Academic Research." The litany of mistakes, backflips, controversies, and denials of India's diverse past by the ruling Bharitiya Janata Party (BJP) is by now well known and too extensive to be rehearsed here in its entirety.
9   FP Staff, "Historians Raise Questions about ICHR's New Boss Prof Y Sudershan Rao."
10 See Bhattacharya, "How Historian Vikram Sampath Uses Decolonisation Rhetoric to Make Hindu Domination Sound Reasonable."
11 For an extended exegesis on the use of historical archives in the efforts to repeal Section 377, see A. Arondekar, "Time's Corpus"; and Kapur, "Unruly Desires, Gay Governance, and the Makeover of Sexuality." For further reading, see Nagar and Dasgupta, "Public Koti and Private Love."
12 When I first conceived of this chapter, it was 2017, and we lived in a pandemic-free world. Since then, much has changed for all of us, but the authoritarian manipulation of our pasts continues unabated in Narendra Modi's India. Now, Modi's propaganda machine routinely merges historical fiction with scientific facts, arguing for the primacy of a Hindu science amid the unfolding health drama in the world. See PTI, "'Cow Urine Is Pure Elixir.'"
13 Stoler, *Along the Archival Grain*, 32–33.
14 Berlant, "On the Case." See also Damousi, Lang, and Sutton, *Case Studies and the Dissemination of Knowledge.*
15 My thinking on the idea of event-making, events in emergence, and all things event-making has benefited from the work of Lauren Berlant. See,

more specifically, "History and the Affective Event" (chap. 2) in *Cruel Optimism*, 51–94. See also Stewart, *Ordinary Affects* and *A Space on the Side of the Road*, as well as the more recent collaboration between Berlant and Stewart, *The Hundreds*. I was also fortunate enough to be invited to think with Berlant, Stewart, Andrew Causey, Susan Lepselter, Barbara Browning, Renee Gladman, Stephen Muecke, Fred Moten, and Erica Rand at a mini-seminar on experimental writing held at the University of Chicago, Experiment in Critical Practice, June 1–2, 2018. I found the seminar to be in equal measure, exasperating, challenging, and meditative in its engagements with historical writing.

16 Berlant, "Genre Flailing."
17 Amin, *Disturbing Attachments*, 19.
18 Goldberg, *The Seeds of Things*, 1–10.
19 The first of many iterations of the question of use and message came at an early presentation I gave on the project at the fiftieth-anniversary celebrations of Goan Liberation in 2011. I was one of a small group of activists and scholars working on caste, and the only one working on sexuality at the conference held in Panjim, Goa. I was repeatedly pushed to speak to how I would use this research to "better" Goan history or produce much-needed hagiographies of the lost women of the Samaj. Much of the critical energy for this chapter came from a decided discomfort with those early demands.
20 Lebow, "Faking What?"
21 I develop this point more carefully in my response to Valerie Traub's work on histories of sexuality. See A. Arondekar, "Thinking Sex *with* Geopolitics."
22 To reiterate a key point I made in my introduction—for most scholars of South Asia, British colonialism remains the lodestone of all historical critique, and Portuguese India serves as an afterthought or mere background material. One has simply to scan the publications of the past few decades or so in colonial South Asian history to notice this trend. The literatures that are available on Portuguese colonialism in South Asia tend to focus more on pre-nineteenth-century histories of trade and labor. Sanjay Subrahmanyam's oft-cited opus *Career and Legend of Vasco Da Gama* would be one good example.
23 My invocation of "timepass" always takes me back to a conversation with one of my queer kin in graduate school. As new and enthusiastic acolytes of queer studies, we were often impatiently asked by suspicious students: "What is a queer poem?" Our answer would be: "A queer poem is a poem that fancies other poems. So it never wishes to settle down." Neither of us can still recall whose words we borrowed in this response, but they were certainly coined by someone infinitely wiser and more prescient than either of us!

24   While print usage of the term in English may indeed only date back to the 1980s, I can easily recall its usage from my own childhood in the 1970s. It is a term whose circulation, like its usage, remains an ever-changing story.

25   For example, we find a reference in 1997 to "a smiling businesswoman who turned a 'timepass' interest into a roaring enterprise." See OED Online, 3rd ed., s.v. "timepass, n. and adj," accessed July 5, 2020, https://oed.com/view/Entry/60968659.

26   See Bedi and Ebrahim, *Timepass*; Jeffrey, *Timepass*; and Fuller, "Timepass and Boredom in Modern India." Protima Bedi's memoirs invoke "timepass" to speak to the perils and pleasures of gendered embodiment as a Hindi film star and actress. Fuller and Jeffrey, on the other hand, proffer more conventional accounts of the homosocial worlds of (largely unemployed) young men who waste time in value/less activities. They rarely address, for example, the postcolonial state's mobilization of "timepass" activities of sexuality and loitering to harass sex workers and queer/trans subjects in public spaces.

27   For more on "timepass" and genres of Hindi cinema, see Rai, *Untimely Bollywood*.

28   The allusion to "nothing" here is of course a nod to Lee Edelman's wonderful essay "Learning Nothing."

29   Gidwani, "Six Theses on Waste, Value, and Commons," 773. In his third thesis, Gidwani writes: "This antithetical aspect of waste, as a logic that stymies the accumulation of property *qua* capital, is mirrored in the various ways it comes to connote not only merely the uncultivated or untended but also the pointless, the misdirected, and the futile; the ineffectual, the foolish, and the worthless; the idle and the improvident; the excessive, prodigal, the improper, the inefficient. As history reveals: time, money, words, things, actions, and nature—all may be wasted, and are disciplined accordingly" (776).

30   Sianne Ngai's formulations on the uncertain value and time of the "gimmick" as object/material are useful to think with here as well. Ngai too pushes us to imagine what deviations from settled practices and readings of productivity would be like, and how we would inhere value other/wise. See Ngai, *Theory of the Gimmick*.

31   Carla Freccero's work on queer spectrality comes to mind here, where the specter is less a force of subversive potential or containment, more a persistent ethical and historical demand. Here the demand, as I alluded to in my introduction, continues to be around refusal and resistance, the resolute mantra of minoritized historiography. Freccero, "Queer Spectrality."

32   After all, as Jacques Derrida reminds us, every example must necessarily fail to do its job (1982, 27).

33 All records of the event were found in an unmarked file at the Mumbai offices of the Gomantak Maratha Samaj. The file was buried in a box containing paperwork on the acquisition of the Samaj building in Girgaum. The available records contain typewritten letters from the Residents and Ratepayers of Girgaum (July 16, 1911) and a response from the Judicial Department (dated November 13, 1911). What is curious about the contents of the file is that the letters contain corrections that have been penciled in, with no indication of whether the letters were revised and re-sent. The official record can be located in the papers of the Judicial Department, Maharashtra State Archives and is titled "Protest by the Rate Payers and Residents of Girgaum, Bombay against the Evil of Women of Bad Repute, 1911," 235.

34 For ease of reading, I have omitted the scare quotes around the term *evil ladies* henceforth, though they are always implied.

35 The select brief invocation of the Samaj I provide here, and in every other chapter, is one that I narrate repeatedly and verbatim in all work that touches on the Samaj's exemplarity. Part of the challenge of writing about a collectivity that is simultaneously known and not known is that historical details become routinized only through their constant repetition.

36 Stephen Best speaks brilliantly to the relationship between such readings in his work on histories of slavery. Drawing from Frances Ferguson's work on tort law, he writes of the pressing desire to recover the subject who existed (or had value) before the injury of slavery. As he writes: "These sorts of historical and political investments (the acquisitive urges, strong claims making, perfective activity) have been hard-baked into the structure of agonistic critique" (39). See Best, *None Like Us*.

37 Steedman, "La théorie qui n'en est pas une." See also Supriya Chaudhuri's wonderful rereading of the Steedman essay in her "Significant Lives."

38 Hortense Spillers invokes this phrase in her juxtaposition of the work of Martin Luther King and Mahatma Gandhi in a short, evocative piece, appropriately titled "Discomfort." Spillers deliberates on "protocols of non-violence" in the face of an increasingly carceral and slave American nation-state and summons "an opening in the chain of necessity" as a possible way out (6, 7).

39 Anagol, *The Emergence of Feminism in India, 1850–1920*, 123–37.

40 Tambe, "Social Geographies of Bombay's Sex Trade"; Legg, "Stimulation, Segregation and Scandal."

41 Tambe, "Social Geographies of Bombay's Sex Trade," 156.

42 I was able to locate this archival source thanks to Ashwini Tambe's brief reference to it. See *Petition Submitted to the Governor and President in Council, Bombay, by Residents of Girgaum and Its Vicinity, 1871*, 125.

43 Ranganathan, *Govind Narayan's Mumbai*, 261–62. The original Marathi text utilizes more lavish and efflorescent language.

44   Raghunathji, "Bombay Dancing Girls," 166.
45   Raghunathji, "Bombay Dancing Girls," 167.
46   Raghunathji, "Bombay Dancing Girls."
47   The Portuguese colonial archives too contain many stories of the wealth of Goan devadasis or bailadeiras. In a small but remarkable essay on the history of *merces* (gifts) within the Portuguese empire in India, Dr. Agnelo Paulo Fernandes tracks the references to bailadeiras and their wealth. He notes, for example, the rich (in all senses of the word) late nineteenth-century history of Caxy Bailadeira, a resident of Goa, who possesses properties and wealth far beyond the imagination of most colonial subjects. See Fernandes, "Curious Case of Goan Orientalism," 8–26.
48   The early records of the National Vigilance Association—keeping an eye on their colonial holdings—mention brothels in Girgaum, near the French bridge, though their focus is more on the presence of white slaves. See National Vigilance Association, *The Vigilance Record*, 150.
49   Bai Monghibai v. Bai Nagubai (1922) 24 BOMLR 1009 and Bai Nagubai v. Bai Monghibai (1926) 28 BOMLR 1143. Other cases that deal with questions of maintenance and similar evil ladies include Bai Appibai v. Khimji Cooverji (1936) 38 BOMLR 77 and Yashvantrav v. Kashibai (1888) ILR 12 Bom 26. Kunal Parker, writing on similar questions, proposes that colonial courts in India augmented devadasi reform through innovative and often unprecedented translations of the law. Legal norms that previously applied to different castes represented within Brahmanical taxonomies were extended to include an innovative set of patriarchal norms with respect to the sexual behavior of Hindu women. For example, the devadasi was cast less as a "temple dancing girl" and more as a "Hindu girl" engaging in sexual activities outside of marriage. Such a shift from the "tradition" of devadasis to the aberration of their sexual practices allowed the courts to legislate against the devadasis as prostitutes without engaging their more complex functions as repositories of art, culture, and religion. According to Parker, these concerns substantially impacted the interpretation of the 1861 Indian Penal code with reference to the devadasis. By focusing on the prostitution of minors dedicated to temples, Parker suggests that devadasi reform groups rerouted provisions intended to protect minors, to nullify adoption by devadasis, and to outlaw any and all dedications of girls to deities. Such a turn to the protection of minors became a crucial part of judicial reform movement aimed at eliminating devadasis. See Parker, "'A Corporation of Superior Prostitutes.'"
50   Dossal, *Theatre of Conflict, City of Hope*. See specifically chap. 7, "Urban Planning or Crisis Management?"

51 "Housing the Poor in a Colonial City." See also Kidambi's *Making of an Indian Metropolis*, 40–47, 70–76.
52 Chopra, *A Joint Enterprise*.
53 In a similar vein, Padma Anagol notes that "residents of various towns and cities often sent complaints to police authorities to remove kalavantins from what they considered respectable neighborhoods and to house them outside the city or town limits." See Anagol, *Emergence of Feminism in India*, 125–26. Anagol cites the example of a complaint carried by Ahmadnagar residents against prostitutes. See *Nagar Samachar*, February 23, 1878, and *Dandio*, March 22, 1879, Vernacular Newspaper Reports (VNR).
54 Kidambi, "Petition as Event." See also Raman, *Document Raj*.
55 Dobbin, "Competing Elites in Bombay City Politics in the Mid-Nineteenth Century." For a broader history of the rise of urban housing in Bombay and more, see Rao, "Community, Urban Citizenship, and Housing in Bombay, ca. 1919–1980." See also Rao's *House but No Garden*. I am grateful to Nikhil for providing early feedback on property disputes in Bombay. For a broader historical view of the twists and turns of the ratepayer/landlord's movement, see also Dossal, "A Master Plan for the City" and *Imperial Designs and Indian Realities*; Batley, "The Need for City Planning"; Haynes, *Small Town Capitalism in Western India*; and Wacha, *Rise and Growth of Bombay Municipal Government*.
56 Edwardes and Campbell, *The Gazetteer of Bombay City and Island*, 1:327–28. For further reading, see Wacha, *Rise and Growth of Bombay Municipal Government*; and Masani, *The Law and Procedure of the Municipal Corporation of Bombay*.
57 Tambe, *Codes of Misconduct*, 60, 168. See also Legg, *Prostitution and the Ends of Empire*.
58 Available property deeds of three such evil ladies—Nandabai Narayan Thakkar, Chandrabai Durgaram Shirodkar, and Mogabai Dattaram Shirodkar, all kalavantins/devadasis and members of the Gomantak Maratha Samaj—indicate properties within the environs of colonial Girgaum. These archives are available as open-access files in the office of the Samaj in Mumbai.
59 Dobbin, "Competing Elites in Bombay City Politics in the Mid-Nineteenth Century," 89.
60 S. M. Edwardes provides the following detailed description of the topography of Girgaum in *The Gazetteer of Bombay City and Island*, 1:41–42: "The Girgaum section is bounded on the North by Girgaum Back road, on the south by Thakurdwar road, on the east by Girgaum Back road and Bhuleshwar road, and on the west by Back Bay and Charni road. Like Chaupati and Phanasswadi its interior portion has arisen upon the side of ancient parts, such as Borbhat and Mugbat, with the old

Girgaum village as its original nucleus. Its most noteworthy buildings are the Muhamadan sanitarium at the corner of Queen's road, the old Police Court on Girgaum back road, the Allbless Bagh on Charni Road and the Portuguese Church opposite the Trans terminus. The latter building which actually lies just outside the sectional limits was founded in 1773 and rebuilt in its present form in 1836. The neighbourhood of Charni road has of late years been taken up to some extend to of the building of middle-class Parsi flats; but the bulk of the section still retains its old character as a Brahman settlement." For one of the most viewed images of colonial Girgaum, see "Bombay, Girgaum Road," cigarette card, George Arents Collection, New York Public Library Digital Collections.

61 A recently curated exhibition by Tejaswini Niranjana and Surabhi Sharma, *Making Music, Making Space*, documents musical histories of Girgaum, giving their audiences a small glimpse of the rich and networked worlds of these naikins and kalavantins. In the exhibition, the audience is also provided with an annotated map of Girgaum that marks all the residences and buildings occupied by collectivities such as the evil ladies. For broader cultural histories of Girgaum, see Adarkar, "Marathi Manus in Girgaon," 145–51; Chandavarkar, "The Perils of Proximity"; Quinn, "Marathi and Konkani Speaking Women in Hindustani Music, 1880–1940."

62 Marathe's account of key events within the emergence and success of the Gomantak Maratha Samaj was in a special issue published in 1980 to commemorate the opening of Dayanand Smruti, a new building dedicated to Samaj meetings and affairs in Panaji Goa. Of note here is that the building housed one of the first women's hostels dedicated to migrant and single women working in Goa. See Marathe, "Gomantak Maratha Samajane Kayleli Samajatli Charvar V Meervlele Yash," esp. 2–3.

63 Punekar and Rao, *Study of Prostitutes in Bombay*, 169, 160. See also Oldenburg, "Lifestyle as Resistance"; and Thatra, "Contentious (Socio-spatial) Relations." For a broader understanding of late-colonial debates on prostitution in Bombay, see Tambe, "Brothels as Families."

64 I am grateful to Shekhar Krishnan, a wonderful chronicler of the varied histories of Bombay, and his deep familiarity with police and municipal archives. Krishnan, for some time, has been attempting to help me gain access to these notorious classified files that, he tells me, have been seen but not catalogued. For a taste of Krishnan's wide-ranging knowledge of colonial Bombay, see http://shekhar.cc/.

65 *Relatório da Comissao de Inquérito à Situaçao dos Emigrantes Indo-Portugueses na India Britannica*. My thanks to Rochelle Pinto for the reference.

66 Durba Mitra has brilliantly reminded us that the exemplarity of prostitutes / evil ladies and their kin is constitutive to the very making of colonial epistemologies and the structure of the archive itself. For more detailed analysis, see chap. 2, "Repetition," in Mitra, *Indian Sex Life*.
67 For more on fiat money and literary forms, see Lindstrom, "Coda."

CHAPTER THREE

Itinerant Sex

Geopolitics as Critique

Consider this geo/history.¹ It is 1947, a year of independence, futurity, violence, genocide, and, yes, fulsome commemoration. The British have left, Pakistan is born, and India breaks free, all in the aftermath of a bloody Partition in the subcontinent. Even as the vagaries of state and faith threaten, the promise and gains of national belonging beckon. Liberation for Goa, Portugal's last stronghold in India, also looms, though a decade or so in the future.² For the Gomantak Maratha Samaj, the collectivity at the center of our investigations here, such new geopolitical forms activate a unique set of challenges and choices. Writing in the September 1947 issue of the *Samaj Sudharak*, B. D. Satoskar reflects on the aftermath of Indian independence for Samaj members and pointedly asks, "Aazchya Hindustanaath gomantakache sthaan kaay?" (What is the status of Goans within today's Hindustan?). The Goans referred to here are specifically Samaj members residing in the territories of Portuguese India. In this editorial, Satoskar, the celebrated author of *Gomantak Prakruti aani Sanskriti* (1951), one of the few widely circulated texts in Marathi encompassing six hundred years of Goan history and culture (1300–1900), details the Samaj's geopolitical "quagmire" (*chakravyuh*).³ Goa will not become part of independent India until 1961, and the pressing question of future allegiances looms large here.

To begin with, Satoskar reminds his readers that their Goa-based Samaj is often hailed as a collectivity "asleep" (*nidrit*) to the potential of political and regional belonging. In his travels to Maharashtra and Karnataka, for example, he is often asked why a devadasi collectivity as "intelligent" (*budhimaan*) as the Samaj refuses to capitalize on its access to social and economic networks within the higher echelons of Goan society. After all, their diverse portfolio of yajemans and benefactors (spanning from landowning Brahmins to Portuguese officials) affords them equal access to both the burgeoning liberation movement growing in Goa *and* Portuguese governmental bureaucracies—two structures, he notes with biting irony, that are completely in contradistinction to one another! Waves of reform and revolution are crashing on every shore, he writes, from the newly independent lands of Hindustan and Pakistan to the fledgling, struggling territory of Goa itself. Yet somehow the Samaj as a *sanstha* (organization) remains detached, uncontaminated by such political energies—driven, it appears to outsiders, primarily by its own self-promotion and reform. Such characterizations of the Samaj, Satoskar avers, can no longer be ignored, especially as the demand for regional belonging grows within and outside Goa. If the Samaj does not choose fidelity to one nation or the other, Satoskar warns, it will be seen as opportunistic, fickle, and inherently untrustworthy as future citizenry.

For Satoskar, Samaj members must thus carefully deliberate on the geopolitical futures that lie ahead of them. Samaj members have the option to continue to migrate not only to the newly independent states of Maharashtra and Karnataka (in western India/Hindustan) but also, he emphasizes, to cities in the newly formed Pakistan. After all, the Samaj's kala (art)—in sexuality and more—traverses religious and territorial hostilities. Yet such mobility, while desirable, also comes at a cost, as there is no guarantee that the independent states of India and Pakistan will continue to endure, or to respect the rights of outsiders. If turmoil were to arise within these newly formed states, Satoskar argues, Samaj members would be vilified as dangerous outsiders—vassals of the Portuguese state in India and Pakistan, or lower-caste devadasis in an independent-but-Brahmin Goa.

A second pressing issue of concern is the financial stability of Samaj members. The sending of remittances back to Goa or to family elsewhere can also be threatened, he sternly reminds his readers, for after all, which free state would like its revenue to flow outward? Last but not least, there is always the option of leaving Goa and embracing the (false) promise of Portuguese citizenship in foreign lands, even as such fidelity demands a painful abdication of culture and language, and their histories of sexuality.[4] And in case his readers, by this point, have settled into the idea of Goa as chosen home, Satoskar quickly dissuades them of that salvific possibility as well. For Satoskar, any "attachment" (*nishta*) to Goa (in its current colonial or future postcolonial form) must be understood against the hegemony of the ruling Brahmin community and the escalating repression of the António de Oliveira Salazar–led Portuguese colonial state.[5] The Samaj's strength, he writes, is that it can be *ikde aani tikde* (here and there), and it must, he continues, resist the *aakarshan* (seductions) of *pranth kiva rajya* (nation or state). Satoskar ends his editorial by urging his readers to wrestle with the rhetorical and political weight of regional forms, not to surrender to their demands, but to examine their place within and without them.[6]

Satoskar's editorial is remarkable on many fronts as it strategically navigates the chakravyuh of sexuality, geopolitics, and history. For a collectivity such as the Samaj that is nonmonogamous and outside of endogamous caste and social forms, the geopolitical too must function less as a locus of containment than as a live landscape of futurity. First, selective itineraries of migration are held up as passages of possibility (India, Pakistan, Portugal), with Luso outposts in Africa (specifically, Mozambique) held carefully at bay. After all, as we know from the many histories of Goan migration across the Indian Ocean, much of the mass migration to African outposts was composed of Catholic subjects (converted and otherwise) and did not include collectivities such as the Samaj. Even sought-after Goan entertainers who flooded venues in Mozambique and Zanzibar, for example, were rarely drawn from devadasi or kalavant traditions.[7] Second, caste lineages are equally maintained and disrupted through references to Brahmin yajemans who allow access and influence (through blood), even as caste status is not guaranteed. That is, Samaj members can claim Brahmins as bio-fathers if needed (as we have seen in previous chapters) without the privilege of the caste status they occupy. Third, the importance of trade is carefully tracked through the references to remittances into and out of Goa, to precisely concatenate the languages of capitalization through which geopolitics enters the holdings of histories of sexuality.

By resisting the historico-political demand for geopolitical allegiance, Satoskar's editorial does not give us access to some bold political gesture. Instead, it reorients our expectations, forging a critical sensibility that signals the value and burden of a promissory geopolitics for sexuality's subjects. Geopolitics (in all its iterations) here provides an inventory of what might be rather than what is or what must be. To be ikde/tikde (here/there) is to eschew the staged lineages that suture subjects to region, to emphasize the violence of (national) origins and to bypass the demands for geopolitical certitude. Scripting a history of sexuality in relation to place, in this instance, is to move past the placations of migrant or citizen, drawing attention instead to a nonrecuperative geopolitics that is abundant, mislaid, and even cagey. Place, region, nation, becomes an origin put into place after the fact, even as such aspirations, as we have seen in the Samaj's own writings, carry no genealogical or historical freight.[8]

Suppose, then, we take Satoskar's editorial not as disruptive but more as constitutive of the ideations of geopolitics as instantiated in histories of sexuality.[9] Geopolitics hangs over any narration of sexuality, like an unreliable ghost. It changes vernaculars, constrains movement, and indeed complicates any fantasy of shared liberation. If there has been a sea change across South Asian studies and sexuality studies in the past few decades, it has been the embrace of more robust geographies of affiliation, instantiated in the languages of networks, oceanic/archipelagic imaginaries, connected histories, and more.[10] Such shifts have troubled the saturated resilience of geopolitical, temporal, and epistemological formations, adding much-needed historical heft to what used to more broadly be described as the "transnational" turn.[11] As I noted in my introduction, these new vernaculars of the geopolitical have equally reordered the grammar of histories of sexuality. No longer content with marking the stifling centrality of geopolitical asymmetries (the oracular status of Euro-American queer studies, for example!), scholars working in/on the global South are now crafting more generative South-South conversations.[12] In their powerful introduction to a special *GLQ* issue on the "queer customary," for example, Kirk Fiereck, Neville Hoad, and Danai Mupotsa demand a queer theory "elaborated from Africa" that refuses any beleaguered "fantasy of representativity." Instead, they call for a critical dispensation that relies less on the liberatory promises of sex and more on "a usable past." Such a turn to a usable past vitalizes and repurposes maligned colonial concepts such as the "customary" and "traditional" within the idea of Africa.[13] A recent collection on "pluriversality" (Walter Mignolo's well-known coinage) and the "geopolitics of knowledge" similarly presses for urgent epistemological transformation. Tired critiques of Western intellectual tradition are to be jettisoned and replaced with place-bound ontologies, epistemologies, and technologies that directly address "questions of development, economic growth, identity, democracy, political power, and self-rule" from within South-South dialogues.[14]

For South Asian studies in particular, it would be difficult to account for the historical commotion the heightened focus on oceanic networks and regions in particular (failed or otherwise) has created. Regions and networks eschew the language of state territoriality; rather, they are seen more as spatial, material, and technological frontiers, effects of porous cross-border counterflows that create informal worlds of peril and possibility. Even as such networked geographies have been fervently (and occasionally shallowly) recuperated through histories of trade, capital, religion, and labor, there has been an equal emphasis on understanding this turn to affiliation as at once novel and familiar. If networks and regions are to be broadly understood as economic, social, religious, and political practices that defuse fictions of bounded nation-states and temporalities, for example, then their emergence can hardly be termed "new," given that such practices have existed for many centuries.[15] On the other hand, there is, as many scholars have argued, something extraordinary and "new" about the current erasure and embrace (in equal measure) of such practices in a post-Fordist, rabid Hindutva era, where nation-states such as the United States and India both cede and appropriate networked technologies and histories. Digital India is also Vedic India.[16]

For sexuality studies, this heightened focus on geographies of affiliation has created more epistemological turbulence than historical analysis. It has served more as a cautionary tale, a reminder that sexuality is always already "a surface network," and "a dense transfer point," legible only through languages of relationality—an effect of an effect, as it were.[17] Within such a well-established Foucauldian vernacular, sexuality has, at its center, epistemes of movement and uncertainty, epistemes that are generative forces of emergence precisely because of the perverse pathways they travel. Bruno Latour, Gilles Deleuze, and Félix Guattari, in particular, have emerged as favored theorists within Europe- and US-based queer studies, through their emphasis on networks as destabilizing assemblages that refuse the causality of forms, focusing more on linkages between objects, bodies, and discourses.[18] Yet even as such an understanding of sexuality has become axiomatic and disruptive of how we think and historicize sex, it can often map geographies of sexuality through more literal forms such as homosexuality that invoke sexuality through the language of rights and representation in fixed places and times.[19] We return to familiar objects, places, and temporalities, forgoing uncertainty, dispersed histories, and contradictory ontologies.

What happens if we refuse to service geopolitics to this end, foregrounding more the critical labor undergirding its emergence? What if the force of geopolitics lies more in its critique than its rehabilitation? The enduring asymmetries of knowledge economies, we well know, have hardly been reversed. The inconvenience of too many languages, too many histories, too many divergent objects of studies colors much of what we continue to do today. As a scholar who works in South Asia, I am always nudged (however gently) to provide glossaries, translations of terms that at least one billion folks else/where inhabit and understand. We still live inside of monolingual and/or metrolingual landscapes, populated by an appetite for geopolitical diversity that nevertheless returns us to the gift of the master language. To be clear, such monolingualism (epistemic and literal) exists as much in the Rest as it does in the West. There remains a dearth of scholarly writing in nonmetropolitan languages across all hemispheres, even as queer/trans subjects flourish and proliferate each and every day. While it is laudable to have scholarship on India, Egypt, Philippines, Brazil (pick your favorite queer else/where) take center stage for a special issue or two (as I cited above), how can such scholarship become central—and not "special"—for queer knowledge? After all, epistemologies of sexuality are always spaced forms, familiar lexical imaginaries, housed within the languages of geopolitics and difference. Reproductive futurism is always geopolitical futurism; queer utopia is equally queer geography, where other worlds are continually reproduced as contexts, exemplars, at best interruptions in a journey that inevitably and necessarily shepherds us back into the diversified holdings of an American studies project. If sexuality's difference is always marked by gender, race, class, caste, and more (jettison that white child, please), it is equally a story of spatialized difference. To put it more ambitiously, could our voyages out forge a queer/trans geopolitics? Or, as my coeditor Geeta Patel and I asked in our special issue, could histories of area be histories of sexuality?[20]

I have called this chapter "Itinerant Sex: Geopolitics as Critique" because I want to imagine a geopolitics that neither salvages nor erases the locational and historical transactions enabled through sexuality. Rather, my meditations call on a figuration of geopolitics that produces epistemic catachresis in the welding of place, focusing more on what precisely makes geographies so worthy of recuperation. I have chosen to go with "itinerant" as the agent provocateur to point to alleys that may also muddle some of the more routinized passages through which divergent geopolitical forms have been recuperated in global histories of sexuality: migration or diaspora, refuge or displacement. Itinerant sex proffers less reliable passages into representation: itinerant as in the sense of those wondrous mendicants in South Asia, such as the fifteenth-century Dalit poet-saint Kabir or the early twentieth-century renegade writer-progressive Miraji, who traversed cross-hatched lineages of geopolitics, gender, and aesthetics troubling the historical seductions of exile and nativism.[21] Here the celebration and/or recuperation of geopolitics holds no purchase, its value as constantly resurrected episteme/object dispersed. Itinerant sex is also a form of capitalization, as suggested by J. C. Van Leur's hoary 1930s research on the Indian Ocean and trade (I'm using him cum grano, of course, merely to make an allegorical point), where he attempts to grapple with Indigenous concepts and bring those concepts into extant discussions. To this end he activated the idea of the peddler, the itinerant merchant, who carried high-value goods from place to place, accruing access and wealth in the very commodification of mobility.[22]

Itinerant sex calls for a historiographical hermeneutics that refuses the seductions of homing devices, of theoretical pathways that suture geopolitics to forms (refused or otherwise) of region, area, nation. The logic of knowing-to-prove we exist (elsewhere), as Katherine McKittrick reminds us, is unsustainable.[23] The Gomantak Maratha Samaj, our geo-history here, is neither familiar nor identitarian nor salvageable. It is more a sprawling, geo-epistemology (here and there) that animates the spaces we seek to occupy. It is knowable less through heroic exemplars—however moving or nimbly organized—than within archival economies that are restless, experimental, and pragmatic, aimed more at the unraveling of space and time. Itinerant sex as heuristic summons attentiveness to places that are ikde aani tikde (here and there), inherently nonrecuperative, not discovered (again). To be ikde aani tikde, as we have seen through the Samaj's history of sexuality, is to focus more on the analytical and political itineraries historiographical methods follow, and the lessons of geopolitics they bypass or leave behind.[24]

IKDE AANI TIKDE: HERE AND THERE

I have modeled this final chapter in attunement to the broader imperatives of this book, veering to an understanding of geopolitics that deliberately strays from a literal understanding of sexuality in/and South Asia. The comportment of my argument thus eschews the repose of place and asks: How can histories of sexuality also be histories of area/region, and what critical lessons are to be learned from such a shift in historical orientation? In lieu of belonging—the seduction that geopolitics so often summons as it incites histories of sexuality—I am interested more in the dispersal of that very provocation. My opening discussion from the Samaj archives provides one such instructive lesson where the abundant sociopolitical kala of an itinerant sex enables myriad geographies of affiliation, even as those affiliations are placed under erasure. The Samaj's sexuality/kala forges a historical lexicon in which genealogies of the past and the future merge into a pragmatic poetics that reads geopolitics anew. Instead of laying claim to geography as established historical value, the Samaj, as I will demonstrate, strategically mobilizes the politics, desires, and identities made possible by the reach of geopolitics.

What does this kind of geopolitical thinking look like? And how is its itinerancy marked within the languages of sexuality and region? By now we have established, for example, that primogeniture/descent, cherished lineages through which histories of kinship and region are scripted, have been thoroughly upended by the Samaj. Given their status as devadasis, Samaj women were, as I noted in my earlier chapter on archives, rarely categorized and criminalized as prostitutes by the Portuguese colonial state. Devadasis in Goa were "given to the goddess," to use Lucinda Ramberg's wonderful formulation, lodged in the messy interstices of sexuality and religiosity, and maintained coercive and noncoercive sexual (and largely monogamous) relationships with Saraswat Brahmin men (and occasionally women). Their offspring were given Brahmin surnames, without Brahmin caste privilege, spawning a structural intransigence and confusion that remained at odds with normative caste hierarchies. Such a corruption of caste as value (the "make.believe" I began with) calls attention to the evidentiary forms that mark sexuality, orienting it toward area and region. Setting the stage for a nonrecuperative historiography of sexuality, the Samaj rends fetishized figurations of caste and family, reaching for what they might yet obtain in geographies accessed through mythologies of origin and belonging.

In obvious ways, the colonial and postcolonial context and content of Goa, as we have also noted, is equally itinerant, the effect of unsettling histories, moving unevenly between the Portuguese and then Indian colonial state. One must contend, for example, with the continued (and, I would venture, startling) narration of Portugal as a "subaltern empire" (in the words of the renowned Portuguese scholar Boaventura de Sousa Santos), as a somewhat benign imperial presence that limped its way into extinction, its histories of exploitation, religious violence, and sheer greed notwithstanding.[25] Speaking on the fiftieth anniversary of Goa's decolonization in 2011, Teotonio de Souza (a renowned historian of medieval Goa) reflected on the former Portuguese enclave's peculiarity, saying that it "had a different colonial experience" in comparison with formerly British India.

De Souza noted that beginning in the sixteenth century, Goa was the nucleus "of a truly global empire that extended from Brazil to Timor to Aden and back to Lisbon; Goans were . . . globalized centuries before the first British merchant showed up in the [Indian] subcontinent."[26] Other elaborate metaphors employed by scholars of the Portuguese empire equally describe Goa lavishly as "a Portuguese outpost, as an island of 'Western civilization' in an Indian sea . . . an Indian region with a rather unusual past."[27] What becomes apparent is that the geopolitics of Goa combines histories of colonization and contemporary globalization as comparable trends, where the connections between the Indian and Atlantic Oceans, as well as the worlds betwixt, are unavoidable. The Portuguese state's extension of citizenship to Goans born before 1961 further consolidates Goa's vexed geopolitical status: it is both *goa dourada* (golden Goa from the Portuguese era) and *goa indica* (Goa of the Indus from the precolonial era). That very same preoccupation with the itinerancy of Goa as geography extends into extant discussions of its history and citizens. It continues to create "existential anxieties within the locals," we are warned.[28] After all, can Goans also be read as Portuguese—Europeans of another color—ask R. Benedito Ferrao and Jason Fernandes, two Goan scholars, instead of traitors to their newly formed relationship with the Indian state?[29]

In the face of such a storied and/or maligned geopolitics, we return once more to Satoskar's editorial from 1947, the year of Indian independence. What happens to the Samaj in the decades that follow, especially in the period leading up to Goa's liberation from Portugal in 1961? How does the Samaj's history of sexuality appropriate, disperse, and survive the apotropaic and propitiatory lure of a geopolitics birthed through freedom struggles? The most salient example of such efforts can be seen in the journey of the much-heralded lower-caste democratic revolution in Goa. Headed by a leading Samaj member, Dayanand Bandodkar and his Bahujan Samaj Party (BSP), lower-caste groups from all over Goa organized to elect the first democratic government of liberated Goa. Within Indian historiography, the rare election of a Bahujan chief minister (*Bahujan* literally means "many, multiple, varied" and is used to designate a broad swath of lower-caste or OBC/Other Backward Castes in India) of a newly liberated state would ordinarily make for riveting scholarly analysis.[30] Instead, with the rare exception of hagiographies commissioned by Bandodkar's own family, there is very little discussion of this otherwise remarkable historical figure.

Such an elision of Bandodkar's contributions to anticaste struggles and the broader history of nationalism within India must be parlayed through the Samaj's itinerant kala. After all, once again there is no easy oppositional cataclysm on offer here. From what we know from the state archives of Goa and the archives of the Samaj, Dayanand Bandodkar was first and foremost a trader who used Samaj lineages of sexuality, kinship, and geopolitics to carve out a business that traversed across South Asia.[31] To simply read his celebrated collaboration with the multiple and often divided Bahujan groups within Goa primarily as the first lower-caste revolution would bypass the convoluted densities of his emergence and merely reinstate the Samaj as exemplary or exceptional. In a recent monograph on Bandodkar, for example, Parag Parabo counters the dismissal of Bandodkar's radical resistance within Indian historiography by applauding his efforts as a capitalist. Parabo avers that "lower caste movements in Goa" were successful precisely because they were led by "capitalists such as Gomantak Maratha Samaj leaders, Rajaram Paigankar and Bandodkar. Such a proximity to trade and capital founded their ability to challenge feudal [Brahmin] setups in Goa."[32] While Parabo is right to signal the relevance of Bandodkar's status as a successful trader to his rise as a political leader, he typically flattens the history of the Samaj to a caricature of reform and revolution. Histories of sexuality are expunged from the mythology of Bandodkar's success, even as the very capital undergirding Bandodkar's success comes from the intimacies of sexuality's trade and networks. Equally absent from Parabo's study is Bandodkar's advocacy of a complicated Hindutva nationalism that moved caste primarily through networks of trade, language, and religion, producing the Bahujan who was as resolutely anti-Catholic as anti-Brahmin. The historical irony here is that today many Goan members of the Samaj aggressively disarticulate themselves from any Bahujan past, claiming upward mobility through their success in arts and industry.

For scholars such as Fernandes, the story of Dayanand Bandodkar's success is complicit with the very promiscuity of Goa's histories of linguistic and regional dissent. Goa, Fernandes writes, remains in a continuous crisis of geo-history, whereby its identity as state/region is unverifiable, embroiled in raucous debates around language, religion, and caste. Nothing in and from Goa appears legible within settled evidentiary regimes of historicity. The migrant upper-caste Brahmins who arrive in Goa are fish-eating "Shenoi Goembab," corrupt versions of their more established Saraswat Brahmin kin in states such as Maharashtra, and as such cast/e in a different mold. And if states are created on the basis of a shared language, Goa refuses even that foundational arrangement as battles rage on about the relationship between dialect, religion, and citizenship. Fernandes reminds us that the Goan Antruz dialect (drawn from Hindu sources) of Konkani in Devanagari script is listed as the official script even as Catholic groups such as the Romi Lipi Action Front argue for official recognition of the Roman script of Konkani. Indeed, Fernandes makes a compelling case for the import of such linguistic wars within the caste history of the Samaj itself. For Bandodkar and the Samaj, the inclusion of the term *Maratha* in their self-nominalization, Fernandes argues, is an alignment with Marathi, a language spoken by multiple Bahujan groups, and a strident refusal of Konkani, seen primarily as a Brahmin Antruz dialect. In a startlingly evocative aside, Fernandes speaks to a skirmish from his field notes that invokes the messiness of such linguistic debates: a member of the Samaj, and an activist for the Devanagari script, is viciously humiliated for his (surprising) allegiance to the script by opponents from the Roman side. To desire Devanagari, the Samaj activist is told, is to desire sexual un/freedom, to submit once again to Brahmin vernaculars of accumulation and extraction.[33] In lieu of a settled geography, we have a geopolitics that is many things at once: an itinerant political form, a language broken and brokered, and an opening into coalitions of solidarity and reform.

GEO/OBJECTS

If it seems, by this point, gratuitous to stress sexuality's ongoing thralldom with geopolitics, I must nonetheless emphasize that the force of geopolitics, which in the aftermath of the Cold War facilitated the very formation of area studies, has not at all abated. This chapter began with a moment of fulsome commemoration—1947—the year of Indian independence, and its afterlives in the lineaments of the Samaj's history in colonial and postcolonial Goa. In what follows, I want to take a historical detour to another equally commemorative moment within global histories of sexuality, to syncopate familiar habits of reading through a subaltern history of itinerant sex. To ask more broadly, how can the Samaj's vast intellectual archive animate a broader history of geopolitics as critique? It is not just that the Samaj's myriad histories bring in something unforeseen about a precise place and time in South Asia. Rather, the Samaj's geopolitical ikde aani tikde stages the movement of the entire book: the epistemic method is not formalized, does not follow quests, does not search for answers or fill in, does not track propitiatory lures, but allows historicist intuition to proffer affiliations, only to then let them go. Thus, one may think of these pages as laying claim to these lessons of geopolitics that inescapably, unavoidably go amiss, in the most generative ways possible. Let me now turn to that story.

In April 2019, as I was in the throes of writing this book, I was invited by the *History Workshop Journal* to write a brief meditation on the impact and legacy of Stonewall from a global perspective. Records of the past provide anthems of the present, and the charge seemed relatively straightforward: speak to the reverberations Stonewall has had as a historical event on the histories of sexuality that animate your scholarship. The oft-cited 1969 Stonewall riots, as has been well documented, continue to occupy a central role in the history of US LGBTQIA movements, even as the event itself has become a multipronged historical character, its script rewritten through erased plot twists around race, transgender, class, and labor concerns. There is no singular historical account of Stonewall, as Americanists and sexuality studies scholars routinely remind us; rather, it is more an event whose afterlives found the conditions of possibility and solidarity for what is often understood as the modern US queer/LGBTQIA movement.

On receiving the invitation, my first response was ungenerous, as I noted to myself that the Stonewall riots had no significant impact on the narration of histories of sexuality in South Asia, beyond their generalized role as an imagined event through which some approximation of global struggles for queerness can be managed. In other words, Stonewall served more as a site of historical metalepsis, I thought, an effect that was miscast as cause within global histories of sexuality. And further, I noted that I was also loath to provide, in saying so, a local historical supplement to Stonewall, to flag historical events of import in South Asia that had been predictably and routinely overlooked by the Euro-Western tilt of queer/sexuality studies. Surely my task must be more complex than merely adding historical events and details that have hitherto been ignored in the historical narratives of sexuality. As I have repeatedly argued for years now, the much-touted scholarly ebullience about the globalization of histories of sexuality has rarely, if at all, shifted the epistemological orientations of Euro/American history. Histories of sexuality in the non-West still serve as exemplars of sexuality's difference/s, their geohistorical and geopolitical locations providing much-needed evidentiary fodder for the global march of sexuality's empire. To fold histories of sexuality in South Asia back into the lineages of Stonewall was surely to reproduce the very asymmetry of geopolitics of the West and the Rest. In other words, I was stonewalling the invitation to think Stonewall globally.

ARE WE THERE YET?

It is March 14, 2019, and I am in Lahore, Pakistan, on the beautiful and eerily bucolic campus of LUMS (the Lahore University of Management Sciences). LUMS is a privately funded, highly respected, and ultra-elite university in Pakistan, with a surprisingly robust focus on the humanities (its name notwithstanding), nestled within the heavily militarized zones that make up the complex urban landscape of Lahore.[34] It is my second trip to Pakistan; the first one came many years ago when I was working in the Sindh archives in Karachi. This time I am here at the invitation of my friends and comrades, the dean of humanities, Kamran Ali, and co-organizers, Omar Kasmani and Nida Kirmani, to give a keynote on my work on the Gomantak Maratha Samaj. The Samaj, as I noted earlier in this chapter, had considered Pakistan as one of its desired destinations of refuge, so there is a poignant symmetry to my return. Boldly conceived as a deliberation titled "Queer Futures: Politics, Aesthetics, Sexualities," the three-day event is being heralded as the first queer conference to be held in Pakistan and promises an invigorating and wide-ranging conversation on Pakistan's myriad queer modalities.[35] The stage is set, and I am raring to go. The journey to Lahore has been beset (unsurprisingly) by a concatenation of histories and collaborations. Indo-Pak relations are once again imploding; airports are hard to get to, and visas even harder to procure. Yet I am finally here, and all that remains now is my short walk to the conference venue. Map in hand, I step outside my guesthouse, hail a "woke"-looking student, and ask him if he can direct me to the venue. Nodding confidently, he says, "You are going to the *musafir* sex conference? Yes, I can show you where that is." I turn to him again, slightly bemused, and say, "No, I am going to the queer conference." Without missing a beat, he rolls his eyes, and says, "*Musafir* sex, queer conference. Same thing, na?"

That playful, throwaway, yet resplendent figuration, "*musafir* sex," stayed with me, akin to "ikde aani tikde," proffering a sight line for an alternate and potentially radical historical orientation: *musafir* means "traveler," "guest," "visitor," "itinerant" (in Arabic, Hindi, Persian, Urdu, and even Romanian, Turkish, and more—though spelled as *misafir*), and coupled with the cruising, moving body of sex, more precisely, queer sex, it summoned a geo/epistemology, a challenge to the historical imagination that surely merited further exploration. What would it mean to "musafir" sex as historical object, to conjure it through a hermeneutics of protean and playful translation? Was musafir sex itinerant sex?

RE/DIRECTIONS

I end with these two scenes because they make differing hermeneutical demands on our settled habits of theorizing and even politicizing histories of sexuality. Both deploy what Gayatri Spivak and Lauren Berlant have described (albeit in divergent geopolitical contexts) as an acute collective historical sense, a historicist intuition that compels the object of gender and sexuality to be summoned at the precise moment of its disappearance or memorialization (which is also, after all, a renewed repetition of loss and absence).[36] In the case of the mandate to think Stonewall as global historical event, the invitation to engage the archival behemoth that is Stonewall within South Asia necessitates a difficult act of translation. Was my goal as a historian of sexuality and South Asia to decenter the primacy of Stonewall with local historical events of import, such as the historical emergence of the Samaj? Or was it more epistemological, to parlay the lessons learned from the Samaj's history to question precisely why historical causality and memorialization works differently within the fabular geography that is South Asia? Did the history of the Stonewall riots create more of a political demand on subaltern collectivities to produce their own seismic historical event, or did it foreground even further the epistemological divide between the West and the Rest? And how did the queer conference in Lahore fit into that conceptual chakravyuh (quagmire)? Was it an origin story that needed to be built up as a moment of repetition and rupture? Was it the local refurbished site of struggle that summoned the spirit of Stonewall? We were on familiar territory (another conference on queer formations) and yet on unfamiliar ground (in a heavily Islamicized space such as contemporary Pakistan).

In the case of the Pakistan conference, we were invited to think of queer futures in locations where they ostensibly have no collective pull. After all, are queer rights Pakistani rights? Are they musafir rights in that they arrive, settle in, commingle, remainders of a persistent sex that can only be configured through chancy deliberations and encounters? As historical event, is the conference the radical archival trace for queer futures, or more emblematic of the quagmire of archival representation? We know that the conference was held at an expensive, elite institution, LUMS, that very few Pakistanis can afford or have access to; yet it was the elitism and protectionism of the institution that allowed for like-minded musafirs to arrive, cohabit, and exchange sex/objects without fear of persecution and censure. I was able to get a visa (despite being a person of Indian origin) because the largesse of the institution procured governmental favors that bypassed my sex/work and focused on my musafir status. I was, as the consul general at the Pakistani embassy in Los Angeles told me, a welcome *mehmaan* (guest), a scholar of Karachi and Sindh, even if my work on Sindh was about homosexuality and its sins.

At stake in both these scenes of reading is the narration of a geopolitics of sexuality, one from within and one from without. At stake also are renditions of subaltern and global histories of sexuality that continually harden certain historical habits of visibility that need to be rethought and traveled anew. How does one break out of such stagings, where the provincial/vernacular clarifies or corrupts the global and/or the hegemonic? After all, Pakistan is as much the minoritized/fetishized geography within South Asia as South Asia is within globalized histories of sexuality, of Stonewall or beyond. How, then, does one translate the richness of a region's myriad politics, theoretical nuances, multilingual aesthetics, without falling prey to historical habits of legibility? To do so, I want to reverse the order of questions at hand. Instead of speaking to the global impact of the Stonewall riots within South Asia, what would it mean to consider the global impact of the first queer conference in Pakistan on our memorialization of the events of Stonewall? If Stonewall has served as a global allegory for a rousing history of sexuality, what does the Pakistan event teach us about sexuality as historical object? How can the vernaculars, temporalities, and spatialities that make "sex" intelligible as object and archive summon itinerant geopolitical forms that are often left behind?

As such, can the Queer Futures conference held in Lahore, Pakistan, serve to model the very historical questions that animate the critical energies of this book? To put it more vulgarly, how can this historical non-event allow us to think histories of region as histories of sexuality? Can the history of a queer event in musafir land become the archival trace for global histories of sexuality? How does the memorialization of the conference "teach" scholars to enter global histories of sexuality? Surely, the Pakistan conference has now become my history without a cause, situated as it is alongside the figuration of Stonewall. Let me end, then, with four readings of musafir sex at the Pakistan conference that should be constitutive historical method for any engagement of sexuality, geopolitics, and abundance.

Location, logistics, and labor: As mentioned at the outset, the conference was mediated through a machinery of bureaucratic, intellectual, and affective labor. Lahore, a piece of a broader geographical puzzle that is Punjab, is a city of myriad histories, idioms, and intellectual genealogies. To stage a conference within such contexts is to embrace the mutable and explosive forms of shifting learning that is South Asia.

Contradictions as promise: The contradictions of holding a conference that heralded queer vernaculars in a place (LUMS) and time (militarization) of peril were neither eschewed nor erased nor naively celebrated. Here the paradox of queer emergence can become the very vernacular through which any history of sexuality must be articulated: a mad balancing act between the forces of censorship, populism, surveillance, and the relentless march of dissident energies. The conference was (as the final wrap-up session acknowledged) equally a success and a failure, yet friendships were forged, sex was had (one hopes), and alliances of profit and pleasure negotiated.

Multi/linguality as comfort: Baloch, Sindhi, Urdu, Punjabi, and English were the languages afloat at the conference. Translations were offered on demand but, more interestingly, rarely accessed. For example, I sat through multiple recitations of verse whose cadences I heard and enjoyed but whose literal meanings eluded me. There was comfort in not knowing, in accepting our contact as a source of constant and uneven multilingual learning. The task of translation here, and as it has always been in South Asia, signified less as project of literalism and more as a project of recomposition and rendition.[37]

Boys are out, or a map for queer (and South Asian) futures: Last but not least, most surprisingly, the central protagonists (or villains) of the conference were not gay men (as I had falsely assumed). No centrality was given to cis/gay men; instead, feminists, lesbians, and trans/subjects took on key roles, not in any orchestrated summoning of safe spaces (as is the practice here in the United States, or even in India) but more as an organic instantiation of the worlds outside the sanitized space of the academic conference. After all, even in terms of the sparse legal rights afforded to sexual minorities in Pakistan, the *khwaja sira* (a term that must be multiply understood as "alternative/third sex," "transgender," and more) have emerged at the forefront of many such battles. We were constantly pushed to imagine khwaja sira lives as origin stories of queer emergence, emanating through messy, rich, and complex genealogies of religion and practice. Queerness here was an embodied, religious, and governmental form—the khwaja sira challenging our very modes of thinking queer futures alongside hitherto unmarked histories and affects.[38]

If these observations read as an excoriation of Euro/American lineages, they are not intended to do so. Rather, I remain focused on the analytical assumptions that forge the grammar of histories of sexuality, on the endeavors to keep sexuality studies attuned to the task of geopolitics, not as exegetical method for clarifying or redeeming asymmetries but as a space of discontinuous, and often impossible learning. However difficult that task may be, it must remain the itinerary of our labors. In this case, instead of acceding to the demand to think a historical event (Stonewall or the Lahore conference) globally, I would like us to rethink the very geo/epistemology founding that invitation. To retune my young Pakistani guide's words from my opening scene in a slightly different tenor: Musafir sex, histories of sexuality? Same thing, na?

NOTES

1. Many of the observations in this chapter are culled from the introduction I cowrote with Geeta Patel for a special issue on geopolitics and queer studies. We called our issue "Area Impossible" to speak to the conversations that were seemingly segregated and unimagined within those two field-formations. The geopolitical then, as it is here, was never summoned to restore meaning to a different place and time. See Arondekar and Patel, "Area Impossible."
2. For a broader review of the violent history of Partition and the establishment of India and Pakistan, see, among others, Gilmartin, "The Historiography of India's Partition"; Butalia, *The Other Side of Silence*; Jalal, *The Sole Spokesman*; Rawat, "Partition Politics and Achhut Identity"; and Zamindar, *The Long Partition and the Making of Modern South Asia*. Goa, for the most part, remained a tricky and complicated geography for the broader Indian independence movement. As Jawaharlal Nehru (the first prime minister of independent India) was known to have famously remarked, "Ajeeb hai ye Goa ke log" (Strange are the people of Goa). It is unclear if and when he uttered these damning words of dismissal. Rumor has it that Nehru muttered these words soon after his Congress Party suffered a humiliating defeat in the first Goa elections; see Keni, "Nehru and Goa." For the variegated history of Goa's liberation struggles, see Cunha's *Goa's*

Freedom Struggle; Kamat, *Farar Far*; Kunte, *Goa Freedom Struggle vis-à-vis Maharashtra 1946–60*, vols. 1–8; Risbud, "Goa's Struggle for Freedom, 1949–1961"; Kelekar, *Panthasth*.

3   Satoskar, *Gomantak Prakriti ani Sanskriti*, vol. 1. See also Dhondo Shirsargar, *Gomantak Suddhicha Itihas*. *Chakravyuh* can also be translated from the Sanskrit and/or Marathi as "labyrinth," a multilayered defensive formation. In this case, I have chosen to go with "quagmire" as my chosen translation for the term as it fits more closely with the broader claims of the editorial.

4   As Thomas Metcalf has argued, the shift from "colonial subject" to "imperial citizen" produced a different worldview, of hybrid positionalities within otherwise rigid colonial hierarchies. Portuguese Goa was a case in point of such shifting positionalities. See Metcalf, *Imperial Connections*.

5   The Acto Colonial passed in 1930 clamped down on the freedoms that had been previously enjoyed by Goans under the Republic. Censorship on all fronts, excessive police surveillance, and an extreme response to any anticolonial sentiment became the rule of the day. Many scholars have argued that it was such escalated levels of political and social repression that led many Goan liberation fighters to look to the Indian National Congress for organizational and financial support. However, it is equally important to note here that the eventual liberation of Goa is still seen by many as an invasion by an overly aggressive and rapacious Indian state. There is no singular history of liberation here. See Cunha, *Goa's Freedom Struggle*; and Benedito Ferrão, "Thinking Goa Postcolonially."

6   Satoskar, editorial, 134–37.

7   To read more on the history of Goan migration to Mozambique and Zanzibar, see P. Gupta, "Disquieting of History" and "Visuality and Diasporic Dynamism." As Gupta carefully points out, Goan migration to Mozambique functioned under the aegis of the Lusophone umbrella, where attachments to a Portuguese Goan Catholic way of life were preserved and recycled. Goan migration to Zanzibar, on the other hand, Gupta reminds us, was less attached to such colonial histories, and more robustly entrepreneurial, invested in imagining new economic and cultural vistas. See also Prinz, "Intercultural Links between Goa and Mozambique"; Frenz, "Transimperial Connections."

8   For historians such as Sumathi Ramaswamy, the origins of place and place-making are fictions of colonial knowledge structures. To refuse such geographies, Ramaswamy argues, is to undo geographies of occupation, making way for more imaginative and political landscapes of possibility. See Ramaswamy, *The Lost Land of Lemuria*. On a related interrogation of belonging and place, see also Sinha, "Premonitions of the Past."

9   In its most basic terms, geopolitics still describes a relationality to global structures of politics, territory, and environment, underwritten by histories of racial capitalism and its afterlives. A broader history of the development of the concept of geopolitics across disciplines can be found in the following texts: Agnew, *Geopolitics*; Coleman, "Geopolitics as a Social Movement"; Hyndman, "Mind the Gap"; and Ó Tuathail, Dalby, and Routledge, *Geopolitics Reader*.

10 Some sample texts marking the shift to geopolitical models of affiliation within South Asian studies and/or sexuality studies: Gupta, Hofmeyr, and Pearson, *Eyes across the Water*; Subrahmanyam, *Explorations in Connected History* and *Setsuzoku sareta rekishi* [Explorations in connected history]; Ho, *Graves of Tarim*; Lowe, *The Intimacies of Four Continents*; Gopinath, *Unruly Visions*; Boellstorff, *Gay Archipelago*; Amar, *The Security Archipelago*.

11 See A. Arondekar, "Geopolitics Alert"; Grewal and Kaplan, "Introduction."

12 A wonderful example of such endeavors can be seen in a recent call for papers for a conference held at Jamia Millia Islamia University, New Delhi, November 23–24, 2020. The call reads as follows: "For too long, we have worked with the Global South as the space of 'experience' and Euro-America as the space of 'thought.' What would it mean to think about both history and thinking as fluid: not premised on terrestrial locations and incarcerated within the nation state or paradigms of area studies. Perhaps we need to start thinking with 'geographies of affinity' rather than the geographies of colonialism and nationalism. The proposed conference, connected to a SPARC-sponsored collaboration between Jamia Millia Islamia and Centre for Indian Studies in Africa, University of the Witwatersrand, aimed to foreground mobility, circulation, and the *longue durée* thinking with movements across the Ocean rather than terrestrial histories." For further details, see the Jamia Millia Islamia website, https://www.jmi.ac.in/.

13 Fiereck, Hoad, and Mupotsa, "A Queering-to-Come." See also Macharia, *Frottage*.

14 Reiter, "Introduction," in *Constructing the Pluriverse*. I would add here that the essays in this collection (like many others that I have cited elsewhere in this book) move beyond the early gestures of Dipesh Chakrabarty's "provincializing Europe." See Chakrabarty's *Provincializing Europe*.

15 Two more recent works that speak to these shifts in geographical imaginaries within South Asia are Amrith's *Crossing the Bay of Bengal* and C. Ghosh's "Cross-Border Activities in Everyday Life." There is a longer list of scholars who very early on moved away from nations to regions as the basis for historiographical analysis. Within Indian Ocean studies, see Chaudhuri, *Trade and Civilization in the Indian Ocean*; McPher-

son, *The Indian Ocean*; and Bose, *A Hundred Horizons*. For work that addressed the foundational connection between dispersed knowledges and aesthetics within South Asia, see Fischer, *Mute Dreams, Blind Owls, and Dispersed Knowledges*. As I noted early on, slavery studies within South Asia has equally complicated the moorings of nation-state formations, as has scholarly work on gender, households, and families. The best example of such scholarship remains Chatterjee's opus, *Forgotten Friends*. Other noteworthy efforts to rethink India and the Indian Ocean as an Afrasian space include A. Burton, *Africa in the Indian Imagination*; and Desai, *Commerce with the University*.

16   For an extended analysis of the connections between digital India, queer subjects, and vedic India, see Dasgupta, *Digital Queer Cultures in India*; and Shahani's forthcoming monograph, *Pink Revolutions*.

17   Foucault, *The History of Sexuality*, 1:103.

18   This brief description is clearly a reductive reading of the work of these influential scholars. I note their centrality primarily to acknowledge the limitations of their work for histories of sexuality of the global South. The epistemological "case studies" that found the arguments of all three scholars invariably emanate from Euro-American lineages and as such do not engage with the prehistory of these concepts within broader strands of global history. My nonengagement with their work should not be seen as a form of reactionary refusal; rather, I am more committed to citational histories that often get elided within queer/sexuality studies. Those citations are at the heart of this project. See Deleuze and Guattari, *A Thousand Plateaus*; and Latour, *Reassembling the Social*. Some notable exceptions are scholars such as Jasbir Puar who complexly navigate such scholarship and its import for histories of occupation, race, and sexuality. Puar's concerns, however, do not extend to historiographical formulations of networks. See Puar, *Terrorist Assemblages*. For a generative history of literary readings of networks, see C. Levine, *Forms*. Levine draws heavily from current debates within global and/or comparative literature, where the concept of "networks" has functioned as an allegory for a more capacious reading practice.

19   See P. Levine, *Prostitution, Race, and Politics*; and Pragna Shah, *Street Corner Secrets*. Durba Mitra's *Indian Sex Life* is one of the few works that provides more epistemic histories of prostitution within South Asia.

20   Many of the intellectual frustrations articulated here can be found in fuller form in my review essay, "Go (Away) West."

21   To access the multitude that is Kabir and Miraji, see chap. 4, "The Anomaly of Kabir," in Milind Wakankar's wonderful *Subalternity and Religion*; and Geeta Patel's pioneering *Lyrical Movements, Historical Hauntings*.

22   Van Leur, *Indonesian Trade and Society*. In many ways, Van Leur's flawed yet comprehensive trade history set the tone for many future histories

of Indian Ocean Trade that foregrounded networks, itinerancy, and movement.

23   McKittrick, *Dear Science and Other Stories*.
24   Some generative theorizations of the concept of "itinerant" within histories of Indian Ocean studies include Pant, "A Poet's Ocean" and "Papering over Racial Capitalism." Through her research on a merchant community in Gujarat, Pant trenchantly speaks to the imagination as a striated landscape of itinerancy that corrupts linear time lines and geographies of history. Specifically, Pant examines modes of Muslim knowledge formations after 1857, especially poetry, family genealogies, travel routes through Indian Ocean ports, and more. Of note, Pant adds, is how such modes of itinerant thinking are equally monetized (by Indian nationalists and more) to sustain the erasures of Gujarati merchant complicity in plantation capitalism, the erasures of Creole life, and gendered and sexualized erasures of women more broadly.
25   De Sousa Santos, "Between Prospero and Caliban." See also Bastos, "Subaltern Elites and Beyond."
26   See de Souza, *Medieval Goa*. The quoted text is from a speech he gave at a conference commemorating the fiftieth anniversary of Goan liberation in 2011.
27   Newman, "Goa," 429.
28   Menezes, "Goa's Golden Jubilee."
29   For an astute analysis of the prickly status of Goans as Europeans, see Menon, "European of Another Color." See also Noronha, "Goan Citizenship Woes, from Karachi to Portugal."
30   For a useful historical primer to the genealogies of Bahujan and other caste monikers such as Dalit, see Karunakaran, "The Dalit-Bahujan Guide to Understanding Caste in Hindu Scripture."
31   See Angle, *Dayanand*; Radhakrishan, "Dayanand Balkrishna Bandodkar, Architect of Modern Goa"; and Salgaonkar, "Amalgam of Leadership Styles."
32   Parabo, *India's First Democratic Revolution*, 11. Parabo's is the only full-length monograph available on Bandodkar. The book's arguments, however, skew too much in Bandodkar's favor and lack adequate critique of the subject of its study. Such a measured reading may be due to the fact that the study was largely made possible through the financial support of the Bandodkar family.
33   Fernandes, "Curious Case of Goan Orientalism," 280–89.
34   LUMS website, https://lums.edu.pk/.
35   LUMS website, https://swgi.lums.edu.pk/events/3-day-queer-futures-workshop-provides-space-important-conversations.
36   Lauren Berlant's theorization of the "historical sense" can be generative here: "How does a particular affective response come to be exemplary of

a shared historical time, in what terms?" See Berlant, "Intuitionists," 845. As she herself notes, such a reading of affective event becomes the centerpiece of her later, oft-cited opus *Cruel Optimism*. See also Spivak, *Critique of Postcolonial Reason*, and her rewriting of Rani of Sirmur in the chapter on history.

37 See Orsini, "How to Do Multilingual Literary History?"; Cort, "Making It Vernacular in Agra"; d'Hubert, "Patterns of Composition in 17th c. Bengali Literature"; and Patel, "Translation's Dissidence" and "Vernacular Missing."

38 For more substantial reading on the *Khwaja Sira*, see Faris Khan's writings on the subject, including "Translucent Citizenship" and "*Khwaja Sira* Activism." See also Kasmani, "Futuring Trans* in Pakistan"; Jaffer, "Spiritualising Marginality"; and Shroff on third-gender legalization in Pakistan, "Colonial Choreography of Queer Value." An additional work in progress comes from the Lahore conference itself: Jameel, "Hijragiri and Translation."

CODA

I Am Not Your Data

Caste, Sexuality, Protest

> I am not your data, nor am I your vote bank,
> I am not your project, or any exotic museum object,
> I am not the soul waiting to be harvested,
> Nor am I the lab where your theories are tested,
> I am not your cannon fodder, or the invisible worker,
> or your entertainment at India habitat center,
> I am not your field, your crowd, your history,
> your help, your guilt, medallions of your victory,
> ....
> So I draw my own picture, and invent my own grammar,
> I make my own tools to fight my own battle,
> For me, my people, my world, and my Adivasi self!
>
> —ABHAY XAXA, "I Am Not Your Data"

So writes Abhay Xaxa, an Adivasi scholar, activist, and artist, in an excerpt from a longer poem titled "I Am Not Your Data" (2011), in what remains one of the most militant and poignant tracts of anticaste aestheticism and politics. Xaxa, member of the Kurukh collective, born and brought up in Jashpur district, Chattisgarh, India, died tragically of a heart attack in March 2020. A stalwart of Adivasi land reform, Xaxa was first and foremost an intellectual who pushed for radical imaginaries that would combat the datafication and dehumanization of his Adivasi and Dalit/Bahujan kin.[1] If one motif hums through his poem, it is the pressing, almost unbearable awareness of the privations of caste and the unction of history. As if to say, between who we are and how we are seen lies an unbridgeable metrics, an archive of algorithmic violence that will not let us breathe. "So I draw my own picture, and invent my own grammar," he writes in his limpid litany of refusals, exhorting us, his readers, to imagine vibrant historical vernaculars for Adivasi and Dalit/Bahujan presence.[2]

For the past decade or so, I have often returned to Xaxa's trenchant exhortations to think through my own intellectual discomfort with the evidentiary regimes that secure pathways to histories of caste and sexuality, to think about what it means to not be data/fodder for a knowledge supply chain that sees minoritized histories only through lineages of loss, erasure, and paucity. As a refutation of such bureaucratized and ethnological imaginaries, I have turned instead to the concept-metaphor of abundance as a heuristic to advance a nonrecuperative history of sexuality that embraces presence without return, or the fear of loss. My turn to abundance appears less as a seductive alternative to the evidentiary mandates of datafied history and more as a gesture toward the shifting demands of such a history, simultaneously iterating and circumventing its ubiquitous claims. As this book repeatedly signals, we have afforded lavish attention to the effacement of histories of sexuality and somehow left their efflorescence woefully undertheorized. A history of sexuality's abundance, like the one that founds the book's argument, full of joyous indiscretions and staged archives, shaped and determined by caste oppression, remains untold. To summon a history of abundance, I suggest, is not to be restored to representation under continuing occupation but to be set adrift upon more intrepid economies of meaning—sometimes harmonious, sometimes dissonant—that come together to upend genealogies of historical recuperation and representation.

What possibly can it mean, then, to invent a historical grammar, as Xaxa notes, to refuse metonymic deployment, to do more than witness, to become—and indeed to inhabit—a different order of presence? Within these pages, our engagement with the lower-caste devadasi collectivity, the Gomantak Maratha Samaj, has given us histories of sexuality that are playful, extensive, creative, a matter of record, folded into archives initiated and indeed sustained by our own productions. Let us rehearse once more—in brief—what we know of the Samaj; after all, its contra/data founds the protocols for the reading of my text. A historical anomaly and rarity in both its archival forms and its content, the Samaj maintains its own continuous archive, embracing rather than disavowing its history of caste and sexuality. Its archives in Mumbai and Panaji are accessible and available to all who care to enter, and those archives are full of the minutiae of subaltern life, an efflorescent and heady mélange of fact and fiction, with archival genres that corrupt and stage verifiability in the form of fake birth records, property deeds, and more. A canny archival pragmatism founds these collections, where the sheer abundance of the materials is less an organizing than a disorganizing force, shot through by questions of pleasure, practice, and subjectivity, agency and ethics. Within these archives, we have encountered evidentiary genres of invention and sustenance, thriving ecosystems of protest, profit, and refusal. We have been prodded into surprise by staged resistive events (the fake halla [attack] in chapter 1), thrilled by the ekphrastic skills of timepass historiography (the question, in chapter 2, of whether sex is apparent or real), and ushered into an itinerant geopolitics (through musafir sex in chapter 3) that refuses to settle.

A second notable feature of the Samaj, we have also learned, is their corruption of the endogamous structures of sexuality and gender that suture caste to power. Endogamy, as Durba Mitra so succinctly argues, founds colonial and postcolonial histories of society in South Asia, a violent structure of caste and conjugality that scaffolds sexuality into zones of domestic and patriarchal containment. For Mitra, the political and epistemological imposition of caste-based endogamy, first by colonial ethnologists/Indologists and then by homegrown Brahmin elites, systematically places nonconjugal sexuality (or what Dr. B. R. Ambedkar calls the problem of the "surplus woman" or excess female sexuality) as the source of civilizational (read Hindu) disarray. To defy endogamy, Mitra writes, is to excavate the sedimented genealogies of its emergence, to speak to its reliance on caste oppression and the management of female sexuality.[3] Any refusal of endogamy equally poses challenges for a Hindu family form in which caste demarcates kin and conjugality determines access to property, inheritance, and livelihood. In bypassing the mandates of endogamy (we have trouble proving who we are, if you recall, says the Samaj secretary), the history of the Samaj proffers a more radical or perhaps more chaotic caste narrative, one where there is no fixed inherited origin and where caste histories are always threatening to dissolve. If endogamy preserves the reproduction of caste as an inherited form through conjugality, then the Samaj's history of itinerant sexuality and nonconjugal kinship makes the permanence of caste both anomalous and temporary. As I noted earlier, Samaj members maintained nonconjugal, sexual, and long-term relationships with their upper-caste Brahmin yajemans and birthed children who were given Brahmin surnames, all outside the prescribed parameters of endogamy and the Hindu family form. Such caste mayhem and breakdown can be seen in the regular ease with which Samaj members are often asked if they are "original or fake Brahmins" at various gatekeeping sites in Goa. For instance, during the course of my early archival work in Shiroda, a small village in southern Goa that hosted the Samaj's first large political gathering, I was often accompanied by an elder from the Samaj, Sunita Chandavarkar. Chandavarkar (whose surname carries the distinctive stench of an upper-caste lineage) facilitated my engagement with local authorities. At each encounter with priests or bureaucrats, she was repeatedly asked to explain the logic of her obviously Brahmin surname, especially given our connections to a devadasi Samaj. Chandavarkar's weary response to such inquiries, uttered with mocking and measured irony, was always the same: "Kaam aamche, naav amche. Khare ki khote, hein kon tharvnaar?" (Our work, our name. Who decides what is original or fake?).[4]

Another unsettling aspect of the Samaj's history is its shifting caste recognition under uneven state laws in India, guided primarily through muddled legislation around devadasi communities.[5] Moving between nominalizations of Dalit, Other Backward Caste (OBC), and Open Category (OC) in Maharashtra, Goa, and Karnataka, respectively, the Samaj's history speaks directly to the biopolitics of caste and sexuality as striated and pliable, less a place of certitude than a signature of persistent unverifiability, where the data for who qualifies as an oppressed caste remains porous, even arbitrary.[6] Ashwini Deshpande and Rajesh Ramachandran, two prominent economists who work on caste and economic disparity in India, foreground the foundational untenability of caste categories in the emerging economic landscape of a divided India, across rural, urban, and gendered lines. For Deshpande and Ramachandran, a shifting caste history such as that of the Samaj would not be surprising, as the parameters for oppressed caste categorizations remain exceedingly varied and unsettled. To be clear, there is no equivocation around the brutalities of caste segregation, discrimination, and violence; what remains less certain are the forms through which caste is legislated and recognized.[7] Such mediated caste knowledges undergird the very judicial categorizations of caste (materialized in the language of rights and representation) where we become data (I tick the OBC box that holds me in reserve), as we identify with the very forms that secure our minoritization. Any robust anticaste scholarship thus requires a balancing act between these two translations of caste: one more fluid and embodied, the other sedimented and regularized within the judicial mandates of the state.

Here I want to suture Xaxa's call for new idioms of protest, refusal, and survival to the Samaj's history of sexuality and caste and proffer two sight lines of epistemic and material protest: First, how can a history of sexuality such as that of the Samaj potentialize nonevidentiary futures for Dalit/Bahujan subjects? How can such histories clog up the data stream, so to speak, on boats of our own archival making? Can we draw pictures, craft verse, imagine worlds that do not translate into captured forms? Second, what happens if we turn to a theorization of radical caste politics, of Dalit/Bahujan imaginaries, as abundance, as *andolan* (protest) visions that cull the creative fury of the *bahu* (expanse) of lower-caste subjects? Ambedkar's "annihilation of caste" remains the horizon, even as attenuation remains the more immediate historical task.[8] After all, the term *Bahujan*, of Pali/Buddhist lineage, refers to a lexical register of transient diversity—present-day Scheduled Castes (Dalits), Scheduled Tribes (Adivasis/Indigenous), Shudra (peasant) castes, and Other Backward Castes—cutting across religion, languages, and geographies. There is little historical clarity around the first political mobilization of the term *Bahujan*. One well-known early usage appears in Vithal Ramji Shinde's oft-cited Marathi manifesto "Bahujan Paksh." Published in 1920, in Baroda's *Jagruti Patra*, Shinde's manifesto served to provide political keywords for his party in the new council elections in Pune (then part of Bombay Presidency in colonial India). For Shinde, the Bahujan (or the backward class), as non-Brahmin people, were deliberately kept away from "knowledge, wealth and power," marked by an inherent subalternity, an inaccessibility to the lines of power and representation that must be addressed and eradicated. As such, he writes, "A caste-specific name like the non-Brahmin party does not foreground the specificity of a Bahujan collectivity that is marked by helplessness and powerlessness. Therefore, if we name this party Bahujan Party or People's Party, which is an appropriate and all-encompassing name, there will be little objection to it."[9]

Even as Shinde's words invite a pragmatic expansion of an anticaste vision that is more inclusive of all lower-caste people, his call remains wedded to electoral politics or "vote banks" (to return to Xaxa), as seen in the postcolonial success and visibility of Bahujan-based political parties, such as the BSP and more.[10] More recently, Gopal Guru cautions against the celebration of Bahujan electoral success as a measure of anticaste projects. Indeed, Guru lambasts the turn to *sarvajan* (people) as an organizing anthem for Bahujan parties, arguing that such language repackages caste oppression as a reform project of the Indian democratic state. A history of sarvajan, Guru underscores, marks the impossibility of Dalit/Bahujan history where the bland recitation of democratic principles (we, the people) flattens Dalit/Bahujan difference and adversity.[11] Instead, Guru and other anticaste scholars, such as V. Geetha, urge a sustained engagement with Dalit/Bahujan intellectual genealogies that speak less to the nationalist rhetoric of the sarvajan and more to the epistemological and agential diversity offered by Dalit/Bahujan pasts and futures.[12] To do so is to leave aside the divisions within Dalit and Bahujan conceptualizations, between anticaste stalwarts such as Kanshi Ram and Dr. B. R. Ambedkar, to focus instead on collective potentiality as an episteme, ethics, and politics.[13] For whenever one encounters the Bahujan, the many, and the more, one is thus engaged with abundance, with the effort to forge supplementary histories that both incite and dissolve the diminishments of their histories.

In what follows, I will provide three staged events of reading, each an archival fragment of histories of caste, sexuality, evidence, and protest, rendered in different rhetorical keys. Each fragment generates a set of protocols for the immanent critique of caste and sexuality, ongoing refutations of clarity and easy categorization. My ambition, for better or for worse, is necessarily diffuse, even didactic: the urgency here is to exude new idioms of the possible. In order to get to my (non)data, you will have to use your imagination.[14]

WE ARE SARASWATS: CASTE

September 2012: A smaller enclave of the Samaj lives in Hubballi-Dharwad, Karnataka, a bustling border city between Maharashtra, Goa, and Karnataka. Here members of the collectivity (150 families or so) are multiply categorized as Dalit or OBC (Other Backward Caste), with a few subgroupings making their way out of lower-caste classifications on the basis of their economic success. As with their counterparts in Maharashtra and Goa, the broader efforts of this smaller group are dedicated to social and economic upliftment of their members, as well as a public embrace of their history of sexuality.[15] Anticaste scholars such as A. Geetha are specifically critical of the Samaj's activities in Karnataka (and to a lesser extent in Goa), arguing that their diffuse caste categorization allows them to disavow their lower-caste Dalit kin who continue to work as devadasis. The Samaj's focus, she argues, remains on the more flamboyant and successful kalavant (artist) caste whose presence and contributions remain central to its history. A. Geetha's claims, while important, are not well grounded in any close engagement with the Samaj's histories or archives; she draws more on interviews with the head of a local devadasi NGO than on available information about the Samaj's outreach to a wide swath of their Dalit kin. More to the point, A. Geeta curiously elides the Samaj's embrace of its histories of sexuality and its devadasi past and present. What remains relevant is her reminder that the Samaj's shifting caste forms make for a variegated and messy arena of reform and recognition.[16]

As such, I am in Hubballi to conduct archival research and to speak to some of the living elders who have wills, property deeds, and various historical memorabilia to share. On the invitation of a member of the Samaj executive council, Uday Badkar, I attend their monthly function held at the Samaj headquarters in the heart of Hubballi. The function is a gathering of celebration and admonition: achievements of *kalakar* (artist) members are lauded, even as the continued social and economic destitution of the community continues to be bemoaned. At this point, I am pulled into the fray by an enthusiastic older devadasi, Nirmalatai, who asks me to speak

C.1 Konkan Saraswat Samaj, Hubli Dharwad, Sanman Karekram for Sri Ram Bhandarkar, a kalakar from the community. Photo: Uday Badkar

on my research and remind the audience of the Samaj's enduring history of sexuality. And, she adds coquettishly, wagging her finger at me, make sure to tell them "namma mahileyaru sundara iddaare" (how beautiful our women are).[17] It is at this point that I notice the very large banner displayed prominently above the stage—a banner written in Kannada, which reads "Konkan Saraswat Samaj."

Baffled at what I conclude is surely a mistake, or at least an aspirational typo, I turn to Nirmalatai and ask her to explain the banner. Surely, I ask, in my best impersonation of a well-behaved historian's "how will this appear in the archives?" mode, you must see how this looks! The banner, I firmly add, suggests that we are a Saraswat Samaj, a Brahmin Samaj, which is clearly not true. Without batting an eyelid, and with a weary nod, Nirmalatai looks at me and says, "Do you see what is next to the banner? That is the image of the Goddess Saraswati, the goddess of learning. In Hubballi, in the Konkan region, we are devotees of Saraswati and committed to learning, and so we are ourselves Saraswat. That right does not belong to the Brahmins!" Bemused by Nirmalatai's casual explanation of what appears to be a rather imaginative leap of self-identification, I turn to Badkar, the Samaj trustee, and ask him the same question. His explanation echoes (albeit with some difference) much of what Nirmalatai has just referenced. Badkar patiently reminds me that the Hubballi branch of the Samaj deliberately chose this name because they believe they migrated from the mystical banks of the river Saraswati and, as such, are her subjects. When pressed on the historical details of this claim, Badkar remains unfazed and states that those details are not relevant because "this is what we believe to be true." And in case I have any further doubts about their legitimacy as a collectivity, he notes with great pride that even the dominant caste community in Hubballi, the Chitrapur Saraswat Brahmin Samaj, has no choice but to respect their nominalization. With an ironic smile, he adds, "They have to accept us because their numbers are shrinking and we are here now." Such acceptance, Badkar reminds me, does not alleviate caste discrimination or segregation; it does, however, fissure proprietary upper-caste claims to visibility and recognition.[18]

There is clearly so much more here to say about this interlude of caste and sexuality and the historical record. After all, from what we have learned about the Samaj's history, such caste "adjustments" rarely materialize economic change, but they appear throughout in the ways the Samaj conjures its own histories of belonging.[19] Caste becomes marked by dissolution, by the very annulment of its evidentiary forms. Regardless of how the Samaj narrates its nominalization, its archival presence in the official archives will now always point to one Konkan Saraswat Samaj, legible for most data-driven research as a Brahmin community. After all, as a registered "Saraswat" collectivity (Registration Number DRZ DAF 56/2009-10), the Samaj will clog up the data stream, corrupting caste lineage as an inherited form. Let me be clear: such castes of hand, if you will, are not to be read as aspirational forms (wanting to be Brahmin), attempts to forge an upper-caste identity. The titular event comports more with the Samaj's broader epistemology, a pretext for a different history of caste, an installation of protest, a reordering of the grammar of recognition and lineage. The Samaj's self-dedicated name, Konkan Saraswat Samaj, hovering somewhere between ordained caste structures and imaginative refurbishment—between evidence and kala (art)—becomes magically liberated from the more burdensome data machine, that stultifying apparatus of rights and representation. Instead, we get translations of sexuality and caste, circulating in a continuous present, that thwart state demands for a compliant and intelligible history.[20]

The data has changed. Who's a Brahmin now?

HUM KAGAZ NAHIN DIKHAENGE/WE WILL NOT SHOW OUR PAPERS: EVIDENCE

Even as protests against the controversial Citizenship Amendment Act (CAA) raged rapidly across India at the end of 2019, till 2020 (the last protest I attended was in Mumbai on March 15, 2020) there was a clear sense that we were facing familiar legal, historical, and political challenges around the linkages between evidentiary regimes and discourses of rights and representation for minoritized subjects (across, caste, religion, labor/sexuality, and more). Passed in December 2019, CAA enacted the virulent logic of earlier efforts to create a National Register of Citizenship (NRC) in the northeastern state of Assam that required all citizens to produce evidence of their citizenship.[21] The prevailing ideology behind both state efforts was the systematic expulsion of the minority Indian Muslim community, whereby CAA would extend citizenship only to non-Muslims fleeing religious persecution in neighboring countries. Meanwhile, Muslims (Indian or otherwise) would be required to prove their citizenship through spurious paper archives that may or may not be recognized. Rahul Rao argues that the anti-CAA protests were significant precisely because they mobilized the seductive language of a secular nationalism (India as diverse, India as democracy) besmirched by the jingoism of a Hindutva, separatist state. For Rao, such protests underscore the difficulties of a resistive politics in India, where the recourse to nationalisms against the state produces "excesses" of its own, including exclusions of region (Kashmir) and indigeneity (Adivasi), to name a select few.[22]

The chant "Hum kagaz nahin dikhaenge" (We will not show our papers) became a rousing anthem of the protests, echoing the challenges evidentiary regimes placed on bodies across regions, generations, and temporalities. Excerpted from Varun Grover's now viral poem, the full paragraph reads:[23]

> Hum samvidhan ko bachaenge,
> Hum kagaz nahin dikhaenge,
> Hum jan gan man bhi gaenge,
> Hum kagaz nahin dikhaenge.
> (We will save the Constitution,
> We will not show [NRC] papers,
> We will sing "Jan Gan Man" [the national anthem],
> We will not show papers.)

For sexuality's subjects, such a demand for *kagaz* (evidence) produced a particularly complex set of legal, ethical, and affective negotiations. The most strident refusals of such kagaz regimes were enacted by trans/ subjects who spoke out against their continuous effacement within legal and societal structures in India. To produce original evidence (kagaz), to "prove" trans lives (who we "really" are), scholars and activists insisted, was to return to familial, legal, and chronological structures of self that were violent and punitive.[24] For Dalit/Bahujan/Adivasi kin (and the segregations of sexuality and caste's subjects here are clearly artificial), the call to documents, verifiable or otherwise, was an acutely exclusionary judicial enactment of caste consolidation. To be legible as paper subjects was to further dehumanize Dalit/Bahujan bodies, already at the peripheries of the state's biopower.[25] For example, my own mother, like so many other caste-oppressed kin in India—like the legendary figure of Aai in Dalit Marathi poet Jyoti Langewar's famous corpus—has no birth certificate, only a memory of a life nourished despite the mandate of that origin story.[26] To refuse kagaz was to forge a history of sexuality and caste that required new languages of political action.

A second noteworthy development of these nationwide protests was of course the exuberant embrace of Dr. Bhimrao Ambedkar alongside a perceptible sidelining of Mahatma Gandhi as national icon. The phrase preceding the chant "Hum kagaz nahin dikhaenge," as we read in the full extract above, was the equally rousing phrase "Hum samvidhan ko bachaenge" (We will save the constitution), a direct homage to Ambedkar's constitutional legacy, his pioneering vision of a radical democracy, all of which centered Dalit and Bahujan histories as places of learning and possibility. The invocation of the constitution (*samvidhan*) here must not be seen as a return to the idea of enshrined truths, or a turn to an evidentiary genre, maligned at the hands of an authoritarian and divisive state. Rather, the call to save or rescue the samvidhan was more a call to what Kalpana Kannabiran has recently termed a constitution as commons—a space of active making and remaking, a coming together of new grammars of subject-making, to create what Rohit De so importantly reminds has always been a people's document.[27] The constitution as commons is not a kagaz full of verifiable data and embodied beginnings; it is more a vocabulary of protest and possibility.

In a space like South Asia, where the idea of evidence is always already a hoax, a jugaad (flexible form), what does it then mean—as we have just seen through the history of the Gomantak Maratha Samaj—to both refuse and mobilize the rhetoric of kagaz? After all, as Matthew Hull, Nayanika Mathur, and Sanjay Srivastava have so persuasively argued, official evidence of existence in colonial and postcolonial South Asia is rarely commensurate with recognizable selves and identities, where the insinuation of paper rationality into lives is the very crux of the matter. Documents fake and fail lives, and their failure incites the variations of duplication, duplicity, and collectivity.[28] Our pandemic times have further heightened these kagaz regimes, as citizens are both composed and jettisoned through a language of evidence that arbitrarily creates insiders/outsiders. I have returned often to these early moments of protest in these past few harrowing months as the jugaad form has become both our salvation and our demise in South Asia—social media secures life at the very moment in which the state refuses its possibility. Unnamed kin die in unnamed spaces, even as the register of COVID-19 deaths and cases climbs up each day. A trans/Dalit comrade in rural Maharashtra (Latur) who could not get their brother into a hospital bed wrenchingly writes me, "Kagaz navhta ga, mhanoon tyache maran lavkar aale" (We didn't have the right papers, sister, that is why he died so prematurely).

I REMEMBER YOU: PROTEST

I remember you, my mother always tenderly says to my partner, Lucy, as she glimpses her across oceans virtual and real every week. My mother is eighty-five, her memory faded and folded into crevices of stories told and untold. Her world, a map of the everyday life of sexuality and caste, charts the realism of autofiction, where the past is always somewhere close at hand. In the pixelated landscape of my video screen, Aai's words linger, a poignant shorthand, and a translated rendering of how she manifests absence. "I remember you" is her English condensation of our shared Marathi phrase—"Mala tujhi aathvan yete"—which makes *aathvan* (memory) an act of personal conjuring, a poignant tethering of past and present. I remember you too, Auntie, Lucy always responds, sealing a treasured ritual of long-distance love that sutures

C.2 Pramila Laxmeshwar, 1947. Photo: Gomantak Maratha Samaj Archives, Mumbai, India

affect to a history of memory. To remember is not to grasp a lost form or surrender to the nostalgia of a less violent past (if there ever was one), but more to aspire to belong. To fashion a world, or at least a version of a world, that brings joy, succor, and the possibility of a reunion.

I have thought of Aai's phrase often this past pandemic year as I've traveled several times to Mumbai to see her, without her beloved Lucy (whose US passport makes it impossible for her to enter a virus-stricken India). I have thought of what it means to remember a history lost and/or unseen in a country besieged by memory disputes, where little separates the factional from the functional. Even as India buckles under the weight of rampant authoritarianism, communalism, casteism, and a general disregard for human life, I remember you. I remember the promises of liberation, the mandate to agitate, organize, and educate. I remember the farmers' protests, the words of Nodeep Kaur, the joyous rhythms of Shaheen Bagh, and the refusals of Bhima Koregaon.

Today, as heartbreak stretches across India, where more fires are lit to cremate than to create, there are more memories to be made. From the searing faces of my Dalit/Bahujan kin who tend the dead in the crematoriums of Hindutva making, to the oxygen-*lungar* (community kitchen) that provides breath to the as yet living, we remember. A cremator "at the Center of India's COVID Hell," the headline reads, weeps; he is, after all, the only witness, the only record of the living dead.[29] Ashu Rai is his name, always a Dalit, yet now the bearer of last rites, of data un/processed, of bodies un/spoken. "Almost everyone asks about my caste because everyone wants a Brahmin to do the rituals and not the Dalits, but they aren't available," Rai says. "We are." Drenched in sweat, bearing wood, he takes one remaining piece of cloth that covers his face and head, and whispers laughingly, "This cloth ... absorbs [my] sweat and ... when I hang it on my shoulder, people think that I am a Brahmin priest." I am a Dalit, I am the record of your loss, I am, I am, I am not your data. I am abundant.[30]

NOTES

1. See Choudhury and Aga, "In Memoriam." See also Sushmita, "Remembering Scholar and Activist Abhay Xaxa."
2. Xaxa's words are a clear tribute to the pioneering work of Dr. B. R. Ambedkar and his insistence on caste as an enduring theoretical calculus and vocabulary. See Ambedkar, *Dr. Babasaheb Ambedkar*.
3. Mitra, "'Surplus Woman.'"

4   Unfortunately, Sunita Chandavarkar passed away tragically due to heart complications in early 2018. Her humor, grace, and knowledge of the Samaj activities remain a founding presence in this book. Like so many subjects who animate the archives of the Samaj, Sunita was an extraordinarily ordinary figure who grew up within a devadasi household and committed herself to a life of possibility, curiosity, and sustenance. She ran a tiny grocery store in central Shiroda, a tiny village in Ponda Taluka, southern Goa, India. My surname, Arondekar, on the other hand, elicited less concern, as it has no perceptible Brahmin connection.

5   TNN, "Commission to Decide on Gomantak Maratha Samaj's Inclusion in OBC."

6   The National Commission for Backward Classes' central list of OBC communities and the statewide list of Scheduled Castes in India reflect many of the shifts in caste nominalizations I have alluded to here. See "Central List of OBC's." See also "List of Scheduled Castes."

7   Deshpande and Ramachandran, "How Backward Are the Other Backward Classes?" See also the current furor over the Maratha quota in Maharashtra, India, where the debate around who constitutes a disadvantaged caste remains an unending debate: Khapre, "Explained: How Marathas Got Reservation, and What Happens Now."

8   Ambedkar, *Annihilation of Caste*. The text was published in 1936 and remains a source of continued inspiration for a broad swath of anticaste collectivities and politics.

9   I have provided a loose translation of Shinde's prose. The original Marathi text of Shinde's article can be found at Tejas Harad's blog *Scattered Pillar*. For a complete (though rough) English translation, see Harad's translated text, June 1, 2019, https://scatteredpillar.wordpress.com/2019/06/01/bahujan-pakshas-manifesto-vitthal-ramji-shinde/.

10 For some sample readings of the rise and success of the BSP, see S. Guha, "From Ethnic to Multiethnic"; and Verma, "Bahujan Samaj Party," 19, 21–22.

11 Guru, "The Indian Nation in Its Egalitarian Conception."

12 Guru and Geetha, "New Phase of Dalit-Bahujan Activity."

13 See Narayan, "Ambedkar and Kanshi Ram."

14 On a related note (and yet somehow requiring perhaps more than this cursory note) is the question of "biodata," that peculiar Indian-English coupling that is regularly foisted on South Asians of all ilk to explain their genealogies of arrival and futurity in any marriage proposal/arrangement. Biodata routinely functions as a placeholder for all histories of caste, sexuality, age, religion, and income. Your biodata solidifies your lineage and smooths your way into conjugality.

15 Information on the membership of the Hubballi-Dharwad branch of the Samaj was obtained from open-access membership lists. Currently,

most members of the Samaj claim OBC status and government benefits (2A) as mandated by the Karnataka State, with a small section categorized as Dalit, and a few families claiming Open Category caste status. All lists and additional materials can be found at the Samaj's office at Sahana, House No. 19, 5s Cross, Chandranath Nagar, Behind Vijay Hotel, Vijaynagar Hubballi-580032. I am grateful to the Badkar family (Uday and Manik) for introducing me to the Samaj archives and membership.

16 Geetha, "Entrenched Fissures." For a more detailed and historical relationship between caste and broader devadasi histories in Karnataka, see Ramberg's wonderful *Given to the Goddess*. It would be important to note here that the devadasi community referenced in Ramberg's work does not have any connections to the Samaj referenced here.

17 Much gratitude to the formidable Prasad sisters, Pratima and Prarthana, for walking me through the linguistic complexities of Kannada and its translated avatars.

18 Badkar's comments were made in Marathi. Translations are mine and are excerpted from many long conversations held during my attendance at the function.

19 Nataraj, "Backward Classes and Minorities in Karnataka Politics."

20 In her forthcoming book on histories of caste and slavery across the Konkan coast, Ananya Chakravarti speaks to connected caste malleabilities and nominalizations such as Kunbi Saraswats that trouble settled historical wisdom. This observation is taken from a talk Chakravarti gave at the Center for South Asian Studies, UCSC, April 12, 2022.

21 A more detailed account of the politics of Assam and its relationship to the amendments to Indian citizenship law can be found in Roy, *Mapping Citizenship in India*.

22 Rao, "Nationalisms by, against, and beyond the State."

23 Grover, "Hum kagaz nahi dikhayenge."

24 One well-circulated video narrative of such refusals can be seen here: "'NRC-CAA-Trans Bill Suicidal for Us': Trans Community Speaks Out | The Quint," produced by *The Quint*, YouTube, January 9, 2020, https://youtu.be/eq-5wXv3p7c. There has also been a considerable amount of rich scholarship on the quandaries of trans/subjects, judicial representation, and activist re/formations. One exemplary essay would be Jain and Gupta, "Law, Gender Identity, and the Uses of Human Rights."

25 Joseph, "Identity Card," 178–79.

26 For more on the pioneering writings and activism of Jyoti Lanjewar, see S. Gupta, "Jyoti Lanjewar." The English translation of her best-known poem, "Aai," can be found on *The Shared Mirror*: Lanjewar, "Mother (Aai)."

27 Kannabiran, "Constitution-as-Commons." Kannabiran also dedicates her essay to the memory of Xaxa. See also De, *A People's Constitution*. A viral

video of Dalit women speaking to the need for a constitution as commons can be seen here: "Samvidhan Bachao Sabha | Hum Kaagaz Nahin Dikhayenge | Barinagar | Jamshedpur | 26 Jan |," YouTube, January 27, 2020, https://youtu.be/bf4by1mpcoc.

28 See Hull, *The Government of Paper*; Mathur, "Transparent-Making Documents and the Crisis of Implementation"; Srivastava, "Duplicity, Intimacy, Community."

29 S. Majumdar, "We Spoke to a Cremator at the Center of India's COVID Hell."

30 Das, "Dalit Cremation Workers and the COVID-19 Pandemic."

ACKNOWLEDGMENTS

I have always disliked the historical common sense that loss is a fundamental ingredient of any subaltern history. That we redeem the deficit of our minoritized pasts through concerted acquisitions of lost pasts has never quite settled. I have turned instead to abundance here—of theories, archives, memories, indiscretions, joy, kinship, care, geopolitics—to proffer a different story of sexuality.

I have been experimenting with the idea of this book for some time. By one recollection, it may have started in 1981, when I was thirteen and first recognized sexuality's myriad fictions and historical forms. There I was, on an enormous stage in Rang Bhavan, at the annual celebration of our community, the Gomantak Maratha Samaj, in Bombay. I had just received a prize for a short story I had written on the Samaj's history. Mostly hagiographical in tone, the story giddily cast the Samaj as a collectivity whose achievements as a lower-caste devadasi community were unparalleled and worthy of recognition. The plot of the story is unremarkable: a young female protagonist, Pramila, bullied by her schoolmates for her caste and devadasi past, turns to her mother for comfort. Her mother regales Pramila with rousing exemplars from the Samaj's archives, exhorting her to imagine the Samaj as a living source more of inspiration than of shame. As the large, raucous, and joyful audience applauded and cheered me on, I recall gleefully thinking stories of sexuality were clearly my ticket to notoriety. And as I read the story aloud, I remember thinking, surely one day, I will write a sequel . . .

A more reliable (and less megalomaniacal!) beginning, however, can be traced to the many conversations I had with my father after my first book came out. Keen to continue thinking sexuality comparatively, across temporalities and empires, I wanted to turn to Portuguese India, specifically Goa, and to our Samaj, as one possible sight line for such histories. After all, there was so much to tell, so many archives available to read and access. Still unconvinced by the innovation of my research, I remember Baba quizzically asking me why such an ordinary history of sexuality would be of interest to anyone. For my Baba, a poet and a mathematician, any history of sexuality was inevitably a shape-shifting chiasmus, one in which value is generated under conditions that require presence and absence from those who appear, only retroactively, as its subjects. For Baba, historical loss and abundance were related in more of a recursive, rather than linear way. Our Samaj's history was thus simply ordinary, unexceptional, pragmatic in its existence and purchase. Baba's early questions forged much of the epistemological groundwork for what eventually became a longer meditation on sexuality's geo/histories. Other early guides and provocateurs from our Samaj who pushed me to ask more risky historical questions include Archanatai Kakodkar, Geeta Manjrekar, Anil Paigankar, Manohar Shirodkar, Adhik Shirodkar, and Sudhatai Bandodkar.

Central to my thinking has been the extraordinary mentorship, tutelage, and wisdom of Geeta Patel, Indrani Chatterjee, and Lauren Berlant. Geeta has always been my intellectual lodestone, a constant guide and poet whose lyricism and humor have made so much of this book possible. I write overly compacted prose, and Geeta's provocations have nudged me to think beyond and across the edges of my own thinking. Geeta read various avatars of each chapter, often smoking her way through multiple cigarettes in thought and consternation, only to return with sound advice and suggestions. Indrani Chatterjee's tough love, generosity, and attention to the mandates of historical archives pushed me in unexpected, rigorous, and rich ways. This is not a book she would write (or perhaps even approve of!), but it is a book that speaks to the arenas of gender and sexuality she opened for so many of us. Lauren Berlant was the first one to think of my twitchy historical sense (as she would call it) as a potential book for her series, Theory Q. Through innumerable phone calls, text messages, and stern emails, Lauren kept me moored to the questions animating this book. Lauren was simply Lauren: impossible, demanding, loving, and endlessly generative. If there is abundance in this book, it owes much to her questions—many of which I never did answer. I miss her.

The writing of this book was sustained by an incredible posse of friends, colleagues, and kin at UCSC. Since the early stirrings of the project, and throughout the painful losses and separations of the pandemic, they have unfailingly extended love, support, bad jokes, food, archival illuminations, and intellectual exchange. Karen Tei Yamashita is that special crazy genius we all need. KT fed me, nurtured my endless quests for meaning (with an eye roll), and gave me a home in Santa Cruz. Ronaldo Wilson's poetry (on and off the tennis court) allowed me the space to find joy (and choreographed "porn") when I needed it most. Gina Dent's intellectual sensibility, love, and fierce friendship have kept me afloat. Vilashini Cooppan sustained me with her exquisite words and khana, while Dard Neuman was exactly the brother and coconspirator I had always wished for. Mayanthi Fernando and Nidhi Mahajan are da special desi ladeez whose spirits soar high—especially over good food and drink—and make radical kinship possible. Other UCSC comrades who extended support and timely intellectual interventions include Jennifer Derr, Marc Matera, Madhavi Murty, Carla Freccero, Juned Shaikh, Rachel Nelson, Mark Anderson, Jody Greene, Debbie Gould, Angela Davis, and Daniel Selden. At UCLA (where I taught from 2017 to 2019), I benefited from the erudition and counsel of Jemima Pierre, Peter Hudson, David MacFayden, Robin Kelley, Ali Behdad, Kathleen McHugh, Jennifer Sharpe, Rachel Lee, and Yogita Goyal. A special thanks to all the graduate students in my multiple seminars on comparative histories of sexuality, slavery, and empire at UCSC and UCLA. Those seminars allowed me to rehearse many of the thorny concerns that are central to this book.

Outside settled institutional contexts, there are many others whose companionship has generated much of the rich texture within these pages. I live in Los Angeles—a city of special dreamers and secret agents—many of who inhabit my life and surround me with magical acts of love and intellectual curiosity. Aneil Rallin, Eve Oishi, Laura Kang, Priya Jaikumar, Thomas Holden, Conor/Connie McTeague, David Rousséve, and Nina Rota are the ultimate mango-tango team. Connie is no longer with us, but I know he's pleased as hell that I made it here. Meha (Memu) Holden grew up alongside this book, and even developed a grudging taste for archives through it all. Bishnupriya Ghosh and Bhaskar Sarkar are the queer family every ho/mo must have. B and B provided that invaluable infrastructure of badass love and thought that helped this queer survive. Bishnu's trenchant critique and Bhaskar's plastic forms are everywhere. My sakhis/sahelis, Raka Ray and Saba Mahmood, the dynamic duo, took me under their wing and shaped my capacity for learning and dissent. Saba, I know, will send me a sign sooner rather than later. Khuda hafiz and shukriya, my sweet dost. Neferti Tadiar and Durba Mitra enthusiastically read many versions of chapters, served as fabulous cheerleaders on speed dial, nudged me into coherence along the way: third-world sistahs forever.

Over the years, many comrades across oceans and time zones have pushed my thinking on the messiness of queer labors and geopolitics: Jasbir Puar, Pete Sigal, David Eng, Lucinda Ramberg, Mrinalini Sinha,

Lakshmi Subramanian, Ritu Birla, Joan Scott, Maya Mikdashi, Ania Loomba, Suvir Kaul, Omnia El-Shakry, Sherene Seikaly, Michael Allan, Afsaneh Najmabadi, Christine Balance, Allan Isaac, R. Zamora Linmark (aka Zack), Judith Surkis, Kris Cohen, Zirwat Chaudhary, Nishita Trisal, Priti Ramamurthy, Kavita Philip, Paul Amar, Robert Diaz, Usha Iyer, Pavithra Prasad, Martin Manalansan, Omar Kasmani, Ishita Pande, Sharika Thiranagama, and Neloufer De Mel. I survived the rigors of writing during the pandemic thanks in large measure to my indomitable El Lay / Vermont Canyon tennis posse: Gustavo Mena, Gabe Moffat, Peter Shin, Ray Wing Lai, Duncan Williams, York Chang, Giulia Corda, Uttara Pant, and Ketaki Pant. Rallies and passing returns animated each (pandemic) day, making words and thought so much more possible.

In India, my research on the Gomantak Maratha Samaj was sustained by an entire network of friends, collaborators, and kin. In 2011, Gopal Guru was my first real audience at a conference celebrating fifty years of Goan Independence, pushing me to center caste oppression and sexuality, even as I wrestled my own hesitations around histories of family and form. Sharmila Rege's 2012 invitation to lecture in Marathi on the Samaj was what ultimately convinced me that this was a book worth writing. My Goan people, kalavants in every way, made every research visit a homecoming of sorts. The Al Zulhaij Collective (Amita Kanekar, Kaustubh Naik, Albertina Almeida, and Dale Menezes), with Jason Fernandes playing the star role, endured my questions, concerns, and archival consternations. Jason was my early guide to Goa's post/colonial histories, over many road trips, meals, and terrible libations. R. Benedito Ferrao (aka Bene), research partner and meu caro amigo, sifted through the detritus of Portuguese and Konkani archival papers, tracking down obscure references and legal cases. Vishwesh Kandolkar and Vanessa reminded me that there was always time for art and architecture. Vivek Menezes, Parag Parabo, Sharon Da Cruz, Alito Siqueira, and Rochelle Pinto were the best interlocutors on Goan history and more. In Bombay (sometimes Mumbai), the "bore mat kar yaar" diva, Paromita Vohra, listened to and read much of what is included in the pages here. Her irrepressible humor, wit, and khana made late-night writing sessions that much more enjoyable. The Bahujan Feminist Collective (Anuradha, Zareena, Shailaja, Chhaya, and Ismat) were committed to a solidarity of conversations that found so much of the book's ethical and political stakes. Sameera Khan, Sameera Iyenger, the Pasha siblings (Dhanu and Manu), Sadanand Mahad, D. Geetha, Anish Gawande, Lata Paik, Monica Almeida, Bhushan Korgaonkar, Surabhi Sharma, Tejaswini

Niranjana, Rohan Shivkumar, Avijit Mukul Kishor, Suryakant Waghmore, and Monica Ballaney made every return home a place of gathering. My cousins, especially Nitin Shirodkar, Kamakshi Gawde, and Manik Shirodkar, were unflagging in their support and enthusiasm for the project. Nitin (bhai)'s research on and celebration of Samaj histories made my work that much easier. Thanks to my brother Ashish Arondekar and his family (Vaishnavi, Neha, and Anisha); perhaps one day my nieces will find their way into this book.

Financial support for this project was generally provided by the following sources: University of California President's Faculty Fellowship in the Humanities and multiple research grants from the Committee on Academic Research, University of California, University of California, Santa Cruz. These sources funded research at libraries, private collections, and national and region archives in India and Portugal. Of particular note is the extraordinary kindness and guidance of trustees at the Gomantak Maratha Samaj Archives, Panaji and Mumbai, and the archivists and staff at the Maharashtra State Archives, Mumbai; Xavier Centre of Historical Research, Goa; Historical Archives of Goa, Central Library, Goa; Heras Institute, Mumbai; Directorate of Archives and Archaeology, Panaji; Biblioteca Nacional, Lisbon, Portugal; and Arquivo Nacional de Torro de Tombo, Lisbon, Portugal. Multiple Devasthan records were made available through the generosity of Samaj networks, too many to be named here.

Much of the architecture of the book took shape in many workshops and seminars, including those at Afterlives of the Postcolonial, the Sharjah Arts Foundation; South Asia Series, Stanford University; Davis Center, Princeton University; Gender Studies Colloquium, Cornell University; Queer Urgencies Symposium, University of Pennsylvania; Queer Futures, Lahore University of Management Sciences (LUMS), Pakistan; Queer Legacies, New Solidarities, Deakin University, Melbourne, Australia; Colonial Sexual Alterity and Histories of the Future, Pérez Art Museum, Miami; Women, Gender, and History Series, University of Texas, Austin; Feminist Inscriptions, Center for Studies in Social Sciences, Calcutta, India; Dalit/Bahujan Feminisms: Anniversary Celebrations, Krantijyoti Phule Center for Women's Studies, University of Pune, India; and Goa: 1961 and Beyond Conference, University of Goa, India. Two anonymous readers and the Theory Q editorial collective provided perceptive, trenchant, and challenging feedback. Ken Wissoker has always been the best editor and ally. His intellectual forbearance, curatorial sensibility, and guidance created space for the book I wanted to write. Tony Wei Ling was the perfect research comrade and assistant whose timely efforts assembled the manuscript into presentable shape. Tony began as a graduate student in a seminar and has now grown to be a cherished reader and interlocutor.

If I imagined a poetics of abundance for our histories, then that poetics begins with my Lucy. Lucy Mae San Pablo Burns (who will always burn me up) lived this book with me, in love and in words. Her presence is inscribed within in more ways than I can know or wish to tally. As always, "mention not/ your homey/ we have the same brain." This book is dedicated to Aai and Baba, Kavita and Ramakant Arondekar, for a lifetime of care, laughter, and imagination. And to all my unreliable and inspirational kin from the Gomantak Maratha Samaj, we continue to make.believe . . .

Earlier versions of some of the arguments and materials in the book have appeared in "Subject to Sex: A Small History of the Gomantak Maratha Samaj," in *South Asian Feminisms: Contemporary Interventions*, ed. Ania Loomba and Ritty Lukose (Durham, NC: Duke University Press, 2012), 244–65; "In the Absence of Reliable Ghosts: Sexuality, Historiography, South Asia," *differences* 25, no. 3 (2015): 98–121; "The Sex of History, or Object/Matters," *History Workshop Journal* (Spring 2020): 1–7; "What More Remains: Slavery, Sexuality, South Asia," *History of the Present* 6, no. 2 (Fall 2016): 146–54; and "Telling Tales: Archives of the Geopolitical," in *Turning Archival: The Life of the Historical in Queer Studies*, ed. Daniel Marshal and Zeb Tortorici (Durham, NC: Duke University Press, 2022), 164–82.

PRIMARY SOURCES

CALL ME RAMA

Call me Rama, he said. I was thirteen, a prickly teenager, with queer feelings and a general disregard for all authority. And here was Baba, once again, trying to reach me through his endless experiments with parental truths. Call me Rama, he said again, with his signature half-smile. I want to be your friend, I want you to talk to me.

I never did call him Rama that day or ever. He remained Baba, a sweet, eccentric, and effortlessly loving parent, the first man of substance I ever knew. From the story of his wanting to witness my birth (a distinctly nonmanly wish in 1968), to his odd refusal of closed shoes, from his dazzling poetic mind to his infatuation with algorithmic jokes that never ended, Baba was always an unfolding and joyful mystery to me. As he was so fond of saying, "Anju, there are always more than two possibilities!" Even my big reveal at twenty-one (of my big bad homo self) elicited the most unusual response. Ah, he said, that's good, but "what are you now going to do for the social justice of gays?" And he promptly reminded me (over the course of many letters and emails) of how more gays should read Babasaheb Ambedkar. With Baba, life was a test case for possibilities, untold and unimagined. Sexuality was just one more possibility to be had, let go, and then revisited again.

Yet that invitation to be with "Rama" has always stayed with me, as a missed opportunity to talk to Baba in a register of abundance that I never did. Especially now, as I compose a history of our community, the Gomantak Maratha Samaj, a lower-caste, devadasi/kalavant collectivity that has shuttled between Goa and Maharashtra for the past two hundred years. As I read through the archives of our Samaj, I encounter "Rama" again. There is the sixteen-year-old writer Rama, who appears in the July 1949 issue of the *Samaj Sudharak* excoriating Brahmin fathers and patrons and calling for an end to the biological determinism of blood relationships. Why must we be forced to love our biological mothers, Rama writes in his first published article, if we are to refuse the blood of our fathers? Can we not fashion the families we desire?, he laments. Then there is the biting editorial titled "Lagn zurvene: Ek manastap" ("Arranging Marriages: An Irritation") (November 1970), where a more mature editor-in-chief Rama (and a father of my two-year-old self) speaks to the contradictions inherent in the efforts of the Samaj to arrange marriages within its own ranks.

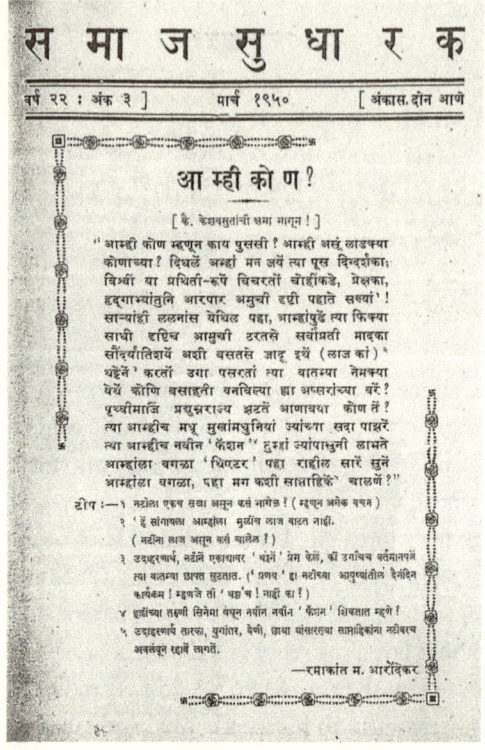

PS.1 Cover of editorial, Ramakant Arondekar, "Aamhi kon" ("Who Are We?"), *Samaj Sudharak*, March 1950. Gomantak Maratha Samaj Archives, Mumbai, India

Even as marriage provides the sanitized resolution to the Samaj's checkered history of sexuality, Rama questions the need for such conventional arrangements. Can we just not forget marriage and just move on?, he writes with great fervor.

Reading Baba amid the pages of our Samaj archives has meant finally saying yes to Rama. It has meant speaking with, and to, a parent who forged an extraordinary life, despite, or because of, the damning calculus of caste, class, and sexuality. Yes, I want to say to Baba, after all this time, I do want to call you Rama, I do want to know you in ways that my young self never could. Will you ask me again, please?

ONLY YOU

Suppose a photograph is a lyric for the future. Suppose a photograph is only you.

My Aai has dementia. Her memory is suffused with the changing shades of a life lost and found. Will I find myself again?, she asks me. A question without a focal point. Each day we spend together, we look at old photographs, feeling the edges of a luminous past folded into family albums. Each day, the same image holds Aai captive: a grainy portrait of her with my aunt, her best friend. Standing tall, she looks straight ahead at the camera, defiant, joyous, youthful. I was staring into the future, she jokingly tells me, and I saw you, only you.

Suppose a photograph is make.believe. Suppose a photograph is a practice of resistance.

I do not know what Aai was thinking in that picture. Neither does she. Not then. Not now. But always, with care, we revisit its forms. Remember, she cajoles me, we can make up our own stories. Once upon a time, a life refused simplicity, eschewed the occupation of description.

I write about histories of subalternity and sexuality, histories that are full of joyous indiscretions and staged archives, shaped and determined by caste oppression. Aai's photograph summons that history of abundance, asking not to be restored to memory but to be set adrift on a voyage of identifications. Perhaps such abundance leaves us inarticulate; perhaps we are daunted by the weight of its promise. It might be time to heed the call and set our photographs free. Only you. Only you.

PS.2 Pramila Laxmeshwar and Leela Shirodkar, 1957

SECONDARY SOURCES

ARCHIVES AND LIBRARIES

Arquivo Nacional de Torro de Tombo, Lisbon, Portugal
Biblioteca Nacional, Lisbon, Portugal
Directorate of Archives and Archaeology, Panaji, Goa, India
Goa State Historical Archives, Panaji, Goa, India
Gomantak Maratha Samaj Archives, Panaji, Goa; and Mumbai, Maharashtra, India
Heras Institute, Saint Xavier's College, Mumbai, India
Maharashtra State Archives, Mumbai, India
Paigini Temple Documents, Parashuram Temple, Paigini, Goa
Pragatik Maratha Samaj Records and Archives, Panaji, Goa, India
Xavier Centre of Historical Research, Alto Porvorim, Goa, India

PUBLISHED SOURCES

Adarkar, Arvind. "Marathi Manus in Girgaon." In *The Chawls of Mumbai: Galleries of Life*, edited by Neera Adarkar, 145–51. New Delhi: Imprint One, 2011.
Agnew, John. *Geopolitics: Re-visioning World Politics*. 2nd ed. London: Routledge, 2003.
Alavedo, A. E. de Almeida. *As communidades de Goa*. Lisboa, 1890.
Alexander, Meena. "Birthplace (with Buried Stones)." *Ploughshares* 35, no. 1 (Spring 2009): 10–12.
Allan, Michael. *In the Shadow of World Literature: Sites of Reading in Colonial Egypt*. Princeton, NJ: Princeton University Press, 2016.
Alloula, Malek. *The Colonial Harem*. Translated by Myrna Godzich and Wlad Godzich. Minneapolis: University of Minnesota Press, 1986.
Amar, Paul. *The Security Archipelago: Human Security States, Sexuality Politics, and the End of Neoliberalism*. Durham, NC: Duke University Press, 2013.
Ambedkar, B. R. *Annihilation of Caste*. Annotated critical ed. New Delhi: Navayana, 2014.
Ambedkar, B. R. *Dr. Babasaheb Ambedkar: Writings and Speeches*. Vols. 1–6, comp. Vasant Moon. Mumbai: Department of Education, Government of Maharashta, 1979. Reprint, New Delhi: Dr. Ambedkar Foundation, 2014.

Amin, Kadji. *Disturbing Attachments: Genet, Modern Pederasty, and Queer History.* Durham, NC: Duke University Press, 2017.

Amrith, Sunil. *Crossing the Bay of Bengal: The Furies of Nature and the Fortunes of Migrants.* Cambridge, MA: Harvard University Press, 2015.

Anagol, Padma. *The Emergence of Feminism in India, 1850–1920.* Burlington, VT: Ashgate, 2005.

Angle, Bikhu. *Dayanand.* Margao: M. S. Prabhu, 1991.

"Aprovando o regulamento das mazannas das devalaias do estado da India." 2nd supplement. Dipiloma Legislative 645 de 30-3-33. Bolletim, Official do Estado da India 27 (1933).

Arnold, David, and Stuart Blackburn, eds. *Telling Lives in India: Biography, Autobiography, and Life History.* Bloomington: Indiana University Press, 2004.

Arondekar, Anjali. *For the Record: On Sexuality and the Colonial Archive in India.* Durham, NC: Duke University Press, 2009.

Arondekar, Anjali. "Geopolitics Alert." *GLQ: A Journal of Lesbian and Gay Studies* 10, no. 2 (2004): 237–40.

Arondekar, Anjali. "Go (Away) West!" State of the Field Review. *GLQ: A Journal of Lesbian and Gay Studies* 28, no. 3 (2022): 463–72.

Arondekar, Anjali. "Subject to Sex: A Small History of the Gomantak Maratha Samaj." In *South Asian Feminisms*, edited by Ania Loomba and Ritty A. Lukose, 244–65. Durham, NC: Duke University Press, 2012.

Arondekar, Anjali. "Thinking Sex *with* Geopolitics." *WSQ: Women's Studies Quarterly* 44, nos. 3–4 (Fall/Winter 2016): 332–36.

Arondekar, Anjali. "Time's Corpus: On Temporality, Sexuality, and the Indian Penal Code." In *Comparatively Queer: Crossing Times, Crossing Cultures*, edited by Jarrod Hayes and William Spurlin, 143–56. New York: Palgrave, 2010.

Arondekar, Anjali. "What More Remains: Slavery, Sexuality, South Asia." *History of the Present* 6, no. 2 (Fall 2014): 146–54.

Arondekar, Anjali, associate ed. (Asia), and Howard Chiang, chief ed. *Global Encyclopedia of Lesbian, Gay, Bisexual, Transgender, and Queer (LGBTQ) History.* Farmington Hills, MI: Charles Scribner's Sons, 2019.

Arondekar, Anjali, and Geeta Patel. "Area Impossible: Notes towards an Introduction." In "Area Impossible," edited by Anjali Arondekar and Geeta Patel, special issue, *GLQ: A Journal of Lesbian and Gay Studies* 22, no. 2 (Spring 2016): 151–71.

Arondekar, Ramakant. "Lagn zurvene: Ek manastap" [Arranging marriages: An irritation]. *Samaj Sudharak*, November 1970.

Arondekar, Ramakant. "Matrudevata aani matruprem" [Mother as God and love for one's mother]. *Samaj Sudharak*, July 1949.

Arunima, G. *There Comes Papa: Colonialism and Transformation of Matriliny.* Hyderabad: Orient Longman, 2003.

Axelrod, Paul, and Michelle Fuerch. "Flight of the Deities: Hindu Resistance in Portuguese Goa." *Modern Asian Studies* 30, no. 2 (May 1996): 387–421.

Azoulay, Ariella Aïsha. *Potential History: Unlearning Imperialism*. London: Verso, 2019.

Bakhle, Janaki. *Two Men and Music: Nationalism in the Making of an Indian Classical Tradition*. New York: Oxford University Press, 2005.

Balachandran, Aparna. "Documents, Digitisation, and History." *South Asia: Journal of South Asian Studies* 45, no. 2 (2022): 339–49.

Banerjee, Prathama. "Writing the Adivasi: Some Historiographical Notes." *Indian Economic and Social History Review* 53, no. 1 (2016): 131–53.

Barak, On. "Archives and/as Battlefields: Political Aspects of Historiographic Revision." *Memory Studies* 12, no. 3 (June 2019): 266–78.

Barker, Joanne, ed. *Critically Sovereign: Indigenous Gender, Sexuality, and Feminist Studies*. Durham, NC: Duke University Press, 2017.

Bastos, Cristiana. "Subaltern Elites and Beyond: Why Goa Matters for Theory and Comparative Studies of Colonialism and Subalternity." In *Metahistory: History Questioning History*, edited by Charles J. Borges, SJ and Michael N. Pearson. Lisbon: Nova Vega, 2007.

Batley, Claude. "The Need for City Planning." *Journal of the Indian Institute of Architecture* 1, no. 1 (April 1934): 11–20.

Bedi, Protima, and Pooja Bedi Ebrahim. *Timepass: The Memoirs of Protima Bedi*. New York: Viking, 1999.

Benedito Ferrão, R. "Thinking Goa Postcolonially." *Muse India* 50 (Summer 2013). https://museindia.com/Home/ViewContentData?arttype=focus&issid=50&menuid=4285.

Berlant, Lauren. *Cruel Optimism*. Durham, NC: Duke University Press, 2011.

Berlant, Lauren. "Genre Flailing." *Capacious: Journal for Emerging Affect Inquiry* 1, no. 2 (2018). https://doi.org/10.22387/CAP2018.16.

Berlant, Lauren. "Intuitionists: History and the Affective Event." *American Literary History* 24, no. 4 (Winter 2008): 845–60.

Berlant, Lauren. "On the Case." *Critical Inquiry* 34, no. 2 (2007): 663–71.

Berlant, Lauren, and Kathleen Stewart. *The Hundreds*. Durham, NC: Duke University Press, 2019.

Best, Stephen. *None like Us: Blackness, Belonging, Aesthetic Life*. Durham, NC: Duke University Press, 2018.

Best, Stephen. "On Failing to Make the Past Present." *Modern Language Quarterly* 73, no. 3 (2012): 453–74.

Best, Stephen, and Sharon Marcus. "Surface Reading: An Introduction." *Representations* 108, no. 1 (Fall 2009): 1–21.

Bhan, Gautam. "For All That We May Become: On the Section 377 Verdict." *The Hindu*, September 7, 2018.

Bhattacharya, Akash. "How Historian Vikram Sampath Uses Decolonisation Rhetoric to Make Hindu Domination Sound Reasonable." *Hindutva Watch*, November 13, 2021.

Bhobe, Gopalkrishna. *Kalavant Gomantak*. Goa: Kala Academy, 1972.

Blouin, Francis X., Jr., and William G. Rosenberg, eds. *Archives, Documentation, and Institutions of Social Memory: Essays from the Sawyer Seminar*. Ann Arbor: University of Michigan Press, 2006.

Bode, Katherine. "The Equivalence of 'Close' and 'Distant' Reading; or, Toward a New Object for Data-Rich Literary History." *Modern Language Quarterly* 78, no. 1 (2017): 77–106.

Boelstorff, Tom. *Gay Archipelago: Sexuality and Nation in Indonesia*. Princeton, NJ: Princeton University Press, 2005.

"Bombay, Girgaum Road." Cigarette card. George Arents Collection, New York Public Library Digital Collections. http://digitalcollections.nypl.org/items/5e66b3e8-ff86-d471-e040-e00a180654d7.

Bose, Sugata. *A Hundred Horizons: The Indian Ocean in the Age of Global Empire*. Cambridge, MA: Harvard University Press, 2009.

Botre, Shrikant, and Douglas Haynes. "Sexual Knowledge, Sexual Anxieties: Middle-Class Males in Western India and the Correspondence in Samaj Swasthya, 1927–53." *Modern Asian Studies* 51, no. 4 (July 2017): 991–1034.

Boxer, C. R. "Fidalgos portugueses e bailadeiras indianas (seculos XVII e XVIII)." In *Revista de Historia* (São Paulo), no. 45 (1961): 83–105.

Brown, Wendy. "Suffering Rights as Paradoxes." *Constellations* 7, no. 2 (2000): 230–41.

Bsheer, Rosie. *Archive Wars: The Politics of History in Saudi Arabia*. Stanford, CA: Stanford University Press, 2020.

Burton, Antoinette. *Africa in the Indian Imagination: Race and the Politics of Postcolonial Citation*. Durham, NC: Duke University Press, 2016.

Burton, Antoinette, ed. *Archive Stories: Facts, Fictions, and the Writing of History*. Durham, NC: Duke University Press, 2005.

Burton, Richard F. *Goa and the Blue Mountains, or, Six Months of Sick Leave*. Berkeley: University of California Press, 1991.

Butalia, Urvashi. *The Other Side of Silence: Voices from the Partition of India*. Delhi: Viking, 1998.

Byrd, Jodi A. "'In the City of Blinding Lights': Indigeneity, Cultural Studies, and the Errants of Colonial Nostalgia." In "Critical Indigenous Theory," edited by Aileen Moreton-Robinson, John Frow, and Katrina Schlunke, special issue, *Cultural Studies Review* 15, no. 2 (January 2009): 13–28.

Carsten, Janet, ed. *Cultures of Relatedness: New Approaches to the Study of Kinship*. Cambridge: Cambridge University Press, 2000.

Caswell, Michelle. *Archiving the Unspeakable: Silence, Memory, and the Photographic Record in Cambodia*. Madison: University of Wisconsin Press, 2014.

Caswell, M. L. "'The Archive' Is Not an Archives: On Acknowledging the Intellectual Contributions of Archival Studies." UCLA, 2021. https://escholarship.org/uc/item/7bn4v1fk

Censo da populaçao do estado da India. December 1, 1900. Quadro VIII Populacao. Concelho de Ponda. Mappa No. 19.

Censo da população do estado da India. Nova Goa: Imprensa Nacional, 1920.

"Central List of OBC's." National Commission for Backwards Classes, updated January 9, 2015. http://www.ncbc.nic.in/User_Panel/CentralListStateView.aspx.

Chakrabarty, Dipesh. *Provincializing Europe.* Princeton, NJ: Princeton University Press, 2000.

Chakrabarty, Dipesh. "The Public Life of History: An Argument out of India." *Public Culture* 20, no. 1 (2008): 143–68.

Chakrabarty, Dipesh. "Subaltern Studies in Retrospect and Reminiscence." *Economic and Political Weekly* 48, no. 12 (March 2013): 23–27.

Chakraborthy, Kakolee. *Women as Devadasis: Origin and Growth of the Devadasi Profession.* New Delhi: Deep and Deep, 2000.

Chandavarkar, Rajnarayan. "The Perils of Proximity: Rivalries and Conflicts in the Making of a Neighbourhood in Bombay City in the Twentieth Century." *Modern Asian Studies* 52, no. 2 (March 2018): 351–93.

Chatterjee, Indrani. *Forgotten Friends: Monks, Marriages, and Memories of Northeast India.* Oxford: Oxford University Press, 2013.

Chatterjee, Indrani. "When 'Sexualities' Floated Free of Histories in South Asia." *Journal of Asian Studies* 71, no. 4 (2012): 945–62.

Chaudhuri, Kirti N. *Trade and Civilization in the Indian Ocean: An Economic History from the Rise of Islam to 1750.* Cambridge: Cambridge University Press, 1985.

Chaudhuri, Supriya. "Significant Lives: Biography, Autobiography, and Women's History in South Asia." Lecture, Wolfson College, Oxford Centre for Life-Writing, June 19, 2019. https://oclw.web.ox.ac.uk/significant-lives-biography-autobiography-and-womens-history-south-asia.

Chaudhury, Zahid. *Afterimage of Empire: Photography in Nineteenth-Century India.* Minneapolis: University of Minnesota Press, 2012.

Chen, Kuan-Hsing. *Asia as Method: Toward Deimperialization.* Durham, NC: Duke University Press, 2010.

Chiang, Howard, and Alvin Wong. "Asia Is Burning: Queer Asia as Critique." *Culture, Theory, and Critique* 58, no. 2 (2017): 121–26.

Chopra, Preeti. *A Joint Enterprise: Indian Elites and the Making of British Bombay.* Minneapolis: University of Minnesota Press, 2011.

Choudhury, Chitrangada, and Aniket Aga. "In Memoriam: Sociologist and Activist Abhay Xaxa." *India Forum*, April 3, 2020. theindiaforum.in/article/memoriam-sociologist-activist-abhay-xaxa.

Chow, Rey. *Entanglements, or Transmedial Thinking about Capture.* Durham, NC: Duke University Press, 2012.

Clarke, Matthew. "'I Am Your Loving Boy-Wife': A Short History of Queer Letter Writing." *Overland* 237 (Summer 2019). https://overland.org.au/2017/10/i-am-your-loving-boy-wife-a-short-history-of-queer-letter-writing/.

Clifford, James. "On Ethnographic Allegory." In *Writing Culture: The Poetics and Politics of Ethnography*, edited by James Clifford and George E. Marcus, 98–121. Berkeley: University of California Press, 1986.

Clifford, James. *Returns: Becoming Indigenous in the Twenty-First Century*. Cambridge, MA: Harvard University Press, 2013.

Cole, Teju. "Finders Keepers." In *Known and Strange Things: Essays*, 176–80. New York: Random House, 2016.

Coleman, Mat. "Geopolitics as a Social Movement: The Causal Primacy of Ideas." *Geopolitics* 9, no. 2 (2004): 484–91.

Connolly, Brian. "Against Accumulation." *J19: The Journal of Nineteenth-Century Americanists* 2, no. 1 (2014): 172–79.

Cooppan, Vilashini. "Time-Maps: A Field Guide to the Decolonial Imaginary." *Critical Times* 2, no. 3 (December 2019): 412.

Cort, John E. "Making It Vernacular in Agra: The Practice of Translation by 17th-Century Jains." In *Telling and Texts: Music, Literature, and Performance in North India*, edited by Francesca Orsini and Katherine Butler Schofield, 61–105. Cambridge: Open Book, 2015.

Coughlan, Sean. "The 200-Year-Old Diary That's Rewriting Gay History." BBC News, February 10, 2020. https://www.bbc.com/news/education-51385884.

Crawford, Margo Natalie. "The Twenty-First-Century Black Studies Turn to Melancholy." *American Literary History* 29, no. 4 (Winter 2017): 799–807.

Cunha, Tristão de Bragança. *Goa's Freedom Struggle: Selected Writings of T. B. Cunha*. Bombay: Dr. T. B. Cunha Memorial Committee, 1961.

Damousi, Joy, Birgit Lang, and Kattie Sutton. *Case Studies and the Dissemination of Knowledge*. New York: Routledge, 2015.

Dandio. March 22, 1879. Vernacular Newspaper Reports (VNR).

Daniyal, Shoaib. "As BJP MP Mounts 'Creamy Layer' Revolt against His Party, What Is Modi Government Thinking?" *Scroll.in*, July 5, 2020. https://scroll.in/article/967984/as-bjp-mp-mounts-creamy-layer-revolt-against-his-party-what-is-modi-government-thinking.

Das, Anita. "Dalit Cremation Workers and the COVID-19 Pandemic." *Medium*, April 1, 2022. https://dalithistorymonth.medium.com/dalit-cremation-workers-and-the-covid-19-pandemic-5d4a500579f8.

Dasgupta, Rohit. *Digital Queer Cultures in India: Politics, Intimacies, and Belonging*. New Delhi: Routledge, 2017.

Dave, Naisargi. *Queer Activism in India*. Durham, NC: Duke University Press, 2012.

De, Rohit. *A People's Constitution: The Everyday Life of Law in the Indian Republic*. Princeton, NJ: Princeton University Press, 2018.

Deer, Patrick. "Beyond Recovery: Representing History and Memory in Iraq War Writing." *MFS: Modern Fiction Studies* 63, no. 2 (Summer 2017): 312–35.

Deleuze, Gilles, and Félix Guattari. *A Thousand Plateaus: Capitalism and Schizophrenia*. Translated by Brian Massumi. Minneapolis: University of Minnesota Press, 1987.

de Mendonça-Noronha, Silvia M. "The Economic Scene in Goa, 1926–1961." In *Goa through the Ages*, vol. 2: *An Economic History*, edited by Teotónio de Souza, 263–84. New Delhi: Concept, 1987.

Deora, M. S. *Liberation of Goa, Daman, and Diu*. Delhi: Discovery, 1995.

Derrida, Jacques. *Of Grammatology*. Translated by Gayatri Chakravorty Spivak. Corrected ed. Baltimore, MD: Johns Hopkins University Press, 1997.

Derrida, Jacques. *Positions*. Chicago: University of Chicago Press, 1982.

Desai, Gaurav. *Commerce with the University: Africa, India, and the Afrasian Imagination*. New York: Columbia University Press, 2013.

Deshpande, Ashwini, and Rajesh Ramachandran. "How Backward Are the Other Backward Classes? Changing Contours of Caste Disadvantage in India." Working paper, no. 233 (Revised), Centre for Development Economics, Department of Economics, Delhi School of Economics, November 2014. https://citeseerx.ist.psu.edu/viewdoc/download?doi=10.1.1.673.4642&rep =rep1&type=pdf).

Deshpande, Prachi. *Creative Pasts: History, Memory, and Identity in Western India*. New York: Columbia University Press, 2007.

de Sousa Santos, Boaventura. "Between Prospero and Caliban: Colonialism, Postcolonialism, and Inter-Identity." *Luso-Brazilian Review* 39, no. 2 (2002): 9–43.

de Souza, Teotonio R. *Medieval Goa: A Socio-economic History*. 2nd ed. Panjim: Goa, 1556; Broadway Book Centre, 2009.

Dever, Maryanne. "Greta Garbo's Foot, or, Sex, Socks, and Letters." *Australian Feminist Studies* 25, no. 64 (2010): 163–73.

DeVun, Leah, and Zeb Tortorici. "Trans, Time, and History." *TSQ: Transgender Studies Quarterly* 5, no. 4 (November 2018): 518–39. https://doi.org/10.1215 /23289252-7090003.

Dhondo Shirsargar, Shankar. *Gomantak Suddhicha Itihas*. Mumbai: Self-published, 1930.

d'Hubert, Thibaut. "Patterns of Composition in 17th C. Bengali Literature." In *Tellings and Texts: Music, Literature, and Performance in North India*, edited by Francesca Orsini and Katherine Butler Schofield. Cambridge: Open Book, 2015.

Dobbin, Christine. "Competing Elites in Bombay City Politics in the Mid-Nineteenth Century (1852–83)." In *Elites in South Asia*, edited by Edmund Leach and S. N. Mukherjee, 79–94. Cambridge: Cambridge University Press, 1970.

Dossal, Mariam. *Imperial Designs and Indian Realities: The Planning of Bombay City, 1845–1875*. Bombay: Oxford University Press, 1991.

Dossal, Mariam. "A Master Plan for the City: Looking at the Past." *Economic and Political Weekly* 40, no. 36 (September 2005): 3897–3900.

Dossal, Mariam. *Theatre of Conflict, City of Hope: Bombay/Mumbai, 1660 to Present Times*. New Delhi: Oxford University Press, 2010.

Dutta, Aniruddha. "Contradictory Tendencies: The Supreme Court's NALSA Judgment on Transgender Recognition and Rights." *Journal of Indian Law and Society* 5, no. 2 (2014): 225–36.

Dutta, Ani, and Raina Roy. "Decolonizing Transgender in India: Some Reflections." *TSQ: Transgender Studies Quarterly* 2, no. 4 (August 2014): 320–37.

Edelman, Lee. "Ever After: History, Negativity, and the Social." *South Atlantic Quarterly* 106, no. 3 (Summer 2007): 469–76.

Edelman, Lee. "Learning Nothing: Bad Education." *differences* 28, no. 1 (May 2017): 124–73.

Edelman, Lee. *No Future: Queer Theory and the Death Drive.* Durham, NC: Duke University Press, 2004.

Edwardes, S. M. *The Gazetteer of Bombay City and Island.* Vol. 1, *1873–1927.* Bombay: Times Press, 1909–10.

Edwardes, Stephen Meredyth, and James M. Campbell. *The Gazetteer of Bombay City and Island.* Vol. 1. Bombay: Times of India Press, 1909.

Eichorn, Kate. *The Archival Turn in Feminism: Outrage in Order.* Philadelphia: Temple University Press, 2013.

El Shakry, Omnia. "'History without Documents': The Vexed Archives of Decolonization in the Middle East." Roundtable. *American Historical Review* 120, no. 3 (June 2015): 920–36.

Eng, David, and David Kazanjian, eds. *Loss: The Politics of Mourning.* Berkeley: University of California Press, 2002.

Fakundiny, Lydia. *The Art of the Essay.* Boston: Houghton Mifflin, 1991.

Fernandes, Jason. *Citizenship in a Caste Polity: Religion, Language and Belonging in Goa.* New Delhi: Orient Blackswan Pvt. Ltd, 2020.

Fernandes, Jason Keith. "The Curious Case of Goan Orientalism." ACT 27—Goa Portuguesa e Pós-Colonial: Literatura, Cultura e Sociedade, 2014.

Ferreiro-Martins, José. *Historia da misericordia de Goa.* Lisbon: Imprensa Nacional, 1910.

Fiereck, Kirk, Neville Hoad, and Danai S. Mupotsa. "A Queering-to-Come." In "Time Out of Joint: Queer and the Customary in Africa," edited by Kirk Fiereck, Neville Hoad, and Danai S. Mupotsa, special issue, *GLQ: A Journal of Lesbian and Gay Studies* 26, no. 3 (June 2020): 363–76.

Fischer, Michael. *Mute Dreams, Blind Owls, and Dispersed Knowledges: Persian Poesis in the Transnational Circuitry.* Durham, NC: Duke University Press, 2004.

Foucault, Michel. *The History of Sexuality, an Introduction.* Vol. 1. Translated by Robert Hurley. New York: Vintage Books, 2012.

FP Staff. "Historians Raise Questions about ICHR's New Boss Prof Y Sudershan Rao." *FirstPost*, July 14, 2014. http://www.firstpost.com/living/historians-raise-questions-about-ichrs-new-boss-prof-y-sudershan-rao-1617971.html.

Freccero, Carla. *Queer/Early/Modern.* Durham, NC: Duke University Press, 2006.

Freeman, Elizabeth. "Still After." *South Atlantic Quarterly* 106, no. 3 (2007): 495–500.

Freeman, Elizabeth. *Time Binds: Queer Temporalities, Queer Histories.* Durham, NC: Duke University Press, 2010.

Freitag, Sandria. "Consumption and Identity: Imagining 'Everyday Life' through Popular Visual Culture." *Tasveer Ghar: A Digital Archive of South Asian Popular Visual Culture*, accessed May 15, 2020. http://scgindia.in/tasveerghar/essay/consumption-identity-everyday-culture.

Frenz, Margaret. "Transimperial Connections: East African Goan Perspectives on 'Goa 1961.'" *Contemporary South Asia* 22, no. 3 (July 2014): 240–54.

Fuentes, Marisa. *Dispossessed Lives: Enslaved Women, Violence, and the Archive*. Philadelphia: University of Pennsylvania Press, 2016.

Fuller, Christopher. "Timepass and Boredom in Modern India." *Anthropology of This Century* 1 (May 2011): 407–9.

Fuss, Diana. *Dying Modern: A Meditation on Elegy*. Durham, NC: Duke University Press, 2013.

Gadihoke, Sabeena. "Selling Soap and Stardom: The Story of Lux." *Tasveer Ghar: A Digital Archive of South Asian Popular Visual Culture*, accessed May 15, 2020. http://www.tasveergharindia.net/essay/soap-stardom-lux.html.

Garlinger, Patrick Paul. *Confessions of the Letter Closet: Epistolary Fiction and Queer Desire in Modern Spain*. Minneapolis: University of Minnesota Press, 2005.

Garroutte, Eva. *Real Indians: Identity and the Survival of Native America*. Berkeley: University of California Press, 2003.

Gatade, Subhash. "Phenomenon of False Caste Certificates." *Economic and Political Weekly* 40, no. 43 (2005): 4587–88.

Geetha, K. A. "Entrenched Fissures: Caste and Social Differences among the Devadasis." *Journal of International Women's Studies* 22, no. 4 (2021): 87–96. https://vc.bridgew.edu/jiws/vol22/iss4/7/.

Ghosh, Bishnupriya. *Global Icons: Apertures to the Popular*. Durham, NC: Duke University Press, 2011.

Ghosh, Sahana. "Cross-Border Activities in Everyday Life: The Bengal Borderland." *Contemporary South Asia* 19, no. 1 (2011): 49–60.

Gidwani, Vinay. "Six Theses on Waste, Value, and Commons." *Social and Cultural Geography* 14, no. 7 (2013): 773–83. https://doi.org/10.1080/14649365.2013.800222.

Gilmartin, David. "The Historiography of India's Partition: Between Civilization and Modernity." *Journal of Asian Studies* 74, no. 1 (2015): 23–41.

Goldberg, Jonathan. *The Seeds of Things: Theorizing Sexuality and Materiality in Renaissance Representations*. New York: Fordham University Press, 2009.

Goldberg, Jonathan, and Madhavi Menon. "Queering History." *PMLA* 120, no. 5 (2005): 1608–17.

Gopinath, Gayatri. *Unruly Visions: The Aesthetic Practices of Queer Diaspora*. Durham, NC: Duke University Press, 2018.

Governo General do estado da India. *Censo da populacao do estado da India*. Vol. 1. December 1, 1910. Nova Goa Imprensa Nacional, 1916, 18–19.

Gramling, David, and Anirudh Dutta. "Translating Transgender." Special issue, *TSQ* 3, nos. 3–4 (2016).

Grewal, Inderpal, and Caren Kaplan. "Introduction: Transnational Feminist Practice and Questions of Postmodernity." In *Scattered Hegemonies: Postmodernity and Transnational Feminist Practices*, edited by Inderpal Grewal and Caren Kaplan, 1–34. Minneapolis: University of Minnesota Press, 1994.

Gross, Tori. "Constructing a Caste in the Past: Revisionist Histories and Competitive Authority in South India." *Modern Asian Studies* 56, no. 6 (2022): 1–39. https://doi.org/10.1017/S0026749X21000573.

Grover, Varun. "Hum kagaz nahi dikhayenge." Lyrics Raag, last modified November 16, 2020. https://lyricsraag.com/hum-kagaz-nahi-dikhayenge-varun-grover/.

Guha, Ranajit. *Elementary Aspects of Peasant Insurgency in Colonial India*. Durham, NC: Duke University Press, 2000.

Guha, Sohini. "From Ethnic to Multiethnic: The Transformation of the Bahujan Samaj Party in North India." *Ethnopolitics* 12, no. 1 (2013): 1–29.

Gupta, Pamila. "The Disquieting of History: Portuguese (De)colonization and Goan Migration in the Indian Ocean." *Journal of Asian and African Studies* 44, no. 1 (2009): 19–47.

Gupta, Pamila. "Visuality and Diasporic Dynamism: Goans in Mozambique and Zanzibar." *African Studies* 75, no. 2 (2016): 257–77.

Gupta, Pamila, Isabel Hofmeyr, and Michael Pearson, eds. *Eyes across the Water: Navigating the Indian Ocean*. Pretoria: Unisa Press, 2010.

Gupta, Srishti. "Jyoti Lanjewar: The Marathi Dalit-Feminist Poet." *Feminism in India*, March 9, 2020. https://feminisminindia.com/2020/03/09/jyoti-lanjewar-marathi-dalit-feminist-poet/.

Guru, Gopal, ed. *Humiliation: Claims and Context*. Oxford: Oxford University Press, 2011.

Guru, Gopal. "The Indian Nation in Its Egalitarian Conception." In *Dalit Studies*, edited by Ramnarayan Rawat and K. Satyanarayana, 31–52. Durham, NC: Duke University Press, 2016.

Guru, Gopal, and V. Geetha. "New Phase of Dalit-Bahujan Activity." *Economic and Political Weekly* 35, no. 3 (January 15–21, 2000).

Halberstam, Judith. *The Queer Art of Failure*. Durham, NC: Duke University Press, 2011.

Hartman, Saidiya. "The Anarchy of Colored Girls Assembled in a Riotous Manner." *South Atlantic Quarterly* 117, no. 3 (2018): 465–90.

Haynes, Douglas. *Small Town Capitalism in Western India: Artisans, Merchants, and the Making of the Informal Economy, 1870–1960*. Cambridge: Cambridge University Press, 2012.

Hayot, Eric. *On Literary Worlds*. Oxford: Oxford University Press, 2012.

Helton, Laura, Justin Leroy, Max Mishler, Samantha Seeley, and Shauna Sweeney. "The Question of Recovery." *Social Text* 33, no. 4 (125) (December 2015): 1–18.

Ho, Engseng. *Graves of Tarim: Genealogy and Mobility across the Indian Ocean*. Berkeley: University of California Press, 2006.

Hull, Matthew. *The Government of Paper: The Materiality of Bureaucracy in Urban Pakistan*. Berkeley: University of California Press, 2012.

Hyndman, Jennifer. "Mind the Gap: Bridging Feminist and Political Geography through Geopolitics." *Political Geography* 23, no. 3 (2004): 307–22.

Ilaiah, Kancha. "Productive Labour, Consciousness, and History: The Dalitbahujan Alternative." In *Subaltern Studies IX: Writings on South Asian History and Society*, edited by Shahid Amin and Dipesh Chakrabarty, 165–200. Delhi: Oxford University Press, 1996.

Jaffer, Amen. "Spiritualising Marginality: Sufi Concepts and the Politics of Identity in Pakistan." *Society and Culture in South Asia* 3, no. 2 (2017): 175–97.

Jain, Dipika, and Debanuj Das Gupta. "Law, Gender Identity, and the Uses of Human Rights: The Paradox of Recognition in South Asia." *Journal of Human Rights* 20, no. 1 (2021): 110–26. https://doi.org/10.1080/14754835.2020.1845129.

Jalal, Ayesha. *The Sole Spokesman: Jinnah, the Muslim League and the Demand for Pakistan*. Cambridge: Cambridge University Press, 1985.

Jameel, Mehlab. "Hijragiri and Translation: A Post-mortem of Lost Genders." Paper presented at *Queer Futures: Politics, Aesthetics, Sexualities*, Lahore, March 15, 2019.

Jangam, Chinnaiah. "A Dalit Paradigm: A New Narrative in South Asian Historiography." *Modern Asian Studies* 50, no. 1 (2016): 399–414.

Jänicke, Stefan, Greta Franzini, Muhammad Faisal Cheema, and Gerik Scheuermann. "On Close and Distant Reading in Digital Humanities: A Survey and Future Challenges." In *Eurographics Conference on Visualization (EuroVis)—STARs*, 83–103. Graz: Eurographics Association, 2015.

Jeffrey, Craig. *Timepass: Youth, Class, and the Politics of Waiting in India*. Stanford, CA: Stanford University Press, 2010.

Jenkins, Laura. "Another 'People of India' Project: Colonial and National Anthropology." *Journal of Asian Studies* 62, no. 4 (November 2003): 1143–70.

John, Mary E., and Janaki Nair. *A Question of Silence? The Sexual Economies of Modern India*. New Delhi: Kali for Women, 1998; London: Zed Press, 2000.

Jolly, Margaretta, and Liz Stanley. "Letters as/Not a Genre." *Life Writing* 2, no. 2 (May 2005): 91–118.

Joseph, S. "Identity Card." Trans. K. Satchidanandan. poetryinternationalweb.net. Poetry International, 2010, accessed December 5, 2019.

Kakodkar, Archana. "Devadasis of Goa." Unpublished paper. 1991.

Kakodkar, Archana. "The Portuguese and Kalavants." Unpublished paper, 1991.

Kamat, Pratima. *Farar Far: Local Resistance to Colonial Hegemony in Goa, 1510–1912*. Panjim: Institute Menezes Braganza, 1999.

Kamble, Uttam. *Devadasi ani Nagnapuja*. Bombay: Lokvangmaya Gruh, 1988.

Kanekar, Amita. "Architecture, Nationalism, and the Fleeting Heyday of the Goan Temple." *Kritika Kultura*, no. 38 (2022): 455–81.

Kannabiran, Kalpana. "Constitution-as-Commons: Notes on Decolonising Citizenship in India." *South Atlantic Quarterly* 120, no. 1 (January 2021): 232–41.

Kapur, Ratna. *Erotic Justice: Law and the New Politics of Postcolonialism.* Portland, OR: Cavendish, 2005.

Kapur, Ratna. "Unruly Desires, Gay Governance, and the Makeover of Sexuality in Postcolonial India." In *Global Justice and Desire: Queering Economy*, edited by Nikita Dhawan, Antke Engel, Christoph Holzhey, and Volker Woltersdorff, 115–31. New York: Routledge, 2015.

Karunakaran, Valliammal. "The Dalit-Bahujan Guide to Understanding Caste in Hindu Scripture." *Medium*, July 13, 2016. https://medium.com/@Bahujan_Power/the-dalit-bahujan-guide-to-understanding-caste-in-hindu-scripture-417db027fce6.

Kasmani, Omar. "Futuring Trans* in Pakistan: Timely Reflections." *TSQ: Transgender Studies Quarterly* 8, no. 1 (2021): 96–112. https://doi.org/10.1215/23289252-8749610.

Kelekar, Ravindra. *Panthasth: Memories of Goa's Freedom Struggle.* Panjim: Rajhauns, 2000.

Keni, Chandrakant. "Nehru and Goa." *Nave Goem*, June 15, 1964.

Kersenboom-Story, Saskia C. *Nityasumaṅgalī-Devadasi Tradition in South India.* New Delhi: Motilal Banarasidas, 1987.

Khan, Faris. "*Khwaja Sira* Activism: The Politics of Gender Ambiguity in Pakistan." *TSQ: Transgender Studies Quarterly* 3, nos. 1–2 (May 2016): 158–64. https://doi.org/10.1215/23289252-3334331.

Khan, Faris. "Translucent Citizenship: Khwaja Sira Activism and Alternatives to Dissent in Pakistan." *South Asia Multidisciplinary Academic Journal* 20 (March 2019). https://doi.org/10.4000/samaj.5034.

Khapre, Shubhangi. "Explained: How Marathas Got Reservation, and What Happens Now." *Indian Express*, May 11, 2021. https://indianexpress.com/article/explained/maharashtra-maratha-quota-supreme-court-verdict-7303546/.

Khedekar, Vinayak. *Gomantak Lok Kala.* Goa: Government Press, 1980.

Kidambi, Prashant. "Housing the Poor in a Colonial City: The Bombay Improvement Trust, 1898–1918." *Studies in History* 17, no. 1 (2001): 58–79.

Kidambi, Prashant. *The Making of an Indian Metropolis: Colonial Governance and Public Culture in Bombay.* Burlington, VT: Ashgate, 2007.

Kidambi, Prashant. "The Petition as Event: Colonial Bombay, 1889–1914." *Modern Asian Studies* 53, no. 1 (2019): 203–39.

Kosambi, Meera, ed. *Women Writing Gender: Marathi Fiction before Independence.* Ranikhet: Permanent Black, 2012.

Krishnan, O. U. *The Night Side of Bombay.* Bombay: Krishnan, 1923.

Kunte, B. G., ed. *Goa Freedom Struggle vis-à-vis Maharashtra 1946–60.* 8 vols. Bombay: Government of Maharashtra, 1978.

Lanjewar, Jyoti. "Mother (Aai)." Translated by Sylvie Martinez, Rujita Pathre, S. K. Thorat, Vimal Thorat, and Eleanor Zelliot. *Shared Mirror* (blog), May 8, 2011. https://roundtableindia.co.in/lit-blogs/?p=1773.

Latour, Bruno. *Reassembling the Social: An Introduction to Actor-Network Theory.* Oxford: Oxford University Press, 2005.

Lebow, Alisa. "Faking What? Making a Mockery of Documentary." In *F Is for Phony: Fake Documentary and Truth's Undoing,* edited by Alexandra Juhasz and Jesse Lerner, 223–37. Minneapolis: University of Minnesota Press, 2006.

Legg, Stephen. *Prostitution and the Ends of Empire: Scale, Governmentalities, and Interwar India.* Durham, NC: Duke University Press, 2014.

Legg, "Stimulation, Segregation and Scandal." Scandal: Geographies of Prostitution Regulation in British India, between Registration (1888) and Suppression (1923). *Modern Asian Studies* 46, no. 6 (2012): 1459–1505.

Levine, Caroline. *Forms: Whole, Rhythm, Hierarchy, Network.* Princeton, NJ: Princeton University Press, 2015.

Levine, Philippa. *Prostitution, Race, and Politics: Policing Venereal Disease in the British Empire.* New Delhi: Routledge, 2013.

Lindstrom, Eric. "Coda: Nature Poets and Fiat Money." In *Romantic Fiat: Demystification and Enchantment in Romantic Poetry.* London: Palgrave Macmillan, 2011.

"List of Scheduled Castes." Department of Social Justice and Empowerment, updated October 26, 2017. http://socialjustice.nic.in/UserView/index?mid=76750.

Love, Heather. *Feeling Backward: Loss and the Politics of Queer History.* Cambridge, MA: Harvard University Press, 2009.

Lowe, Lisa. *The Intimacies of Four Continents.* Durham, NC: Duke University Press, 2015.

Macharia, Keguro. *Frottage: Frictions of Intimacy across the Black Diaspora.* New York: New York University Press, 2019.

Macharia, Keguro. "Queer African Studies: Personhood and Pleasure." *Gukira* (blog), May 3, 2013. https://gukira.wordpress.com/2017/05/03/queer-african-studies-personhood-pleasure/.

Mahmood, Saba. *Politics of Piety: The Islamic Revival and the Feminist Subject.* Princeton, NJ: Princeton University Press, 2005.

Majumdar, Neepa. *Wanted Cultured Ladies Only! Female Stardom and Cinema in India, 1930s to 1950s.* Urbana-Champaign: University of Illinois Press, 2009.

Majumdar, Suprakash. "We Spoke to a Cremator at the Center of India's COVID Hell." *Vice,* April 27, 2021. https://www.vice.com/en/article/y3dggy/we-spoke-to-a-cremator-at-the-center-of-indias-covid-hell.

Mani, Lata. *Contentious Traditions: The Debate on Sati in Colonial India.* Berkeley: University of California Press, 1998.

Marathe, N. A. "Gomantak Maratha Samajane Kayleli Samajatli Charvar V Meervlele Yash" [The struggles and successes of the Gomantak Maratha Samaj]. *Gomantak Maratha Samaj* 5, no. 2 (May 1980): 1–30.

Marglin, F. A. *Wives of the God-King: Rituals of Devadasi of Puri.* Delhi: Oxford University Press, 1985.

Masani, Sir Rustom Pestonji. *The Law and Procedure of the Municipal Corporation of Bombay.* Bombay: Times Press, 1921.

Masood, Javed. "Catering to Indian and British Tastes: Gender in Early Indian Print Advertisements." *Tasveer Ghar: A Digital Archive of South Asian Popular Visual Culture,* accessed May 15, 2020. http://scgindia.in/tasveerghar/essay/catering-indian-british-tastes.

Mathur, Nayanika. "Transparent-Making Documents and the Crisis of Implementation." *PoLAR* 35, no. 2 (November 2012): 167–85.

"Matriz Poinguinim." Unpublished land documents at the Sub-Treasury Office. Chauri, Canacona, Goa, and Paigini Temple Documents (in Marathi, Modi, and Portuguese) located at the Parashuram Temple, Paigini, Goa.

Mbembe, Achille. "The Power of the Archive and Its Limits." In *Refiguring the Archive,* edited by Carolyn Hamilton, Verne Harris, Michèle Pickover, Graeme Reid, Razia Saleh, and Jane Taylor, 19–27. Dordrecht. Boston: Kluwer Academic, 2002.

McClintock, Anne. *Imperial Leather: Race, Gender, and Sexuality in the Colonial Conquest.* New York: Routledge, 1995.

McGowan, Abigail. "Modernity at Home: Leisure, Autonomy, and the New Woman in India." *Tasveer Ghar: A Digital Archive of South Asian Popular Visual Culture,* accessed May 15, 2020. http://scgindia.in/tasveerghar/essay/modernity-leisure-autonomy-woman.

McKinnon, Susan, and Cannell Fenella, eds. *Vital Relations: Modernity and the Persistent Life of Kinship.* Santa Fe, NM: School for Advanced Research Press, 2013.

McKittrick, Katherine. *Dear Science and Other Stories.* Durham, NC: Duke University Press, 2021

McPherson, Kenneth. *The Indian Ocean: A History of People and the Sea.* New Delhi: Oxford University Press, 1993.

"Memorial de Poinguinim (Canacona)." 1849–73, 1880, 1867–1906. Historical Archives of Goa, Panjim, Goa.

Menezes, Vivek. "Goa's Golden Jubilee." *The Caravan,* November 30, 2011. https://caravanmagazine.in/perspectives/goas-golden-jubilee.

Menon, Nivedita. "European of Another Color: Why the Goans Are Portuguese." *Kafila,* August 31, 2013. https://kafila.online/2013/08/31/europeans-of-an-other-colour-why-the-goans-are-portuguese-r-benedito-ferrao-jason-keith-fernandes/.

Metcalf, Thomas. *Imperial Connections: India in the Indian Ocean Arena, 1860–1920.* Berkeley: University of California Press, 2007.

Miller, Christopher. *Impostors: Literary Hoaxes.* Chicago: University of Chicago Press, 2018.

Mitra, Durba. *Indian Sex Life: Sexuality and the Colonial Origins of Modern Social Thought.* Princeton, NJ: Princeton University Press, 2019.

Mitra, Durba. "'Surplus Woman': Female Sexuality and the Concept of Endogamy." *Journal of Asian Studies* 80, no. 1 (February 2021): 3–26.

Morgan, Jennifer. "Accounting for the 'Most Excruciating Torment': Gender, Slavery, and Trans-Atlantic Passages." *History of the Present* 6, no. 2 (Fall 2016): 184–207.

Morris, Rosalind. *In the Place of Origins: Modernity and Its Mediums in Northern Thailand*. Durham, NC: Duke University Press, 2000.

Moten, Fred. "Black Optimism / Black Operation." Manuscript of lecture delivered in Chicago, October 19, 2007.

Muñoz, José Esteban. *Cruising Utopia: The Then and There of Queer Futurity*. New York: New York University Press, 2019.

Muñoz, José Esteban. "Race, Sex, and the Incommensurate: Gary Fisher with Eve Kosofsky Sedgwick." In *Queer Futures: Reconsidering Ethics, Activism, and the Political*, edited by Elahe Haschemi Yekani, Eveline Kilian, and Beatrice Michaelis, 103–16. Farnham, VT: Ashgate, 2013.

Nagar, Ila, and Debanuj Dasgupta. "Public Koti and Private Love: Section 377, Religion, Perversity and Lived Desire." *Contemporary South Asia* 23, no. 4 (2015): 426–41.

Nagar Samachar. February 23, 1878. Vernacular Newspaper Reports (VNR).

Narayan, Badri. "Ambedkar and Kanshi Ram: Similar, Yet Different." *LiveMint*, October 14, 2009. https://www.livemint.com/Opinion/hXyHXD1PKogjgSs6hI3VxH/Ambedkar-and-Kanshi-Ram-similar-yet-different.html.

Nataraj, V. K. "Backward Classes and Minorities in Karnataka Politics." In *Division, Deprivation, and the Congress*, vol. 1, edited by Ramashray Roy and Richard Sisson. New Delhi: Sage, 1990.

National Vigilance Association. *The Vigilance Record: Organ of the National Vigilance Association*. London: W. A. Coot, 1887.

Navaro-Yashin, Yael. "Make-Believe Papers, Legal Forms, and the Counterfeit: Affective Interactions between People and Documents in Britain and Cyprus." *Anthropological Theory* 7, no. 1 (2007): 79–98.

Newman, Robert. "Goa: The Transformation of an Indian Region." *Pacific Affairs* 57, no. 3 (1984): 429–49.

Newman, Robert. "Konkani Mai Ascends the Throne: The Cultural Basis of Goan Statehood." *Journal of South Asian Studies* 11, no. 1 (1988): 1–24.

Newman, Robert Samuel. *Of Umbrellas, Goddesses, and Dreams: Essays on Goan Culture and Society*. Mapusa: Other India Press, 2001.

Ngai, Sianne. *The Theory of the Gimmick: Aesthetic Judgment and Capitalist Form*. Cambridge, MA: Harvard University Press, 2020.

Niranjana, Tejaswini, and Surabhi Sharma. "Making Music, Making Space." http://www.indiaifa.org/events/making-music-making-space-june-15-17-2015-studio-x-mumbai.html.

Noronha, Frederick. "Goan Citizenship Woes, from Karachi to Portugal." *Telegraph India*, January 16, 2020. https://www.telegraphindia.com/india/goan-citizenship-woes-from-karachi-to-portugal/cid/1736529.

Nyong'o, Tavia. *Afro Fabulations: The Drama of Black Life*. Durham, NC: Duke University Press, 2018.

Nyong'o, Tavia. "Situating Precarity between the Body and the Commons." *Women and Performance* 23, no. 2 (2013): 157–61. https://doi.org/10.1080/0740770X.2013.825440.

Oldenburg, Veena Talwar. "Lifestyle as Resistance: The Case of the Courtesans of Lucknow." In "Speaking for Others/Speaking for Self: Women of Color," edited by Lynn Bolles and Rayna Rapp, special issue, *Feminist Studies* 16, no. 2 (Summer 1990): 59–287.

Omvedt, Gail. *Cultural Revolt in a Colonial Society: The Non-Brahman Movement in Western India: 1873 to 1930*. Bombay: Scientific Socialist Education Trust, 1976.

Orsini, Francesca. "How to Do Multilingual Literary History? North India in 15th and 16th Century." *Indian Economic and Social History Review* 49, no. 2 (2012): 225–46.

Ó Tuathail, Gearóid, Simon Dalby, and Paul Routledge, eds. *The Geopolitics Reader*. 2nd ed. London: Routledge, 2007.

Paigankar, Rajaram Rangoji. *Mee kon*. Vols. 1–2. Margao: Gomantak Chapkhana, 1969.

Paik, Shailaja. "Amchya jalmachi chittarkatha (The Bioscope of Our Lives): Who Is My Ally?" *Economic and Political Weekly* 44, no. 40 (October 3–9, 2009): 39–47.

Pandey, Gyanendra. "Can There Be a Subaltern Middle-Class? Notes on African-American and Dalit History." *Public Culture* 21, no. 2 (2009): 321–42.

Pandey, Gyanendra, ed. *Unarchived Histories: The "Mad" and the "Trifling."* London: Routledge, 2013.

Parabo, Parag. *India's First Democratic Revolution: Dayanand Bandodkar and the Rise of the Bahujan in Goa*. Hyderabad: Orient BlackSwan, 2015.

Parker, Kunal. "'A Corporation of Superior Prostitutes': Anglo-Indian Legal Conceptions of Temple Dancing Girls, 1800–1914." *Modern Asian Studies* 32 (1998): 559–663.

Patel, Geeta. *Lyrical Movements, Historical Hauntings: On Gender, Colonialism, and Desire in Miraji's Urdu Poetry*. Stanford, CA: Stanford University Press, 2001.

Patel, Geeta. *Risky Bodies and Techno-Intimacy: Reflections on Sexuality, Media, Science, Finance*. Seattle: University of Washington Press, 2017.

Patel, Geeta. "Translation's Dissidence: Miraji Becomes Sappho." In *Dissident Aesthetics: A Critical Humanities for Our Times*, edited by Brinda Bose. London: Bloomsbury, 2017.

Patel, Geeta. "Vernacular Missing: Miraji on Sappho, Gender, and Governance." *Comparative Literature* 70, no. 2 (June 2018): 132–44.

Pawar, Urmila, and Meenakshi Moon. *We Also Made History: Women in the Ambedkarite Movement*. Delhi: Zubaan, 2008.

Pérez, Rosa Maria. "The Rhetoric of Empire: Gender Representations in Portuguese India." *Portuguese Studies* 21 (Autumn 2005): 126–34.

Phadke, Narayan Sitaram. *Ajace tarun stree-purush va tyanpudhil prasna* [Contemporary youth and the problems before them]. 1931. Reprint, Pune: K. S. Gupta, 1947.

Phadke, Narayan Sitaram. *Jadugaar* [The magician]. Pune: Venus Prakashan, 1928.
Phadke, Narayan Sitaram. *Kulabyachi dandi* [The lighthouse at Colaba]. 1925. Reprint, Pune: Kulakarni Granthagara, 1971.
Phadke, Narayan Sitaram. *Manas-mandir* [The temple of the mind]. Kolhapur: School and College Book Stall, 1935.
Phadke, Narayan Sitaram. *Sex Problems in India: Being a Plea for a Eugenic Movement in India and a Study of All Theoretical and Practical Questions Pertaining to Eugenics.* Bombay: D. B. Taraporevala Sons & Co., 1927.
Phadke, Narayan Sitaram. *Sex Problems in India, a Scientific Exposition of Sex Life and Some Curious Marriage Customs Prevailing in India from Time Immemorial to the Present Day.* Bombay: D. B. Taraporevala Sons & Co., 1929.
Pinney, Christopher. *The Coming of Photography in India.* London: British Library, 2008.
Pinto, Celsa. "Women's Inheritance Rights: Conflict and Confrontation." In *Goa: Images and Perceptions,* 29–37. Panjim: Prabhakar Bhide, 1996.
Pinto, Rochelle. *Archives and Access.* Updated January 2020. https://publicarchives.wordpress.com/877-2/.
Pinto, Rochelle. *Between Empires: Print and Politics in Goa.* New York: Oxford University Press, 2007.
Povinelli, Elizabeth. *Economies of Abandonment: Social Belonging and Endurance in Late Liberalism.* Durham, NC: Duke University Press, 2011.
Povinelli, Elizabeth. "Radical Worlds: The Anthropology of Incommensurability and Inconceivability." *Annual Review of Anthropology* 30 (2001): 319–34.
Povinelli, Elizabeth. "The Woman on the Other Side of the Wall: Archiving the Otherwise in Postcolonial Digital Archives." *differences* 22, no. 1 (2011): 146–71.
Pragna Shah, Svati. *Street Corner Secrets: Sex, Work, and Migration in the City of Mumbai.* Durham, NC: Duke University Press, 2014.
Prakash, Rohini. "The Social and Cultural Dimensions of Migration: The Case of a Village in India." PhD diss., University of Michigan, 1984. ProQuest, http://search.proquest.com/docview/303325742/.
Prinz, M. "Intercultural Links between Goa and Mozambique in Their Colonial and Contemporary History." In *Goa and Portugal: Their Cultural Links,* edited by Charles Borges and Helmut Feldmann. New Delhi: Concept, 1997.
Probyn, Elspeth. "Suspended Beginnings of Childhood and Nostalgia." *GLQ: A Journal of Lesbian and Gay Studies* 2, no. 4 (1995): 439–68.
"Prostitution in Bombay." Minutes of Evidence of Prostitution Committee, Maharashtra State Archives. Mumbai: Home Department, 1921. File 469-III.
"Protest by the Rate Payers and Residents of Girgaum, Bombay against the Evil of Women of Bad Repute, 1911." *Judicial Department Volume 208/1911.* Maharashtra State Archives.
PTI. "'Cow Urine Is Pure Elixir': To Fight Coronavirus, Hindu Mahasabha Hosts 'Gaumutra Party.'" *Outlook India,* March 15, 2020. https://www.outlookindia.com/website/story/india-news-cow-urine-is-pure-elixir-to-fight-coronavirus-hindu-mahasabha-holds-gaumutra-party/348809.

Puar, Jasbir. *Terrorist Assemblages: Homonationalism in Queer Times.* Durham, NC: Duke University Press, 2007.

Punekar, S. D., and Kamala Rao. *A Study of Prostitutes in Bombay (with Reference to Family Background).* 1962. Reprint, Bombay: Lalwani, 1967.

Quinn, Jennifer Post. "Marathi and Konkani Speaking Women in Hindustani Music, 1880–1940." PhD diss., University of Minnesota, 1982.

Radhakrishan, N. "Dayanand Balkrishna Bandodkar, the Architect of Modern Goa." PhD diss., University of Goa, 1994.

Radhakrishnan, Waman. *Purushatra.* Panjim: Rajhauns, 1998.

Raghunathji, K. "Bombay Dancing Girls." *Indian Antiquary* 13 (June 1884): 165–78.

Rai, Amit. *Untimely Bollywood: Globalization and India's New Media Assemblage.* Durham, NC: Duke University Press, 2009.

Raman, Bhavani. *Document Raj: Writing and Scribes in Early Colonial South India.* Chicago: University of Chicago Press, 2012.

Ramaswamy, Sumathi. *The Lost Land of Lemuria: Fabulous Geographies, Catastrophic Histories.* Berkeley: University of California Press, 2005.

Ramberg, Lucinda. *Given to the Goddess: South Indian Devadasis and the Sexuality of Religion.* Durham, NC: Duke University Press, 2014.

Ranganathan, Murali, ed. and trans. *Govind Narayan's Mumbai: An Urban Biography from 1863.* Delhi: Anthem, India, 2012.

Rao, Nikhil. "Community, Urban Citizenship, and Housing in Bombay, ca. 1919–1980." *South Asia* 36, no. 3 (2013): 415–33.

Rao, Nikhil. *House but No Garden: Apartment Living in Bombay's Suburbs 1898–1964.* Minneapolis: University of Minnesota Press, 2013.

Rao, Rahul. "Nationalisms by, against and beyond the State." *Radical Philosophy* 2, no. 7 (Spring 2020): 17–28.

Rawat, Ramnarayan. "Partition Politics and Achhut Identity: A Study of the Scheduled Castes Federation and Dalit Politics in UP, 1946–48." In *The Partitions of Memory: The Afterlife of the Division of India,* edited by Suvil Kaul. Delhi: Permanent Black, 2001.

Rawat, Ramnarayan, and K. Satyanarayana. "Dalit Studies: New Perspectives on Indian History and Society." In *Dalit Studies,* edited by Ramnarayan Rawat and K. Satyanarayana. Durham, NC: Duke University Press, 2016.

"Receita e despeza de Poinguinim." 1868–72, 1873–77, 1877–81, 1882–1903. Historical Archives of Goa, Panjim, Goa.

Rege, Sharmila. "'Real Feminism' and Dalit Women: Scripts of Denial and Accusation." *Economic and Political Weekly* 35, no. 6 (February 5–11, 2000): 492–95.

Reiter, Bernd, ed. *Constructing the Pluriverse: The Geopolitics of Knowledge.* Durham, NC: Duke University Press, 2018.

Relatório da Comissao de Inquérito à Situaçao dos Emigrantes Indo-Portugueses na India Britannica. Nova Goa: Imprensa Nacional, 1931.

Rice-Sayre, Laura. "Veiled Threats: Malek Alloula's Colonial Harem." *boundary 2* 15, nos. 1/2 (Autumn 1986–Winter 1987): 351–63.

Ricoeur, Paul. *Freud and Philosophy: An Essay on Interpretation*. New Haven, CT: Yale University Press, 1970.

Rifkin, Mark. *When Did Indians Become Straight: Kinship, the History of Sexuality, and Native Sovereignty*. New York: Oxford University Press, 2010.

Risbud, Seema. "Goa's Struggle for Freedom, 1949–1961: The Contributions of National Congress (Goa) and Azad Gomantak Dal." PhD diss., Goa University, 2003.

Risley, Sir Herbert Hope. *The People of India*. Calcutta: Thacker, Spink & Co., 1908.

Rizki, Cole. "Trans-, Translation, Transnational." *TSQ: Transgender Studies Quarterly* 8, no. 4 (November 2021): 532–36.

Rizzo, Lorena. "Gender and Visuality: Identification Photographs, Respectability, and Personhood in Colonial Southern Africa in the 1920s and 1930s." *Gender and History* 26, no. 3 (November 2014): 688–708. https://doi.org/10.1111/1468-0424.12092.

Roy, Anupama. *Mapping Citizenship in India*. New Delhi: Oxford University Press, 2010.

Rubinoff, Arthur. *India's Use of Force in Goa*. Delhi: Popular Prakashan, 1971.

Sa, Cabral e. "Here Lived Batabai." *Goa Today*, accessed July 9, 2005. http://www.goacom.org/goatoday/2003/jan/CoverStory.htm.

Saksena, H. S., K. K. Seth, and A. K. Biswas. "Study on Issue of False Scheduled Caste / Scheduled Tribe Certificates." Lucknow: Director for Scheduled Castes and Scheduled Tribes. National Commission for Scheduled Castes and Scheduled Tribes, Government of India (1988).

Salgaonkar, Seema P. "Amalgam of Leadership Styles: A Case Study of First Chief Minister of Goa." *Indian Journal of Political Science* 73, no. 1 (2012): 141–48.

Salmi, Hannu. "Cultural History, the Possible, and the Principle of Plenitude." *History and Theory* 50 (May 2011): 171–87.

Samaj Sudharak / Gomant Shardha. Samaj, Mumbai branch.

Sangari, Kumkum, and Sudesh Vaid, eds. *Recasting Women: Essays in Colonial History*. New Delhi: Kali for Women, 1989.

Sarkar, Rameshchandra. "Dedication to the Altar: The Devadasi Tradition in Goa." In *Goa: Cultural Patterns*, edited by Sharayu Doshi. Bombay: Marg, 1983.

Satoskar, B. D. Editorial. *Samaj Sudharak*, September 1947.

Satoskar, B. D. *Gomantak Prakriti ani Sanskriti*. Vol. 1, 2nd ed. Pune: Subhda Saraswat, 1988.

Schmitt, Cannon. "Interpret or Describe?" In "Description across the Disciplines," edited by Stephen Best, Heather Love, and Sharon Marcus, special issue, *representations* 135 (Summer 2016): 102–18.

Scholberg, Henry. *Bibliography of Goa and the Portuguese in India*. New Delhi: Promila, 1982.

Seikaly, Sherene. "How I Met My Great-Grandfather: Archives and the Writing of History." *Comparative Studies of South Asia, Africa, and the Middle East* 38, no. 1 (May 2018): 6–20.

Shahani, Nishant. *Pink Revolutions: Globalization, Hindu Fundamentalism, and Queer Triangles in Contemporary India*. Forthcoming.
Shankar, Jogan. *Devadasi Cult: A Sociological Analysis*. New Delhi: Ashish, 1990.
Sharpe, Jenny. *Immaterial Archives: An African Diaspora Poetics of Loss*. Evanston, IL: Northwestern University Press, 2020.
Shashishekhar. "Harvelele patr " [Lost letters]. *Samaj Sudharak* (August–December 1940).
Shirodkar, P. P. *Goa's Struggle for Freedom*. New Delhi: Ajanta, 1988.
Shroff, Sara. "The Colonial Choreography of Queer Value." *Zed Books*, August 22, 2017. https://www.zedbooks.net/blog/posts/the-colonial-choreography-of-queer-value/.
Simpson, Audra. *Mohawk Interruptus: Political Life across the Borders of Settler States*. Durham, NC: Duke University Press, 2014.
Sinfield, Alan. *Faultlines: Cultural Materialism and the Politics of Dissident Reading*. Oxford: Clarendon, 1992.
Singh, Pritam. "Numbers as a Means to Power: Politics of Caste as a Census Category in Colonial India c. 1871–1941." *Economic and Political Weekly* 57, no. 18 (April 2022): 63–68.
Sinha, Mrinalini. *Colonial Masculinity*. Manchester: Manchester University Press, 1995.
Sinha, Mrinalini. "Premonitions of the Past." *Journal of Asian Studies* 74, no. 4 (2015): 821–41.
Soneji, Davesh. *Unfinished Gestures: Devadasis, Memory, and Modernity in South India*. Chicago: University of Chicago Press, 2012.
Spillers, Hortense. "Discomfort." *boundary 2* 41, no. 2 (2014): 6–7. https://doi.org/10.1215/01903659-2685962.
Spivak, Gayatri Chakravorty. *A Critique of Postcolonial Reason: Toward a History of the Vanishing Present*. Cambridge, MA: Harvard University Press, 1999.
Spivak, Gayatri Chakravorty. *Outside in the Teaching Machine*. New York: Routledge Classics, 2008.
Squires, David. "Roger Casement's Queer Archive." *PMLA* 13, no. 2 (2017): 596–612.
Srinivasan, Amrit. "Temple 'Prostitution' and Community Reform: An Examination of the Ethnographic, Historical, and Textual Context of the Devadasis of Tamil Nadu, South India." PhD diss., Cambridge University, 1984.
Srivastava, Sanjay. "Duplicity, Intimacy, Community: An Ethnography of ID Cards, Permits, and Other Fake Documents in Delhi." *Thesis Eleven* 113, no. 1 (December 2012): 78–93.
Steedman, Carolyn. "La théorie qui n'en est pas une, or, Why Clio Doesn't Care." In "History and Feminist Theory," special issue, *History and Theory* 31, no. 4 (December 1992): 33–50.
Stewart, David. "The Hermeneutics of Suspicion." *Journal of Literature and Theology* 3 (1989): 296–307.
Stewart, Kathleen. *Ordinary Affects*. Durham, NC: Duke University Press, 2007.

Stewart, Kathleen. *A Space on the Side of the Road*. Princeton, NJ: Princeton University Press, 1996.

Stoler, Ann Laura. *Along the Archival Grain: Epistemic Anxieties and Colonial Common Sense*. Princeton, NJ: Princeton University Press, 2010.

Stoler, Ann Laura. "Colonial Archives and the Arts of Governance: On the Content in the Form." In *Refiguring the Archive*, edited by Carolyn Hamilton, Verne Harris, Michèle Pickover, Graeme Reid, Razia Saleh, and Jane Taylor, 83–100. London: Kluwer Academic, 2002.

Stoler, Ann Laura. "On Archiving as Dissensus." In "Palestine: Doing Things with Archives." Special issue, *Comparative Studies of South Asia, Africa, and the Middle East* 38, no. 1 (2018): 43–56.

Strathern, Marilyn. *Relations: An Anthropological Account*. Durham, NC: Duke University Press, 2020.

Subrahmanyam, Sanjay. *Career and Legend of Vasco Da Gama*. Cambridge: Cambridge University Press, 1997.

Subrahmanyam, Sanjay. *Explorations in Connected History: From the Tagus to the Ganges*. Delhi: Oxford University Press, 2012.

Subrahmanyam, Sanjay. *Explorations in Connected History: Mughals and Franks*. Delhi: Oxford University Press, 2012.

Subrahmanyam, Sanjay. *Setsuzoku sareta rekishi* [Explorations in connected history]. Translated by Masahiko Mita and Nobuhiro Ota. Nagoya: University of Nagoya Press, 2009.

Supplemento ao Numero 30 do Boletim Official do Governo. Recenseamento Geral do Populacao do Estado da India. Realizado EM 17 de Fevereiro de 1881. Nova Goa Imprensa Nacional 1882. Mappa No. 8.

Sushmita. "Remembering Scholar and Activist Abhay Xaxa, Whose Death Is an Irreparable Loss to Adivasi Movements." *The Caravan*, June 27, 2020. https://caravanmagazine.in/amp/communities/remembering-abhay-xaxa-whose-death-is-a-loss-to-adivasi-movements.

Tadiar, Neferti X. M. "Ground Zero." In "Area Impossible," edited by Anjali Arondekar and Geeta Patel, special issue, *GLQ: A Journal of Lesbian and Gay Studies* 22, no. 2 (April 2016): 173–81. https://doi.org/10.1215/10642684-3428699.

Tambe, Ashwini. "Brothels as Families: Reflections on the History of Bombay's Kothas." *International Journal of Feminist Politics* 8, no. 2 (June 2006): 219–42.

Tambe, Ashwini. *Codes of Misconduct: Regulating Prostitution in Late Colonial Bombay*. Minneapolis: University of Minnesota Press, 2009.

Tambe, Ashwini. "From Romance to Reproduction: Pre- and Post-independence Covers in a Marathi Women's Magazine." *South Asia: Journal of South Asian Studies*, 43, no. 1 (January 2020): 1–31.

Tambe, Ashwini. "Social Geographies of Bombay's Sex Trade." In *Bombay before Mumbai: Essays in Honour of Jim Masselos*, edited by Prashant Kidambi, Manjiri Kamat, and Rachel Dwyer. Oxford: Oxford University Press, 2019.

Tanoukhi, Nirvana. "Surprise Me If You Can." *PMLA* 131, no. 5 (2016): 1423–35.

Thapan, Meenakshi. "Embodiment and Identity in Contemporary Society: Femina and the 'New' Indian Woman." *Contributions to Indian Sociology* 38, no. 3 (October 2004): 411–44. https://doi.org/10.1177/006996670403800305.

Thapar, Romila. "The Appointment of a Historian Whose Work Is Unfamiliar to Most Historians Shows Scant Regard for the Impressive Scholarship That Now Characterises the Study of Indian History and This Disregard May Stultify Future Academic Research." *India Today*, July 11, 2014. http://indiatoday.intoday.in/story/romila-thapar-smriti-irani-old-history-baiters-of-bjp/1/370799.html.

Tharu, Susie. "The Impossible Subject-Caste and the Gendered Body." *Economic and Political Weekly* 32, no. 22 (June 1996).

Thatra, Geeta. "Contentious (Socio-spatial) Relations: Tawaifs and Congress House in Contemporary Bombay/Mumbai." *Indian Journal of Gender Studies* 23, no. 2 (2016): 191–216.

Thatra, Geeta. "Dalit Chembur: Spatializing the Caste Question in Bombay, c. 1920s–1970s." *Journal of Urban History* 48, no. 1 (2022): 63–97.

"Tilulos de Poinguinim." 1874–82. Historical Archives of Goa, Panjim, Goa.

Tipnis, Y. N. "Kala-Sangeet" [Kala of music]. *Samaj Sudharak* (June 1937): 99–101.

TNN. "Commission to Decide on Gomantak Maratha Samaj's Inclusion in OBC." *Times of India*, August 4, 2018. https://timesofindia.indiatimes.com/city/goa/commission-to-decide-on-gomantak-maratha-samajs-inclusion-in-obc/articleshow/65265086.cms

"Tombo Segundo B da Communidade da Aldea de Poinguinim." 1889–97, 1898, 1889–1918. Unpublished land documents at the Communidade Office, Chauri, Goa.

Traub, Valerie. *Thinking Sex with the Early Moderns*. Philadelphia: University of Pennsylvania Press, 2016.

Trichur, S. Raghuraman. "Politics of Goan Historiography." *Lusotopie* 2000: 637–46. http:// www.lusotopie.sciencespobordeaux.fr/somma2000.html.

Underwood, Ted. "A Genealogy of Distant Reading." *DHQ: Digital Humanities Quarterly* 11, no. 2 (2017).

Van Leur, J. C. *Indonesian Trade and Society: Essays in Asian Social and Economic History*. The Hague: W. van Hoeve, 1955.

Verenkar, Sanjiv. *Prerarna Rukh*. Ponda, Goa: Verenkar, 2021.

Verma, A. K. "Bahujan Samaj Party: Beyond Uttar Pradesh." *Economic and Political Weekly* 44, no. 7 (February 14–20, 2009).

Visweswaran, Kamala. *Fictions of Feminist Ethnography*. Minneapolis: University of Minnesota Press, 1994.

Wacha, Dinsha Edulji. *Rise and Growth of Bombay Municipal Government*. Madras: G. A. Natesan & Co., 1913.

Waghmore, Suryakant. "The Dominant Victim?" *Seminar* 727 (March 2020). https://www.india-seminar.com/2020/727/727_suryakant_waghmore.htm.

Wakankar, Milind. "The Question of a Prehistory." *interventions* 10, no. 3 (2008): 285–302. https://doi.org/10.1080/13698010802444694.

Wakankar, Milind. *Subalternity and Religion: The Prehistory of Dalit Empowerment in South Asia*. New Delhi: Routledge, 2010.

Weld, Kirsten. *Paper Cadavers: Archives of Dictatorship in Guatemala*. Durham, NC: Duke University Press, 2014.

Williamson, Elizabeth. "Abundance and Access: Early Modern Political Letters in Contemporary and Digital Archives." Lecture, Digital Humanities Conference: "Puentes/Bridges," Mexico City, June 26–29, 2018.

Xaxa, Abhay. "I Am Not Your Data." *Shared Mirror* (blog), September 19, 2011. https://roundtableindia.co.in/lit-blogs/?tag=abhay-xaxa.

Yule, Henry, and A. C. Burnell. *Hobson-Jobson: The Anglo-Indian Dictionary (1886)*. Hertfordshire, UK: Wordsworth Editions, 1996.

Zamindar, Vazira Fazila-Yacoobali. *The Long Partition and the Making of Modern South Asia: Refugees, Boundaries, Histories*. New York: Columbia University Press, 2007.

INDEX

abundance: archival, 8, 11, 17, 36, 44–45, 56; Dalit histories as, 20; as heuristic, 25, 69–71, 80, 113–14; linguistic, 94, 105; radical caste politics as, 116–17, 124; sexuality as/and, 2–3, 5. *See also* ikde aani tikde; kala/art; timepass

access: archival, 14–16, 21, 28n32, 30n54, 46, 69, 88, 113; to caste value, 7, 92, 119–20, 125n15; institutional, 10, 38, 79, 90–92, 104, 116, 122; linguistic, 105; to property, 96–97, 114; religious, 19

Adivasi, 20, 113, 116, 121

Ambedkar, Bhimrao, 114, 116–17, 122, 124n2, 135

archive: access to, 10, 14–5, 17, 21, 28n32, 30–31, 46, 69, 113–14; colonial, 13, 35, 38–39, 45, 49, 66, 69–71, 74–79, 89n66; economies and value, 3–4, 6–10, 16, 23–25, 27n17, 28n32, 34, 36, 41, 45–46, 49, 53, 61n44, 64, 67–68, 71, 80–81, 97; of Gomantak Maratha Samaj, 6–9, 13, 15–17, 45–46, 52–56, 69–72, 78–80, 90–93, 98, 100, 113; as historical futurity, 3–4, 8–9, 22–23, 34, 45, 66, 104, 116, 137; preservation of, 3, 6, 8, 21, 45, 59n32, 114; staging of, 4, 16, 40–45, 72, 80, 114, 117–20; trace, 23, 27n14, 66–67, 71–73, 80, 104. *See also* access, archival; data; evidentiary forms

Arondekar, Ramakant, 55–56, 62n56, 136

asymmetry, 3, 18, 93–94, 102, 106

attachment: to archival form, 42; to community, 9–10; genealogy, 67; to Kapalikas, 18; to language of loss, 1–4, 21; to Portuguese India, 68, 91–92; to region, 24; to sexuality, 14–15, 43

Bahujan, 98–9, 100, 112–13, 116–17, 121–22, 124

bailadeiras, 11, 38, 86n47. *See also* dance

bande, 12, 37. *See also* chede

Berlant, Lauren, 26n9, 67, 82n15, 103, 110n36

Best, Stephen, 2, 13, 81n3, 85n36,

bio-: -data, 125n14; parentage, 40, 54–55, 92, 136; -politics, 115; -power; 121. *See also* conjugality; inheritance; kin

Brahmin: hegemony, 24, 92; land-ownership, 91; language and vernaculars, 100, 115; Saraswat, 12–13, 37–40, 55, 97–99, 119; structures of sex, 54, 86n49, 97, 114

caste: certification, 7–10; data, 79, 112–17, 120, 124; endogamy and, 92, 114; membership, 7–8, 13, 30n53, 43–45, 54, 115, 125n15. *See also* Bahujan; make.believe; OBC

Chandavarkar, Sunita, 116, 125n4

Chatterjee, Indrani, 18, 31n60, 64, 82n7, 108n15

chede, 12. *See also* bande

circulation: of archival materials, 15–17; of historical narrative, 13, 46, 72; of value, 75, 80, 120

collectivity: of evil ladies, 79; Gomantak Maratha Samaj, 6, 24, 71, 90; Kurukh, 112; migrant, 77; political, 116; reproduction of, 9, 25; Saraswat, 119–20

conjugality, 72, 114, 125n14

critique: anticolonial, 5, 17; of caste and sexuality, 117; geopolitics as, 94–95, 100; loss as, 1–2; of nationalist epistemology, 19–20; of "show and tell" historiography, 17, 19, 21, 72; as Western intellectual tradition, 64; of Western intellectual tradition, 93

Dalit: art/kala, 11–13, 38, 42–43, 46–9, 74, 86n49, 91, 112, 118–20; diaspora, 11, 14; historiography, 18–20; 46–48, 114–16; literature, 16, 18, 46, 50–54, 95, 121; performance, 12, 14–15, 29n46, 30n51, 48, 121; politics, 19, 31n60–64, 43, 99, 116–17, 127n27; Studies, 18–19, 29n44, 31n64, 116–17. *See also* Bahujan; caste; ESBC; OBC; subaltern

dance: bayadere or nachnis, 11–13, 29n41, 38, 43, 86n47. *See also* devadasi; kalavants/kalavantins; music

data: and archival research, 21, 81n4; and caste, 115–16, 120, 124; as ethnographic episteme, 79, 113, 125n14; Xaxa, Abhay, 112. *See also* evidentiary forms; kagaz

devadasi: and conjugal structures, 14, 70–74, 97; Goan histories of, 12–14, 31n55, 36–41, 44, 56; Gomantak Maratha Samaj, 6, 12–16, 19n46, 36, 48, 87n58, 91, 118; labor, 6, 11–14, 43, 74, 117; reform, 16, 44, 46, 86n49; Southern Indian histories of, 15, 29n48, 126n16. *See also* caste; Gomantak Maratha Samaj; kala/art; sexuality

diaspora, 11, 14

El Shakry, Omnia, 35, 58n10

endogamy, 92, 114. *See also* caste; kin; inheritance; sexuality

epistemology: and/against exemplarity, 22, 34, 71, 89n66; and geopolitical difference, 4, 6, 18, 93, 96; in histories of sexuality, 80, 94–95, 100–102, 119; of loss, 2–3, 53; malleability of, 53, 62n50, 66, 120; non-evidentiary, 19, 49–52, 116; non-recuperative, 8, 36, 42, of race and rule, 11, 18; timepass as, 68, 72;

ESBC, 10. *See also* Adivasi; OBC; Dalit

evidence: of caste lineage, 7; genres/forms of, 4, 8, 16, 35, 45–46, 52, 61n44, 77, 114, 119, 122; and loss, 1–2, 21–23; regimes of, 22, 99, 101, 113, 120–21; transactive value of, 7–10, 21–25, 33–36, 42, 54, 65, 76–77, 80, 97. *See also* archive; evidentiary forms; exemplar; veracity (genres)

evidentiary forms: certificate, 7–10, 121; editorial, 24, 54–55, 74, 90–92, 98, 136; fiction, 9, 16, 40, 45–48, 52–54, 80, 82n12, 114, 123, 129; jugaad/duplicate, 9, 122; letters, 7, 30n53, 52–54; 61n44, 62n50, 70, 72, 85n33; name, 7, 14, 43, 54, 76, 97, 114–16, 119–20, 122–24; photograph, 25n1, 49, 60n37, 60n40, 72, 118, 123, 137; origin story, 2, 21, 34, 36, 43, 52, 55, 57n5, 92–93, 103, 106, 107n8, 121; petition, 77. *See also* archive; data; halla/attack; kagaz; make.believe; veracity (genres)

exemplar: archival, 22–23, 34–35, 66–69, 96, 129; as epistemology, 68, 71–73; ordinariness, 85n35; relegation to, 64, 72, 92; of sexuality, 67, 76, 80–81, 92, 101

genealogies: of caste, 12, 18, 114; of family histories, 25, 55, 72, 110n24; of inheritance, 78; intellectual, 17, 26n9, 105, 117; of modernity, 20; of past and future, 97, 125n14; of religion and practice, 106; of representation, 25, 56, 60n37, 113; of sexuality, 66–67, 72, 114

genre: archival, 15–16, 28n32, 45–46, 52, 72, 75, 114; evidentiary, 4, 8, 16, 22–23, 35, 52–56, 77, 122; "Genre Flailing" (Berlant), 67; historiographical, 22; narrative, 6, 59n25, 63, 84n27. *See also* evidence (genres/forms of); evidentiary forms; veracity (genres)

geographies: of affiliation, 93–94, 97, 108n12; of "elsewheres," 4, 34–35; as history, 6, 13–14; imaginary, 22, 108n15; itinerant, 98; networks: 21, 91–94, 99, 109n18, 109n22; queer, 95; settled, 100, 107n8; social, 74, 78, 106n2; as value, 24

geopolitics: as form/method, 4, 15, 22–24, 35–38, 90–96, 100–106; itinerant, 97–98, 114; as site, 3, 6, 34–35, 67; stakes of, 63–64; as value, 99

Ghosh, Bishnupriya, 49, 61n41

Global South, 33–34, 108n12, 109n18; elsewheres, 5, 26n8, 34, 64, 67, 96; South–South comparison, 93

Goa, 6–15, 29nn42–46, 29–30nn49–50, 31n55, 36–44, 54–56, 75, 79–80, 83n19, 86n47, 90–92, 97–100, 106n2, 107nn4–7, 115, 117

Gomantak Maratha Samaj: archives of, 7–9, 16–17, 22–24, 30n53, 31n56, 45–56, 61n42,

67–72, 81, 85n33, 87n58; as collectivity, 25, 38, 59n27; figures of, 29n44, 29n46, 30n51, 73, 83n19; history of, 6, 11–5, 29n47, 42–44, 48, 58n20, 78–80, 88n62, 90–93, 96–103, 113–20, 122; *Samaj Sudharak*, 16, 46–49, 51–56, 60n34, 61n42, 90, 135–36

halla/attack, 37–8, 40–44, 72, 114
hermeneutics, 1, 3, 23, 27n15, 32n74, 34, 42, 45, 63–67, 71, 80, 96, 103
heuristic, 6, 25, 36, 69, 96, 113. *See also* epistemology; evidentiary form, jugaad

ikde aani tikde/here and there, 92, 96, 100, 102. *See also* itinerant; musafir; queer
Ilaiah, Kancha, 19
Indigenous: concepts, 96; elites, 11; studies, 17–21. *See also* Adivasi
inheritance: caste lineage as, 114, 120; of loss, 8, 22, 32n71; of property, 14, 78
itinerant: archival forms, 34; heuristics, 6, 110n24; musafir, 102–3; sex, 24, 94–99. *See also* ikde aani tikde; musafir; queer

kagaz, 120–22
kala/art, 11–15, 36, 41–43, 48, 73–74, 91, 96–99, 120
kalavants / kalavantins, 11–13, 15, 36–43, 48, 54–56, 73, 79, 92, 118. *See also* devadasi; Gomantak Maratha Samaj
kin, 55, 99, 114, 117–18, 122, 124. *See also* collectivity
Konkani, 15, 79, 100

liberation: of British India, 55; of Goa, 29n49, 90, 98, 107n5; histories, 42; movements, 24, 44, 91; shared fantasy of, 93, 124
loss: in/as history, 1–8, 15, 17–22, 32n71, 34, 42–45, 63–68, 71, 80, 97, 113, 124; language of, 26n4, 56; repetitions of, 63, 103

queer: history, 9, 52, 56, 57n1, 61n44, 66–73; musafir, 102; readings, 45, 64, 83n23, 84n31; studies, 26n4, 93–95, 101–5; subjects, 2, 24, 44, 65, 84n26; as term, 6. *See also* musafir

make.believe, 7–10, 52, 137
Maratha, 6, 10, 38, 43, 59n27, 100, 125n7. *See also* Gomantak Maratha Samaj
Marathi, 15, 29n46, 30n53, 38, 43, 48, 52–54, 58n12, 59n27, 75, 85n43, 88n61, 90, 100, 107n3, 116, 121, 123, 125n9
Mitra, Durba, 81n4, 89n66, 109n19, 114
Mumbai/Bombay, 7–8, 14, 16, 28n29, 31n56, 39, 43–48, 54, 60n34, 69–71, 74–79, 85n33, 87nn55–60, 113, 116, 120, 123–24
musafir, 102–6, 114. *See also* itinerant; queer; timepass
music, 12, 15, 29n46, 43, 48, 88n61. *See also* dance; kala/art; kalavants/kalavantis

OBC, 7, 10, 13, 58n20, 98, 115, 117, 125n6, 125n15. *See also* Dalit; Gomantak Maratha Samaj

Paigankar, Rajaram Rangoji, 16, 31n55, 36–43, 46, 53–54, 79, 99
Panaji, 6, 16, 31n56, 43–45, 88n62, 113
Patel, Geeta, 2, 26n11, 34, 57n4, 95, 106n1, 109n21, 111n37
Phadke, Narayan Sitaram, 52, 61–62
Povinelli, Elizabeth, 2, 64
presence, 3–4, 7–11, 14–19, 24–25, 45, 49, 55, 60n33, 62n57, 65–66, 69, 73–75, 79, 86, 97, 113, 118, 120
problem event, 23, 66, 79–80. *See also* exemplar
protest, 24, 31n61, 69, 114, 116–17, 120–24

Ramberg, Lucinda, 29n48, 126n16
reproduction: as copy, 8–9; futurity, 43–45, 53–54, 56, 95; lineages of, 68; of modernity, 20; protocols of, 4–5, 25

Satoskar, B. D., 29n47, 90–93, 98, 107n3
sexuality: as capital, 72; and evidence, 121–22; Gomantak Maratha Samaj and, 13–16, 42–48, 52–55, 69, 97–100, 115–19; histories of, 1–10, 22–25, 33–36, 61n45, 65–67, 72–73, 80–81, 91–92, 96, 101–6, 112–17; and slavery, 17–18, 64; Studies, 94–95, 108n10, 109n18; and timepass, 84n26

Shiroda/Seroda, 11–12, 43–44, 115
slavery: Atlantic, 21–12, 27n13; devadasi, 6, 12–13; histories of, 1, 31n59, 32n74, 35, 57n5, 64–65, 85n36, 86n48; South Asian and Indian Ocean, 17–18, 108n15, 126n20. *See also* Devadasi; subaltern
Spillers, Hortense, 73, 85
Spivak, Gayatri, 5, 52, 59n30, 61n43, 103, 110n36
staging: of halla/attack, 40–45, 72–73; "hermeneutics of perfidiousness," 42; of historical narrative, 2, 10, 21, 48, 92, 100, 104; of incommensurability, 5; of record or archives, 4, 16, 40–45, 55, 80, 113–14, 117–20; of sexuality, 6, 95, 102. *See also* archive, staging of; kala/art
subaltern: "Can the Subaltern Speak" (Spivak), 5; empire, 97; evidentiary practices, 8, 10, 34, 100; lives and pasts, 2–3, 103, 114, 116; middle-class, 59n31; (non)oppositionality, 41, 44–46; Studies, 19–20, 23, 27n17, 82n7, 109n21
Subrahmanyam, Sanjay, 83n22, 108n10
surplus: archival, 8, 17; Derridean supplement as, 62n57; ordinary, 6; "surplus woman" (Ambedkar), 114

Tambe, Ashwini, 74, 88n63
timepass, 68–69, 72, 81, 82n23, 84nn25–27, 114

value: archival/evidentiary, 8, 16, 28n32, 41, 46–49, 53, 61n44, 67–68, 80–81, 85n36; of caste, 10, 97; devaluation, 3–4, 17, 34, 36, 64, 69; epistemological, 27n17; form, 9, 23–24, 33, 45, 76; of geopolitics, 92, 96; loss as, 3, 61n44, 68, 71; of music, 48; of property, 75–78; of sexuality, 5, 10, 25, 73, 110n38; timepass and waste, 84n26, 84n29, 84n30
veracity: archive, 23, 42, 66–67; genres, 23, 46; narrative, 41; and sexual knowledge, 62n49. *See also* data; evidentiary forms; kagaz
vernaculars: elitist, 19; of geopolitics, 93; of loss, 2; press, 39, 74, 87n53; postcolonial, 68; of reading, 65; of self-making, 10; of sex, 24, 94; theoretical, 5, 27n28, 94
violence, 18, 43, 64, 85n38, 90, 92, 97, 106, 113–15, 121, 124

Wakankar, Milind, 18

Xaxa, Abhay, 112–13, 116, 126n27

www.ingramcontent.com/pod-product-compliance
Lightning Source LLC
Chambersburg PA
CBHW031453160426
43195CB00010BB/968